Professional Inn Guide

All Inspected
8OO Photographs

Second Edition

By Wendy and Jon Denn

Colburn Press
P.O. Box 356
Montvale, NJ 07645

February 1995

COLBURN PRESS
P.O. Box 356
Montvale, NJ 07645

Copyright © 1995 by Colburn Press

DESIGNED BY JON DENN

MANUFACTURED IN THE UNITED STATES

10 9 8 7 6 5 4 3 2 1

LIBRARY OF CONGRESS CATALOGING IN PUBLICATION DATA
93-73540
ISBN
0-9634187-9-3

Front Cover Photo: 2439 Fairfield A Bed and Breakfast: Photo by Larry Posey
Back Cover Photo: Food shot, Southern Hotel: Photo by Tom Bagley, Styling by Gail Greco
Back Cover Photo: Exterior, The Lodge at Sedona: Photo by Dave Tate
Table of Contents Photo: F. W. Hastings House Old Consulate Inn: Photo by Don Pier-Portland

Text printed on Recycled Paper

Table of Contents

F. W. Hastings House Old Consulate Inn, Port Townsend, WA

Welcome

Your desire as an inn traveller for a getaway experience that fulfills your fantasy, while meeting your expectations of safety, cleanliness, and maintenance, has catalyzed this guide's creation.

Many innkeepers across North America have been eager, not only to be inspected, but to develop demanding standards for themselves and their peers. What you find here are some of the inns who have invited inspections, have passed, and are members of Professional Association of Innkeepers International (PAII pronounced pie as in mom's apple).

You will not find here any evaluation of hospitality and "innkeeper friendliness." The adventure of inn travel is the people you meet. Some will be distant, some will hover in an attempt to discover how they might help fulfill your dreams for this trip, some will be exactly what you want. What one person loves in an inn's decor or style of operation another will hate. Only you can be the judge of these intangibles and you can only judge for yourself, not for everyone else.

Bed-and-breakfast/country inns are the heart of a country, countryside, and community. Innkeepers actively participate in their local community with a strong dedication to its improvement while committed to preserving those parts of history and the environment that entice you to visit their favorite spot on earth, their hometown.

At a bed-and-breakfast/country inn, you are not a room number. You are a person. Curl up and read a book in a quiet alcove, or chat with other guests while enjoying a cup of coffee sitting around the fireplace. Find a romantic hideaway or enjoy the fellowship of playing out a mystery weekend. A small inn is like you always pictured "home" — hearty breakfasts in a sunny nook, freshly baked cookies, lemonade on the porch, watching a glorious sunset, finding that great local restaurant, a hidden antique shop, strolling along a hidden beach. Innkeepers routinely take guests on the ragged edge of burnout, provide them a quiet place to be themselves and find one another again — then return those same guests to their world of appointments, meetings, and traffic — refreshed and relaxed.

PAII is the recognized national trade association for the serious country inn/bed-and-breakfast innkeeper. For the past five years PAII has encouraged state associations to develop and implement standards, by consulting with association leaders, providing sample standards, offering workshops for association leaders, and speaking at their association meetings. The linkages among volunteer-run state associations have been fostered by PAII through the PAII International Conferences for the Keepers of the Small Inn, and in the quarterly *Association Leaders Update*.

In assuring your safety as a guest, staff and members of PAII have also worked with the American Hotel & Motel Association, American Automobile Association, National Restaurant Association and the American Culinary Federation.

PAII's mission is to support the innkeeper in the field by publishing the well-read monthly newsletter, *innkeeping*, as well as numerous other publications specific to the business of innkeeping. In-depth workshop programs, and serving as the central clearinghouse for research on the small inn, along with its extensive resource files accessible on the member-only hotline — are all ways PAII serves the active and preparing innkeeper.

Yes, innkeepers have paid to be in the *Guide* and there are fine inns that are not listed. If they presently meet the requirements of one of the organizations whose criteria PAII has accepted, you may find them by contacting the group directly. (See the following pages.)

For the first time, the Professional Association of Innkeepers International has commissioned a Guide of member bed-and-breakfast/country inns who have passed an outside inspection. The conscientious efforts of these lodging gems are impressive, yet each one markets its properties separately. A coordinated national forum was needed to announce and celebrate the high standards being implemented and monitored in the bed-and-breakfast/country inns industry — thus your *Professional Inn Guide*.

Pat Hardy & Jo Ann M. Bell • Co-Executive Directors • Professional Association of Innkeepers International • Santa Barbara • CA •
November 1993

TWO DIFFERENT CRITERIA were used in approving inspections: one for consumer-driven, independent inspecting groups and one for innkeeper-run associations. *For independent inspecting groups,* PAII reviewed the group's standards and reputation, as well as randomly visiting properties inspected under these programs. The three organizations included in this category have established themselves in the public's and innkeepers' minds as being conscientious and responsible in their inspection process. The following descriptions were written by the specific organizations themselves. Not all of an organization's members are in the *Professional Inn Guide*. Readers are encouraged to contact each directly for a complete listing.

■ *American Automobile Association (AAA)*

Properties are listed in AAA TourBooks without charge. Each property must be inspected annually by one of AAA's full-time inspectors. The inspection ensures that properties meet AAA's minimum listing requirements. Properties are rated from one to five diamonds. The diamond rating represents the overall quality of the property when compared to other properties within the same classification (e.g., bed and breakfast). TourBooks are available exclusively to AAA members, at no charge, from their local club. American Automobile Association • 1000 AAA Drive • Heathrow • FL • 32746-5063

■ *American Bed & Breakfast Association (ABBA)*

The American Bed & Breakfast Association sets national standards for the bed & breakfast industry. Compliance with these standards is established by an annual on-site inspection of each property which is both rigorous and thorough. Consumer ratings are awarded after each inspection and they are intended to give readers a true and objective feel for the overall quality of the property, the level of hospitality, cleanliness, and how well the building and its contents are maintained. All members of the American Bed & Breakfast Association agree to comply with the association's Code of Ethics and agree to help resolve any guest complaints in a spirit of cooperation. American Bed & Breakfast Association • P.O. Box 1387 • Midlothian • Virginia • 23113 Phone: 804/379-ABBA (2222) • Fax: 804/379-3627

■ *Mobil Travel Guide (Mobil)*

Mobil Travel Guide has been rating establishments for 38 years. The rating system has been perceived to be the most critical of the rating publications. Mobil accepts no advertising and offers no memberships to the *Guide*. Listings are free of charge, and properties that are accepted for review will be inspected between the months of late March through July 1st of the inspection year. Every establishment will not be chosen for inspection. The decision on this matter is made by the editorial department for the *Guide*. Comments about any listed property are welcomed: *Mobil Travel Guide* • 4709 Golf Road, Suite 803 • Skokie • IL • 60076

■ *National innkeeper-run organization*

Independent Innkeepers Association (IIA)

In accordance with IIA's stated purpose of maintaining the highest standards of innkeeping, each member is required to participate in a quality assurance program. This program provides for mandatory periodic inspections of every inn by specialists personally trained to provide thorough, unbiased and honest evaluations. The evaluation visit is for two consecutive nights, whenever possible, to permit the evaluator to get a full picture of the inn's operation. The visits, of course, are unannounced. Independent Innkeepers Association • Box 150 • Marshall • MI • 49068 • 800/344-5244

■ *State innkeeper-run organizations*

For state innkeeper-run associations, the following requirements have been met:

• PAII's review and approval of the association's standards and inspection forms (yearly). • Association standards are published and available for review by the public. • On-site inspections are completed every two years (minimum) or performed initially and followed with an ongoing, approved guest-comment card monitoring system. • Associations using comment card systems in lieu of follow-up inspections, must present written guidelines, annual reports, and card tallies to PAII. • On-site inspections must be performed by trained inspector(s) consisting of either one person who is not as association member, or at least two members of the association, preferably three. • Each association agrees that *Guide* readers may contact the association for additional information, and to comment on their experiences at its member *Guide*-participating inns. • Colburn Press will forward all reader inquiries to the associations . • Each association agrees to promptly and effectively (within 30 days) handle accolades and complaints about its association members. • If a complaint is registered about a specific inn, the state association agrees to forward to Colburn Press and PAII headquarters written confirmation that such has been handled in a prompt and effective manner.

State innkeeper-run associations meeting these requirements are listed below. Not all of the association's members are listed in the *Professional Inn Guide*. Readers are encouraged to contact the association for a complete listing.

Bed and Breakfast Innkeepers of *Colorado*, P.O. Box 38416-Dept.-94, Colorado Springs, CO 80937 — *8416-BBIC*

Illinois Bed and Breakfast Association, POB 82, Port Byron, IL 61275 — *IBBA*

Indiana Bed & Breakfast Association, 3729 Old St. Rd. 32W, Crawfordsville, IN 47933 — *IBBA*

Kansas Bed and Breakfast Association, Rt. 1, Box 93, Wakenney, KS 67672 — *KBBA*

Maryland Bed and Breakfast Association, POB 23324, Baltimore, MD 21203 — *MBBA*

Lake to Lake Bed and Breakfast Association (*Michigan*), POB 428, Saugatuck, MI 49453 — *Lake to Lake*

Missouri B&B Association, 146 S. Third, St. Genievieve, MO 63670 — *BBIM*

Montana Bed and Breakfast Association, POB 7721, Kalispell, MT 59901 — *MBBA*

New Mexico Bed and Breakfast Association, 122 Grant Ave., Santa Fe, NM 87501 — *NMBBA*

North Carolina Bed & Breakfasts & Inns, PO Box 1077, Asheville, NC 28802 — *NCBBI*

Oregon B&B Guild, POB 3187-P, Ashland, OR 97520 — *OBBG*

South Carolina Bed & Breakfast Association, 278K Harbison Blvd. # 120, Columbia, SC 29212, SCBBA

Bed and Breakfast Inns of *Utah*, POB 3066, Park City, UT 84060 — *BBIU*

Bed and Breakfast Association of *Virginia*, POB 791, Orange, VA 22960 — *BBAV*

Washington B&B Guild, 2442 NW Market St. #PI, Seattle, WA 98107 — *WBBG*

Wisconsin B &B Homes & Historic Inns Association, 405 Collins St., Plymouth, WI 53073 — *WBBHHIA*

ALL COMMENTS about Inns inspected by the above organizations should be directed to the inspecting organization.

Dedication

To all of the Innkeepers who have committed themselves to their Inns, their communities, and their guests...who have submitted to critical inspections of their Inns and examination of their hospitality skills in order to continually raise their levels of professionalism and to meet the expectations of travellers...*we salute you*!

And to the guests, who have stayed at Inns when everything has been perfect, as well as during protracted restorations and overdue renovations...who have eaten gourmet delights and fallen soufflés...we dedicate our efforts so that you may continue to discover and enjoy this wonderful world of Inn Travel.

ACKNOWLEDGEMENTS

This guide is the result of the tireless efforts of many people. We are grateful to the Innkeepers who urged us to create this book and to all of them whose kind words and generosity of spirit throughout the months kept us moving forward. Without the unwavering support of Sandy Dragona and all the named and unnamed photographers this would not have been possible. Special thanks to George and Roberta Gardner, Tom Bagley and Gail Greco, for their friendship, magnificent photography and willingness to share their expertise.

Accessibility; TDD	Bowling	Fax
Accessibility; wheelchair	Breakfast; continental	Fireplace; in-room
Afternoon Tea	Breakfast; full	Fishing
Antiquing	Business services	Fitness area
Aquarium	Carriage rides	Game room
Art gallery	Children; appropriate for	Gaming nearby
Auto Racing	City area	Gardens
Ballooning	Common area	Golf
Bar; beer and or wine	Cookouts	Hay rides
Bar; bring your own bottle	Country area	Hiking
Bar; full service	Credit Cards; not accepted	Historic, landmark/site/or area
Beach	Croquet	Horseback riding
Biking	Computer services	Horseracing
Billiards	Dancing	Hot tub; in room
Bird Watching	Day trips	Hot tub; common use
Boating	Dinner served to the public	Hunting

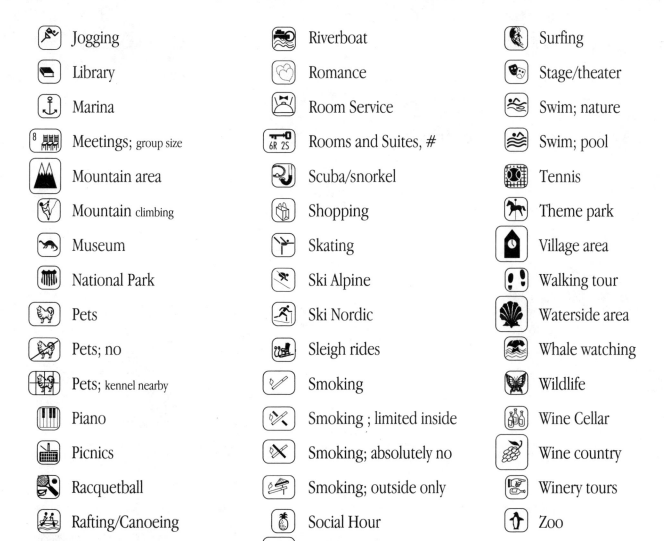

Jogging

Library

Marina

Meetings; group size

Mountain area

Mountain climbing

Museum

National Park

Pets

Pets; no

Pets; kennel nearby

Piano

Picnics

Racquetball

Rafting/Canoeing

Restaurant row

Riverboat

Romance

Room Service

Rooms and Suites, #

Scuba/snorkel

Shopping

Skating

Ski Alpine

Ski Nordic

Sleigh rides

Smoking

Smoking ; limited inside

Smoking; absolutely no

Smoking; outside only

Social Hour

Suburban area

Surfing

Stage/theater

Swim; nature

Swim; pool

Tennis

Theme park

Village area

Walking tour

Waterside area

Whale watching

Wildlife

Wine Cellar

Wine country

Winery tours

Zoo

Each listing is full of useful information, here is your key to a world of hospitality.

Inn Specific Information

Number of rooms-Number of Suites
5R 6S

Full Breakfast available

Continental breakfast,

Full bar service

Beer and Wine only

Bring Your Own Bottle
BYOB

Dinner served to the public

Fireplace in at least one room

Hot tub in at least one room

Appropriate for children

Smoking allowed

No smoking allowed

Smoking outside only

Limited smoking inside

Pets allowed

No pets allowed

Kennel nearby

Meetings for the ideal size group
10

CC Credit Cards Accepted. Visa is V, Mastercard is M, American Express is X, Discover is Dv, Diners is Dn, En Route is En, JCB is J.

CC No Credit Cards Accepted.

Price ranges

$ under $79 per night
$$ $80-109
$$$ $110-159
$$$$ $160-199
$$$$$ $200 and up

*Packages

AP American Plan (includes three meals a day)
MAP Modified American Plan (Includes Breakfast and Dinner)
EP European Plan (room only)
B&B Bed and Breakfast (includes breakfast)
followed by $/$$ (low season/high season), (to-from year round)

City, Address, Zip, Phone & Fax #'s and Innkeepers

Price Ranges (off/in season)(to-from)

Name of the Inn

Accessibility & Packages *

Photo #1

Photo #2

Direction to Inn

Text Description

Inspection and Approval Source(s)

General Locale

MOUNTAINS

WATERSIDE

SUBURBAN

VILLAGE

COUNTRY

WINE COUNTRY

CITY

Top Eight Activities

At and around the Inn
indicated by
International Symbols
The key is on the
previous spread.

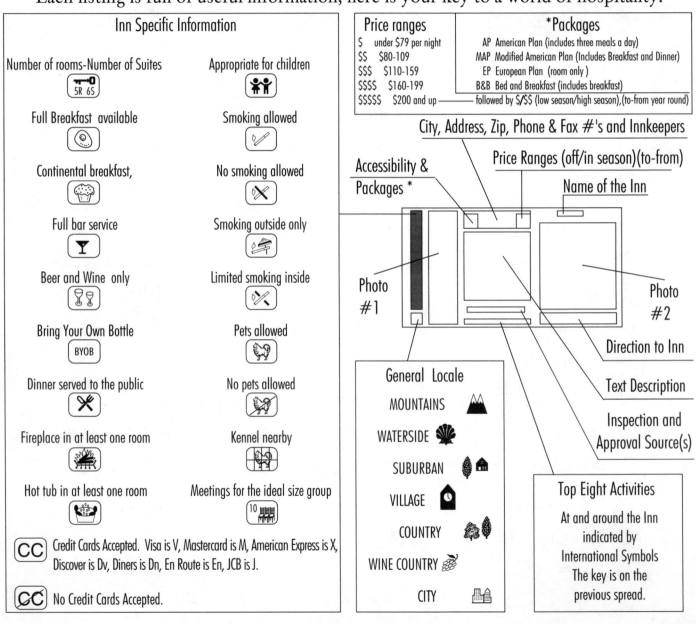

Relay Numbers: TTY (800) 548-2546, VCE (800) 548-2547

Anniston

B&B

1604 Quintard Avenue, 36202
(205) 236-0503, Fax (205) 236-1138
Innkeepers: Beth & Fain Casey

The Victoria, A Country Inn

$/
$$$

Built in 1888 and listed on the National Historic Register, the Inn wears her name well. Restored and expanded in 1985, the Inn features a three-story turret, beautiful stained and etched windows, a conservatory and colonnaded verandas, and original hardware, mantels, flooring, and woodwork. Nestled on a hill, the Inn is surrounded by trees and well-groomed flower beds and is insulated from the sounds of the downtown traffic. Each guest room is decorated individually with brass, wicker, and pine or mahogany furnishings. You are welcomed by many amenities and a caring staff.

Approved by: AAA

From I-20, at the Oxford-Anniston interchange, go north on Quintard Ave. four miles. The Inn is on the left.

Relay Numbers: TTY (800) 770-8973, VCE (800) 770-8255

Fairbanks, AK

7 Gables Bed & Breakfast

B&B

4312 Birch Lane, 99708
(907) 479-0751, Fax (907) 479-2229
Innkeepers: Paul & Leicha Welton

$/
$$$$

This Tudor home is spacious and features a custom, energy-efficient design. The entrance through the floral solarium into the antique, stained-glass decorated foyer with its indoor waterfall is just part of the Inn's unique architecture. Other features, including cathedral ceilings, a wedding chapel, and a wine cellar, create an environment of elegance. A gourmet breakfast is served daily. Laundry facilities, Jacuzzis®, bikes, boats, and luggage storage are available. Each room has a dormer, cable TV, and phone. The Inn is centrally located.

Approved by: AAA, ABBA

Take Parks Highway to Geist Road to Loftus Road. South on Loftus Road for 3 blocks, and left on Birch Lane.

3R 1S

BYOB

7

V,M,X DN

Pearson's Pond Luxury Inn

Juneau, AK

B&B   4541 Sawa Circle, 99801-8723 $$/
(907) 789-3772, Fax (907) 789-6722 $$$
Innkeepers: Steve & Diane Pearson

Here you will find spectacular scenery and complete relaxation just minutes away from the Glacier Bay departures and the major attractions. Your suite retreat has all the private comforts of home, including stocked kitchenettes. You may dine ensuite or alfresco and reflect on life with the healing sounds of nature and wildlife. You will soothe your cares in a starlit spa amid lush gardens, sparkling fountains or snowflakes, and a glacial duck pond left by the nearby retreating, world-famous Mendenhall Glacier. Perfect for anyone, this is a photographers and birders delight!

Approved by: AAA, ABBA

Drive toward the campground at the glacier, following the (Mendenhall) Loop Rd. for 2 miles. Turn onto River Rd. (left from the airport; right from the ferry). Turn right onto Kelly/Whitewater Ct. and left onto Sawa Circle.

Arizona

N
W • E
S

Relay Numbers: TTY (800) 367-8939, VCE (800) 842-4681

Flagstaff

The Inn at 410

B&B
410 North Leroux, 86001
(800) 774-2008, or (602) 774-0088
Innkeepers: Howard & Sally Krueger

$$

On a hill overlooking historic, downtown Flagstaff, this Inn offers four seasons of hospitality in a charming 1907 home. It is elegantly furnished with antiques, stained glass, and touches of the Southwest. The spacious, sunny living room and lovely garden gazebo provide a peaceful ambiance. The Innkeepers pamper you with their personal attention including oven-fresh cookies and a delicious, healthy breakfast. They will help you plan day trips to Native American ruins and villages or help you to find magnificent views of the Grand Canyon and other natural wonders.

Approved by: AAA, ABBA

From I-40, exit 195B north onto Milton. From I-17 continue north onto Milton. Follow Milton under the railroad overpass and curve to the right onto Santa Fe. Turn left at the first stoplight; Humphreys Street. At Dale, turn right. Turn left at Leroux. Inn is on the right.

Phoenix

Maricopa Manor

B&B
15 West Pasadena Avenue, 85013
(602) 274-6302, Fax (602) 263-9695
Innkeepers: Mary Ellen & Paul Kelley

$$/
$$$

Private suites, spacious common rooms, patios, decks, and the Gazebo Spa offer an intimate, old-world atmosphere in an elegant, urban setting. The Inn is in the heart of the Valley of the Sun, convenient to restaurants and museums as well as civic and government centers. The Spanish-styled Inn, built in 1928, houses beautiful art, antiques, and a warm Southwestern hospitality. Each suite is distinctive and offers TV, books, telephone, and private entrance. Some have a fireplace, private decks, and patios. The unique "Breakfast in a Basket", is delivered to your suite.

Approved by: AAA, Mobil

From I-17, East on Camelback Road to 3rd Avenue. Left on 3rd, 1 block to Pasadena Avenue. Right to the Inn at 15 West Pasadena.

Photo by Ginger

Prescott

B&B

204 N. Mt. Vernon Avenue, 86301
(602) 778-0886, Fax (602) 778-7305
Innkeepers: Sybil & John Nelson

$$

Mt Vernon Inn

Step back in time at this Inn nestled among towering shade trees in the center of Arizona's largest Victorian neighborhood. You will delight in the climate with occasional snow in mild winter, colorful wildflowers and greenery in spring, brisk breezes and comfortable nights in summer, and fall foliage of gold and maroon. You may enjoy a host of outdoor sports, relax in front of the sitting room fire with a fine collection of old movies on the VCR, or linger on the Greek Revival porch in the warm weather. Start your day with freshly-baked breads, granola, and light, healthy specialties.

Approved by: AAA

Take I-10(N) to Rt. 17. At Cordes Junction, take Rt. 69 to Prescott. From I-10 at Quartzsite, take Rt. 60 to Rt. 71 to Rt. 89(N) to Prescott. The Inn is between Gurley Street and Sheldon Street.

Sedona

B&B

255 Rock Ridge Drive, 86336
(602) 282-7640
Innkeepers: Fran & Dan Bruno

$$$

Bed & Breakfast at Saddle Rock Ranch

History, romance, antiques, and elegance combine in this country estate. Used for location filming of many old westerns, the lovingly-restored home features flagstone floors, beamed ceilings, and rock and adobe walls. Romantic rooms have woodburning fieldstone fireplaces, private baths, and famous views. Furnishings are often family antiques; linens by Laura Ashley. Deluxe service includes terry robes, scrumptious breakfasts, saucer-size cookies, and afternoon snacks beside the parlor fireplace or sparkling pool and spa. Special packages and 4-wheel drive tours are available.

Approved by: AAA

On 3 acres of hillside above the town of Sedona. Off of Airport Road.

Sedona

B&B

125 Canyon Circle Drive, 86336
(800) 453-1166, Fax (602) 284-2114
Innkeepers: Chuck & Marion Yadon

$$/$$$$

Canyon Villa Bed & Breakfast

Photo: Tom Bagley

Nestled in the shadows of Bell Rock and Courthouse Butte is this beautiful Bed & Breakfast. The 10 luxurious rooms have spectacular views of the brilliant, red rock cliffs from balconies or patios. Every room is individually decorated, yours could be Victorian, Southwestern or Santa Fe style, with relaxing whirlpool tubs and large, fluffy robes to make you feel right at home. Every morning you will be greeted by the wonderful aroma of fresh-baked bread, muffins, or cinnamon rolls that complement your gourmet breakfast. At Canyon Villa, you'll arrive as a guest and leave as a friend.

Approved by: AAA, ABBA, Mobil

Off Route 179 in the Village of Oak Creek, turn west on Bell Rock Blvd. One block, then turn north on Canyon Circle Drive to Inn.

Sedona

B&B

150 Canyon Circle Drive, 86351
(800) 228-1425, Fax (602) 284-0767
Innkeepers: Carol & Roger Redenbaugh

$$/$$$$$

Graham Bed & Breakfast Inn

Photo: Jeanne Westenberg

A very special Bed-and-Breakfast experience awaits you here...awesome red rock views from the pool and Jacuzzi® or your private balcony; beautifully decorated theme rooms with fireplaces, whirlpool tubs, TV/VCR's; special touches in every guest room, consistent with the room's theme, including wonderful bed linens, comfy robes, night lights, and flowers. Choose a video from the Inn's collection or a book from the "take a book, leave a book" library. Each morning after Roger's fresh roasted coffee and Carol's gourmet breakfast, enjoy this Inn's very helpful area orientation program.

Approved by: AAA, Mobil

Two blocks west of Highway 179 on Bell Rock Blvd. in Village of Oak Creek.

11R 2S

BYOB

25

V,M

Sedona

B&B

125 Kallof Place, 86336
(800) 619-4467, Fax (602) 204-2128
Innkeepers: Barb & Mark Dinunzio

$$/
$$$$

The Lodge At Sedona

Photo: Dave Tate

High desert breezes sweep through the canyon carrying the fragrance of pine. This elegantly rustic Lodge offers secluded privacy on 2 1/2 wooded acres with beautifully appointed guest rooms, suites, and ample common areas. The two-story Lodge, accented with earthy, country pine antiques and red rock views, provides a comfortable and nurturing ambiance. Some rooms have decks and one suite has a double Jacuzzi®. A full breakfast is served on the morning porch where the food is only over shadowed by the peaceful outdoor view. A promise of comfort and graciousness welcomes you here.

Approved by: AAA

Kallof Place is two miles west of the intersection of US 89A and AZ 179.

4R 1S

BYOB

V,M

Sedona

B&B

65 Piki Drive, 86336
(800) 801-2737, Fax (602) 204-2230
Innkeepers: John & Linda Steele

$$/
$$$$

Territorial House

Photos: Jeanne Westenberg

The native stone and cedar house, decorated to depict Sedona's territorial era, offers choices of private balconies, a whirlpool tub, or a fireplace. The covered veranda and the stone fireplace in the great room welcome you at the end of the day. Native trees and shrubs surrounding the Inn attract birds and wildlife. The serene setting makes the Inn ideal for that special romantic getaway. The aroma of fresh-baked breads whets the appetite for the full, hearty breakfast served around the harvest table. The Innkeepers gift to you is their friendly, western hospitality.

Approved by: AAA

At the junction of 89A and 179, go 3.1 miles to Dry Creek Road. Turn north for .2 mile, then turn left onto Kachina. Stay left for .4 mile to Piki. Turn left onto Piki. The Inn is the 2nd house on the left.

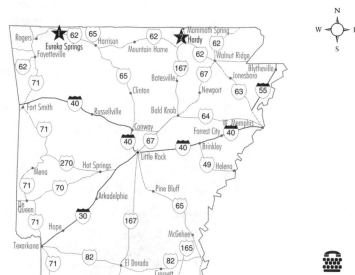

Relay Numbers: TTY (800) 332-5580, VCE (800) 482-5400

3R 3S

BYOB

16

V,M,X
DN,DV

Eureka Springs

B&B

515 Spring Street, 72632
(501) 253-7444, (800) 562-8650

$$$/
$$$$

Innkeepers: Ned Shank & Crescent Dragonwagon

Dairy Hollow House

There is always a friendly Innkeeper to welcome you and perhaps on a cool day the smell of hot apple cider with cinnamon. Dairy Hollow's rooms and suites are in two homes (an 1880's Farmhouse and a late 40's Bungalow) on either side of a peaceful, wooded, green valley just a mile from quirky, historic, downtown Eureka Springs. You'll relish the breakfast-in-a-basket delivered right to your door each morning. Dinner in the elegant, sensual restaurant with old-fashioned service and fresh up-to-the-minute Nouveau 'Zarks cuisine cannot be missed!

Approved by: AAA, Mobil

Photo: (Left) Alison Misch, *Organic Gardening*, (Right) Alan Smith

Turn off Highway 62 downhill to Historic District. Bear left at Y downtown to stay on Spring Street. Continue 1.4 miles. Inn is on the right.

Hardy, AR

B&B

511 Main Street, 72542
(501) 856-2983
Innkeepers: Peggy & David Johnson

$/
$$

Olde Stonehouse B&B

Located in the foothills of the Ozarks, this historic, native-stone house greets you with large porches, jumbo rocking chairs, and a warm fireplace. It has comfortable antique furnishings, ceiling fans, and queen beds as well as an in-town location, one block from Spring River and the shops of quaint Old Hardy Town. Secluded honeymoon suites have fireplaces. Exceptional antique and craft shopping, country music theaters, dinner theater, Indian Culture Center, and the Veteran's Military Museum are nearby. Picnic baskets are available upon request.

Approved by: AAA, ABBA

From Springfield/Branson, MO. Highway 60 (E) to Highway 63(S) (150 miles). Memphis, TN - I-55 (N) to Highway 63 (W) (135 miles). Little Rock, AR - Highway 167 (N) (150 Miles).

Alameda, CA

B&B

900 Union, 94501
(510) 521-4779, Fax (510) 521-6796
Innkeepers: Royce & Betty Gladden

$/
$$$

Garratt Mansion

You'll find this elegant Victorian (circa 1893) only 15 miles from downtown San Francisco or Berkeley, on the island of Alameda. Peruse the rich architecture of the neighborhood, take the ferry or rapid transit to "The City" for sightseeing, or retreat to your comfortable room. Breakfasts reflect the abundance the area provides. Throughout the afternoon there are fresh, chocolate-chip cookies, and your choice of hot or cold beverages. Anticipating your needs is what the Innkeepers do best.

Approved by: ABBA

From Highway 880, take the High St/Alameda Exit. West on High Street. Go 5 blocks, then turn right on Central. Go 1 1/2 miles, then turn left on Union. Continue 4 blocks. The Inn is located on the left.

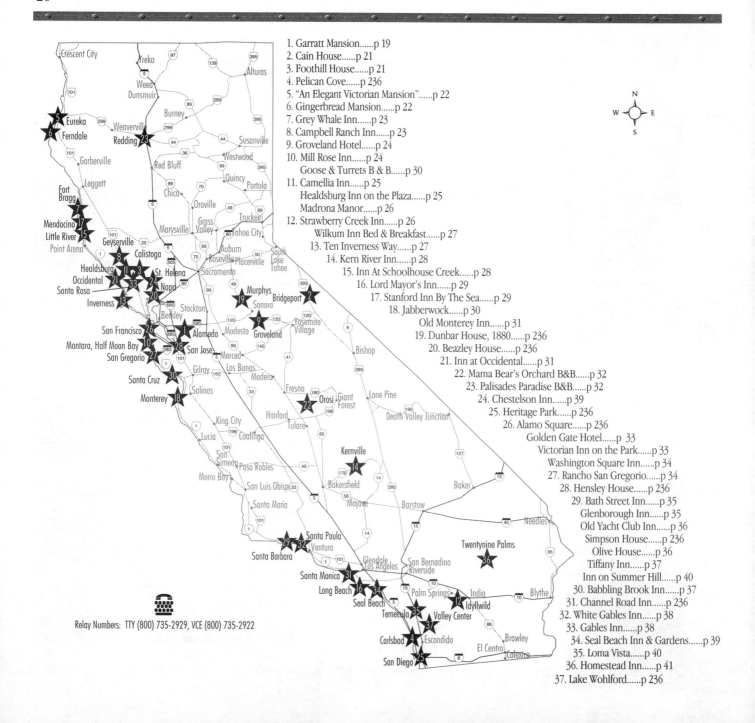

1. Garratt Mansion......p 19
2. Cain House......p 21
3. Foothill House......p 21
4. Pelican Cove......p 236
5. "An Elegant Victorian Mansion"......p 22
6. Gingerbread Mansion......p 22
7. Grey Whale Inn......p 23
8. Campbell Ranch Inn......p 23
9. Groveland Hotel......p 24
10. Mill Rose Inn......p 24
    Goose & Turrets B & B......p 30
11. Camellia Inn......p 25
    Healdsburg Inn on the Plaza......p 25
    Madrona Manor......p 26
12. Strawberry Creek Inn......p 26
    Wilkum Inn Bed & Breakfast......p 27
13. Ten Inverness Way......p 27
14. Kern River Inn......p 28
15. Inn At Schoolhouse Creek......p 28
16. Lord Mayor's Inn......p 29
17. Stanford Inn By The Sea......p 29
18. Jabberwock......p 30
    Old Monterey Inn......p 31
19. Dunbar House, 1880......p 236
20. Beazley House......p 236
21. Inn at Occidental......p 31
22. Mama Bear's Orchard B&B......p 32
23. Palisades Paradise B&B......p 32
24. Chestelson Inn......p 39
25. Heritage Park......p 236
26. Alamo Square......p 236
    Golden Gate Hotel......p 33
    Victorian Inn on the Park......p 33
    Washington Square Inn......p 34
27. Rancho San Gregorio......p 34
28. Hensley House......p 236
29. Bath Street Inn......p 35
    Glenborough Inn......p 35
    Old Yacht Club Inn......p 36
    Simpson House......p 236
    Olive House......p 36
    Tiffany Inn......p 37
    Inn on Summer Hill......p 40
30. Babbling Brook Inn......p 37
31. Channel Road Inn......p 236
32. White Gables Inn......p 38
33. Gables Inn......p 38
34. Seal Beach Inn & Gardens......p 39
35. Loma Vista......p 40
36. Homestead Inn......p 41
37. Lake Wohlford......p 236

Relay Numbers: TTY (800) 735-2929, VCE (800) 735-2922

Bridgeport

B&B

340 Main Street, 93517
(619) 932-7040, Fax (619) 932-7419
Innkeepers: Chris & Marachal Gohlich

$$-
$$$

The Inn has been lovingly restored, with an attention to elegance and comfort. In the evening, after checking-in to your individually, decorated room, you may come down for social hour. Complimentary wine and cheese is served from 5-7 pm daily. The smell of fresh ground coffee will greet you in the morning. After a country breakfast, the pristine beauty of the valley, lakes, and streams await you, for hiking, boating, fishing, hunting, and cross-country skiing. The Inn is less than one hour away in either direction from downhill skiing and Nevada gaming.

Approved by: AAA, ABBA, Mobil

The Cain House

         On Highway 395.

Calistoga (Napa Valley)

B&B

3037 Foothill Blvd., 94515
(800) 942-6933, Fax (707) 942-5692
Innkeepers: Doris & Gus Beckert

$$$/
$$$$$

The Inn is located a half mile north of Calistoga where one finds health spas, mineral and mud baths, and superb restaurants. The Inn is a turn-of-the-century farm house surrounded by trees and wild life. Suites and a luxurious cottage are available, and each is individually decorated with antiques. All suites have private entrances, private bathrooms, a fireplace, and small refrigerator. Air conditioning is available for summer use. Each evening you will enjoy hors d'oeuvres and a complimentary bottle of wine. A gourmet breakfast is served each morning.

Approved by: Mobil

Foothill House

       Take Highway 29 north from Napa to Calistoga. This becomes Highway 128 at the intersection of Lincoln Ave. Continue north on 128 for 1 1/2 miles. The Inn will be on the left.

Eureka

B&B

1406 C Street, 95501

(707) 444-3144

$$/$$$

Innkeepers: Doug & Lily Vieyra

This elegantly restored, 1888 National Historic Landmark is filled with luxurious accommodations. You will enjoy spectacular Victorian architecture outside and authentically furnished opulence inside. The Parlors, Library, and Sitting Room are decorated with family antiques and are wonderful places to read, play games, or relax and converse with others. The guest rooms are individually decorated with your comfort in mind. The Innkeepers are congenial, spirited hosts and will pamper you with a festive breakfast and interesting conversation in a tranquil setting.

Approved by: AAA, Mobil

"An Elegant Victorian Mansion"

From Hwy. 101, travel south on C Street for 10 blocks to the intersection of 14th and C Street.

Ferndale

B&B

400 Berding Street, 95540

(800) 952-4136

$$$/$$$$

Innkeeper: Ken Torbert

Exquisitely turreted, carved, and gabled, the Gingerbread Mansion Inn is truly a visual masterpiece. Completely decorated with antiques and surrounded by formal English gardens, it offers all who stay a chance to step back in time to experience Victorian elegance at its best. The Inn is located in the fairytale village of Ferndale, which has been designated a State Historic Landmark because of all of the well-preserved Victorian homes, shops, and galleries. Nearby are Redwood parks, coastal beaches, and little-known backroads to explore.

Approved by: AAA, ABBA, IIA, Mobil

Gingerbread Mansion Inn

Photo: Pat Cudahy

Take Fembridge/Ferndale Exit. Turn onto bridge. Follow highway into Ferndale. Turn left onto Brown Street (at Bank of America).

8R 6S

BYOB

25
V,M,X
DV,JCB,EN

Fort Bragg

B&B

615 North Main Street, 95437
(800) 382-7244, Fax (707) 964-4408
Innkeepers: John & Colette Bailey

The Grey Whale Inn

$/
$$$

A Mendocino Coast landmark since 1915, this romantic Inn was established in 1978. The extra-wide hallways and doorways and turn-of-the-century, high ceilings contribute to the Inn's spacious, posh comfort. With its classic-revival architecture, the four-story Inn stands proud amidst unsurpassed coastal beauty. Each room is unique and provides the utmost in privacy. Decor is pleasantly eclectic: antiques and reproductions, country quilts, and local art. The Inn is within strolling distance to restaurants, galleries, shops, the Skunk Train, and beaches.

Approved by: AAA, ABBA, IIA, Mobil

Photos: Leona Walden

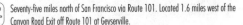 160 miles NW of San Francisco on Pacific Coast Highway 1, via Highways 101(N), 128 (W), 1 (N) to Fort Bragg.

5R

10
V,M

Geyserville

B&B

1475 Canyon Road, 95441
(800) 959-3878, or (707) 857-3476
Innkeepers: Mary Jane & Jerry Campbell

Campbell Ranch Inn

$$$

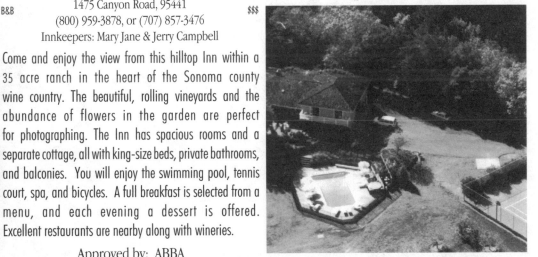

Come and enjoy the view from this hilltop Inn within a 35 acre ranch in the heart of the Sonoma county wine country. The beautiful, rolling vineyards and the abundance of flowers in the garden are perfect for photographing. The Inn has spacious rooms and a separate cottage, all with king-size beds, private bathrooms, and balconies. You will enjoy the swimming pool, tennis court, spa, and bicycles. A full breakfast is selected from a menu, and each evening a dessert is offered. Excellent restaurants are nearby along with wineries.

Approved by: ABBA

Seventy-five miles north of San Francisco via Route 101. Located 1.6 miles west of the Canyon Road Exit off Route 101 at Geyserville.

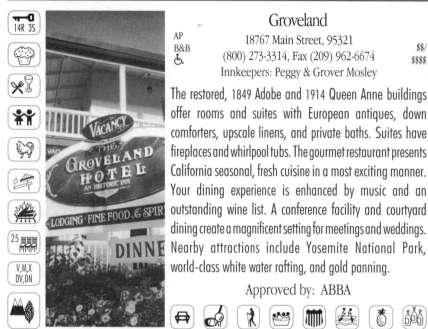

Groveland

Groveland Hotel

AP
B&B
&

18767 Main Street, 95321
(800) 273-3314, Fax (209) 962-6674
Innkeepers: Peggy & Grover Mosley

$$/
$$$$

The restored, 1849 Adobe and 1914 Queen Anne buildings offer rooms and suites with European antiques, down comforters, upscale linens, and private baths. Suites have fireplaces and whirlpool tubs. The gourmet restaurant presents California seasonal, fresh cuisine in a most exciting manner. Your dining experience is enhanced by music and an outstanding wine list. A conference facility and courtyard dining create a magnificent setting for meetings and weddings. Nearby attractions include Yosemite National Park, world-class white water rafting, and gold panning.

Approved by: ABBA

14R 3S

From the San Francisco Bay area, take Highway 680 to 580 (E). At Tracy, take Highway 120 to Groveland Highway 120. Highway 120 is also Main Street in Groveland.

Half Moon Bay

Mill Rose Inn

B&B

615 Mill Street, 94019
(800) 900-7673, Fax (415) 726-3031
Innkeepers: Eve & Terry Baldwin

$$$$-
$$$$$

This wonderfully romantic Inn invites you to spend a night or a weekend in the comfortable luxury of an English country garden by the sea. All the conveniences of a World-class hotel and the charm and gracious services of a small, Country Inn are beautifully combined. You are within walking distance of the ocean and the historic old town district, renowned for boutiques, galleries, and fine restaurants. Uncompromising attention to detail and quality, as well as the pervading sense of tranquility and warm caring service, will transform your visit into an unforgettable experience.

Approved by: AAA

6R 6S
BYOB

From Highway 280 or 101 take Highway 92 (W) to Half Moon Bay. Turn left at first signal onto Main Street, then take first right onto Mill Street. Inn is located 2 blocks west on right side.

Photo: Thomas Haworth

Healdsburg

B&B

211 North Street, 95448
(707) 433-8182, Fax (707) 433-8130
Innkeepers: Ray & Del Lewand

$-
$$$

Camellia Inn

An 1869 Italianate Victorian townhouse, the Inn sits on one half acre. Antiques fill the spacious bedrooms, each with its own private bath. Several rooms have whirlpool tubs for two, gas fireplaces, or private entrances. Double parlors with twin, marble fireplaces and a dining room with a massive, mahogany mantle return you to the elegance of yesteryear. A delicious breakfast buffet is served and afternoon refreshments are offered in the parlor or by the pool. The Inn is on a quiet, residential street, within walking distance of fine restaurants, wine tasting rooms, and shops.

Approved by: Mobil

From San Francisco, take Hwy. 101(N) to Central Healdsburg Exit and turn right onto North Street. From Calistoga, take Hwy. 128 to Alexander Vly Rd. and turn left onto Healdsburg Ave. Follow to North Street.

Healdsburg

B&B

110 Matheson Street, 95448
(800) 431-8663, or (707) 433-6991
Innkeepers: Genny Jenkins & LeRoy Steek

$$$/
$$$$

Healdsburg Inn on the Plaza

This historic Wells Fargo Building of 1900 is now a quiet Inn where history and hospitality meet. There are gift shops and an art gallery for browsing on the main floor. A grand staircase in the gallery takes you to the guest suites; all with private baths, some with fireplaces and tubs for two. Each room is furnished with American antiques and decorated in the colors of the sunrise or the sunset. The solarium and the roof garden provide a charming spot for afternoon coffee and cakes as well as breakfast. There are books and games, a television and VCR, soft music, and fresh-baked cookies.

Approved by: Mobil

Take Hwy. 101(N) from San Francisco to Healdsburg. Exit at the Central Healdsburg exit onto Healdsburg Ave. Turn right onto Matheson. The Inn is on the left.

18R 3S

Healdsburg

B&B

1001 Westside Road, 95448
(800) 258-4003, Fax (707) 433-0703
Innkeepers: John & Carol Muir

$$$-
$$$$$

Madrona Manor

Deep in the wine country, this Inn conveys a sense of homey elegance with country ambiance and gracious hospitality. Guests find the enveloping warmth one feels at a friend's home combined with elegant decor, stately antique furniture, luxurious amenities, thick terry robes, and an expansive breakfast buffet. You feel you have been transported to a European country estate. Todd Muir's Restaurant at the Inn is equal to any in San Francisco, offering fabulous cuisine, plus a gold-medal-winning wine list. An elegant place to stay in the Sonoma Wine Country.

Approved by: IIA

65 miles north of San Francisco; 12 miles north of Santa Rosa. 2nd Healdsburg Exit. Sharp left turn under freeway on Mill Street.

9R 1S

Idyllwild

B&B

26370 Highway 243, 92549
(800) 262-8969, Fax (909) 659-3202
Innkeepers: Diana Dugan & Jim Goff

$/
$$$

Strawberry Creek Inn

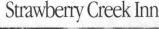

The Inn is only a short, 15 minute stroll along the creek to the village. The cedar-shingled Inn is homey and attractive with its stained glass and dormer windows and surrounding giant oak and stately evergreens. Decks offer restful, hammock settings from which to view the grounds and wildlife. Inside, the Inn is equally relaxing with the large living room, fireplace, comfortable couches, piano alcove, and extensive library. The glassed-in dining porch overlooks a colorful garden. Individual rooms are appointed with country antiques and crafts.

Approved by: AAA, Mobil

On the approach to town from the south on Highway 243, the Inn is located just past South Circle Drive.

Idyllwild

P. O. Box 1115, Hwy. 243 at Toll Gate Road, 92549

(800) 659-4086, or (909) 659-4087

B&B

Innkeepers: Annamae Chambers & Barbara Jones

$/ $$

Wilkum Inn Bed & Breakfast

Set in a pine and cedar forest against a spectacular backdrop of towering mountains and sheer rock faces, this Inn offers you an "at home" feeling. The warmth of lace curtains, handmade quilts, and family antiques is enhanced by the pine interior and original wood stair railing. You may be tempted to curl up in front of the river rock fireplace with a good book. The comfortable guest rooms reflect the Innkeepers attention to detail. Breakfast treats may include crêpes, waffles, or the very special abelskivers. There are always hot drinks available and afternoon snacks.

Approved by: AAA

From I-10 at Banning, take Idyllwild off-ramp. Follow Hwy. 243 to Idyllwild. From the south, take Hwy. 74 to Mt. Center, follow Hwy. 243 to Idyllwild. The Inn is 3/4 mile south of the village.

Inverness

B&B

10 Inverness Way, 94937

(415) 669-1648

Innkeeper: Mary Davies

$$$

Ten Inverness Way

The Inn for books, long walks, and cottage gardens. There are at least four full days of varied hiking at Point Reyes National Seashore, and you can end your day with a soak in the hot tub and great food at local restaurants. Then sprawl out and cozy up in the living room with a good book and a mug of herbal tea to send you to sleep. The beds are so comfortable that the Innkeepers have to lead you by your nose to the sunroom for breakfast. Count on good, strong coffee and specialties like Banana Buttermilk Buckwheat Pancakes.

Approved by: Mobil

From Highway 1 in Olema, turn onto Bear Valley Road. Go 3 miles to stop sign, left on Sir Francis Drake. Go 4 miles to Inverness, left on Inverness Way.

6R

BYOB

12

V,M

Kernville

B&B
119 Kern Drive, 93238
(619) 376-6750
Innkeepers: Jack & Carita Prestwich

$/
$$

Kern River Inn

This stately two-story B&B with a wraparound porch is located on the wild, scenic Kern River in the quaint, western town of Kernville in Sequoia National Forest. The casual, country decor reflects the personalities of the owners. Generous used brick, river and field rocks, and oak accents are found throughout. Each room is individually decorated and named for local or historical events or landmarks. Breakfast specialities are "GIANT" homebaked cinnamon rolls, stuffed french toast or sweetheart waffles.

Approved by: AAA

          55 miles Northeast of US 99 via State Highway 178(E) or 45 miles west of State Highway 14 via 178(W).

Little River

EP
7051 N. Highway 1, 95456
(707) 937-5525
Innkeepers: Linda Wilson & Peter Fearey

$/
$$$

The Inn at Schoolhouse Creek

Facing the Pacific Ocean like a small, rural community, the Inn has offered lodging to coastal visitors since the 1930's. Separate cottages and rooms all have ocean views, most have fireplaces, and some kitchens are available. Located on 10 acres of spectacular gardens, meadow, and forest with a creek, the sense of quiet and peace of this country environment offers relaxation at its best. Charming country-style decor, exceptionally clean rooms, and complete privacy best describe this spot just three miles south of the historic village of Mendocino.

Approved by: AAA

          The Inn is on Coast Hwy. 1, just south of Little River (three miles south of Mendocino and six miles north of the junction of Hwy. 128 and Coast Hwy. 1).

Long Beach

B&B

435 Cedar Avenue, 90802
(310) 436-0324, Fax (310) 436-0324
Innkeepers: Laura & Reuben Brasser

$$

Lord Mayor's Bed & Breakfast Inn

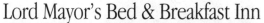
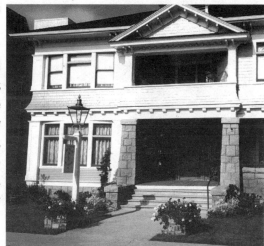

The welcome sign in front is the first clue to the warm and comfortable experience that you will enjoy once you pass through the door. The Mayor no longer lives at the Inn but the hospitality begun years ago still lingers and is enhanced by the Innkeepers. Every room is unique and every corner reflects the elegance of the early 1900's. You will wake up to the aroma of Laura's cinnamon coffee cake and a scrumptious breakfast. A good night's sleep and fine food; what a lovely way to start your day of business or pleasure.

Approved by: ABBA

From the 710 Freeway, exit on the 6th Street downtown off-ramp. Go 4 streets to Cedar Street, turn right. The Inn is 1 1/2 blocks down.

Mendocino

Highway 1 & Comptche-Ukiah Road, Box 487, 95460

B&B   (800) 331-8884, Fax (707) 937-0305 $$$$

Innkeepers: Joan & Jeff Stanford

Stanford Inn By The Sea

The Stanford's elegantly rustic lodge is quintessential Mendocino. Atop a meadow sloping to the sea, the Inn combines paneled rooms and woodburning fireplaces with amenities found at the finest hotels. The expansive grounds are home to the Innkeepers' California Certified Organic nursery and Big River Llamas. If you decide not to spend all of your time snuggled in front of the fireplace, the Inn's Catch A Canoe & Bicycles, Too! offers fine mountain bikes for exploring the headlands and canoes and kayaks for trips along the scenic Big River Estuary.

Approved by: AAA

At the intersection of Coast Hwy. 1 and Comptche-Ukiah Road.

Montara

B&B   835 George Street, P. O. Box 937, 94037-0937 $$
(415) 728-5451, Fax (415) 728-0141
Innkeepers: Raymond & Emily Hoche-Mong

Only 20 minutes from the San Francisco Airport, the Inn is also just 1/2 mile from Pacific beaches. The 1908 villa features four-course breakfasts, comfortable beds, afternoon tea with savouries, and quiet gardens with a hammock, bocce ball court, and mascot geese. This is a convenient headquarters for day excursions to San Francisco, Silicon Valley, Berkeley, Monterey Aquarium, Carmel, or Sausalito. Your well-travelled hosts are pilots who have lived in the South and in Europe; places whose customs and cuisines are reflected in the food and the hospitality at the Inn.

Approved by: AAA

Goose & Turrets B & B

From San Francisco take Freeway 101(S) to Freeway 280(S) to Hwy. 1(S) for 12 miles to Montara. From San Jose take Freeway 280(N) to Hwy. 92(W) to Half Moon Bay. Go north 8 miles to Montara.

Monterey

B&B   598 Laine Street, 93940 $$-
(408)372-4777 $$$$
Innkeepers: Jim & Barbara Allen

This Inn has secluded gardens overlooking Monterey Bay complete with waterfalls . "Cannery Row" is just four blocks below, and the Monterey Bay Aquarium, restaurants, shops, and ocean are within easy walking distance. Seals and sea lions can be heard from the patio and sun porch, and a view of the bay can be seen from all three floors. Each room is as unique as its name, all of which come from the poem "Jabberwocky." Surely "things are not always as they seem" here, but that's what makes the Inn special. Enjoy a full breakfast by the fireplace, hors d'oeuvres, and cookies.

Approved by: Mobil

The Jabberwock

Take 1 (S) to 68 (W). Follow road through forest for 2 1/2 miles. Turn right at Prescott (stoplight). Go to Pine, turn right to Hoffman. Turn left, go 4 blocks to Laine. The Inn is located on the right corner.

Monterey

B&B

500 Martin Street, 93940
(800) 350-2344, or (408) 375-8284
Innkeepers: Ann & Gene Swett

$$$$$

Old Monterey Inn

Surrounded by over an acre of English gardens, this award-winning Inn is an exclusive retreat hidden amidst the trees. The Tudor-style mansion is tastefully blended with many modern comforts. Each room has a private bath and comfortable sitting area. Many have woodburning fireplaces, stained glass windows, or sky-windows. A gourmet breakfast is served each morning as well as complimentary afternoon tea and evening wine and hors d'oeuvres. The Inn offers a full concierge service for restaurant reservations, bay cruises, and tickets to the aquarium.

Approved by: AAA, IIA, Mobil

Photos: Grant Huntington

Take highway 1 to the Soledad-Munras exit (from the north). Cross Munras Ave., then right on Pacific Street—From the south take the Munras exit, make an immediate left on Soledad Drive, then a right on Pacific Street. Either way, proceed 1/2 mile to Martin St. on your left.

Occidental

B&B

3657 Church Street, P. O. Box 857, 95465
(800) 522-6324, Fax (707) 874-1078
Innkeeper: Jack Bullard

$$$$

Inn At Occidental

This elegant Victorian Inn is one of the secrets of the Sonoma Wine Country. It is a secluded place surrounded by country-side and redwoods of unsurpassed beauty. It is the perfect spot for rejuvenating the mind and body, yet is only one hour north of the Golden Gate Bridge near the Sonoma Coast. The Inn is furnished with original art and antiques and offers a sunny, English cottage garden with overstuffed lounges. Enjoy warm days and cool nights...wicker rockers on the porch and down comforters. For the adventuresome, there is kayaking, golf, local wineries, enzyme baths, and hiking.

Approved by: AAA

Photos: Tom Rider

Take Rt. 101(N) to Petaluma and then Rt. 116(W) to Sebastopol. Follow Rt. 12 toward Bodega Bay for 6.4 miles. Turn north at the sign to Freestone and Occidental. Go 3.7 miles to the stop sign. Turn right up the hill to the Inn.

Orosi

B&B

42723 Road 128, 93647

(800) 530-BEAR, or (209) 528-3614

Innkeepers: Lita Fernandez & Betty Bernard

$/ $$$

Mama Bear's Orchard

While staying here you will wake up to the aroma of freshly brewed coffee and the sound of roosters crowing in the distance. In the garden, flowers surround you as birds sing, water trickles in the Koi pond, and a multitude of hummingbirds feed. The scrumptious country breakfast includes Betty's homemade jams, jellies, pastries, and bread along with fresh eggs from the chickens. Outside, the baby goat loves attention, the ducks frolic in the pond, and the rabbits munch away. The Inn is located at the foot of the Sierras, a stepping stone to the Sequoia Kings Canyon National Park.

Approved by: AAA

From San Francisco, take Hwy. 99(S) to the Manning Ave. exit. Go east past Reedley to Hwy. 63, (about 18 miles). Turn right onto Hwy. 63 and go past Avenue 428. The Inn is on the right before Avenue 424.

Redding

B&B

1200 Palisades Avenue, 96003

(916) 223-5305

Innkeeper: Gail Goetz

$/ $$

Palisades Paradise B&B

You will feel as though you are in Paradise when you watch the magnificent sunsets from the Bluffs overlooking the Sacramento River. Enjoy breath-taking views of the Sacramento River, the city, and the surrounding mountains from this beautiful, newly-decorated, contemporary home with its garden spa, fireplaces, wide screen TV-VCR, and warm atmosphere. Palisades Paradise is a serene setting for a quiet hideaway, yet it is conveniently located one mile from shopping, fine dining, and Interstate 5. Water-skiing and river rafting are nearby.

Approved by: ABBA

From I-5 (N) take Hilltop Exit. Go left (N) 1 mile. Turn left onto Palisades Avenue. From I-5 (S), take Lake Blvd. Exit, turn right and go .4 miles. Left onto Palisades Avenue. Inn is 1.5 miles on right.

San Francisco

B&B

775 Bush Street, 94108
(415) 392-3702, Fax (415) 392-6202
Innkeepers: John & Renate Kenaston

$-
$$

Golden Gate Hotel

This is a charming, European-style Bed and Breakfast Hotel with a friendly, cozy atmosphere, birdcage elevator, wicker and antique furnishings, and fresh flowers! The Nob Hill location is ideal for walking. The Inn is just two blocks up from Union Square and central to about all San Francisco has to offer. The cable cars to Fisherman's Wharf and Ghirardelli Square stop on the corner, and the south gate of Chinatown is just two blocks east. Continental breakfast and afternoon tea are served in the Parlor, and tours pick up from the Hotel.

Approved by: ABBA

The Golden Gate Hotel is centrally located in the heart of San Francisco, 2 blocks north of Union Square on Bush Street between Mason and Powell. Approach from Mason Street as Bush is one-way running west (Mason) to east (Powell).

San Francisco

B&B

301 Lyon Street, 94117
(800) 435-1967, Fax (415) 931-1830
Innkeepers: Lisa & William Benau

$$/
$$$

Victorian Inn on the Park

This registered, historic landmark, also known as the "Clunie House," was built in 1897, Queen Victoria's Diamond Jubilee year. Its restoration seeks to retain and revive late 19th century elegance. The Inn is located adjacent to Golden Gate Park in an area famed for its noble Victorians. You are welcomed into the Inn's elegant parlor for a romantic and unforgettable experience. Enjoy the warmth of the fire and the essence of the 1890's. All of the guest rooms are unique, and each reflects Victorian San Francisco. Breakfast is a special time as the Innkeepers help you plan your day.

Approved by: Mobil

From San Francisco Airport, take 101 (N) towards Golden Gate Bridge Exit onto Fell Street. Go 1 mile west on Fell Street and turn right onto Lyon Street.

San Francisco

Washington Square Inn

B&B

1660 Stockton Street, 94133
(800) 388-0220, Fax (415) 397-7242
Innkeeper: Brooks Bayly

$$-
$$$$

This is a special place for those who care about quiet and comfort with liberal dashes of elegance. The Inn offers the charm and hospitality of a Country Inn, just one block from Telegraph Hill in the heart of the historic North Beach area. You will enjoy flaky croissants, fresh juice and fruit, and coffee served in bed or at the table by the hearth. Afternoon tea and hors d'oeuvres are available for guests as well as their visitors. Each guest room has been individually decorated and furnished with English and French antiques. For the business or leisure traveller, the Inn is a delight.

Approved by: ABBA

From the SFO Airport, go north on Hwy. 101 toward Bay Bridge. Exit at 4th St., go one block on Bryant and turn left onto 3rd St. Cross Market St. and turn left onto Columbus. Turn right onto Stockton. The Inn is at the corner of Stockton and Filbert.

San Gregorio

Rancho San Gregorio

B&B

Route 1, Box 54, 94074
(415) 747-0810, Fax (415) 747-0184
Innkeepers: Bud & Lee Raynor

$$

Graceful arches and a red tile roof characterize this Mission-style Inn set on a hillside with 15 wooded acres and a creek. Built as a family home in 1971, the Inn's rural setting and American oak antiques reflect the casual elegance of an early California lifestyle in the days of the Spanish land grants. Enjoy friendly hospitality with complimentary beverages, snacks, and a harvest breakfast feast that includes products grown on the ranch. The Inn is close to miles of beaches and redwood hiking trails. San Francisco, Santa Cruz, and most Bay locations are within one hour.

Approved by: AAA, ABBA, Mobil

Located on Hwy. 84(E), 5 miles from Hwy. 1 and west 15 miles from 280 Freeway.

Santa Barbara

Bath Street Inn

B&B

1720 Bath Street, 93101
(805) 682-9680 or (800) 778-BATH
Innkeepers: Susan Brown & Lynn Kirby

$$-
$$$

This 1890 Queen Anne Victorian is located close to the heart of downtown Santa Barbara. With its big comfortable chairs, roaring fire, and friendly golden retriever, the Inn reflects the casual, relaxing style of its owner. The guest rooms are a charming mix with the luxury and comfort of added modern amenities. Enjoy a home-cooked breakfast in the dining room or out in the garden. Later in the day, visit with other guests over tea or a glass of wine and dine at one of the fabulous restaurants nearby.

Approved by: AAA

        From South: Exit 101 on Arrellaga; left on Bath to 1720.
From North: Exit 101 on Carrillo. East to Bath; left to 1720.

Santa Barbara

Glenborough Inn

B&B

1327 Bath Street, 93101
(800) 962-0589, Fax (805) 564-2369
Innkeepers: Michael, Steve, and Ken

$$/
$$$$

The Inn with its three homes, reflecting Victorian and California Craftsman eras, is referred to by many guests as "Santa Barbara's most romantic Bed and Breakfast Inn." Luxuriate in the privately-reserved garden spa and pamper yourself with a hot, gourmet breakfast served in your room or in the gardens. Relax around the parlor fireplace or in the gardens as you enjoy a refreshment or quiet moment. The Inn is located in the heart of Santa Barbara, three blocks from fine shops, restaurants, museums, theatres, nightlife, and just 13 blocks to the beach.

Approved by: AAA, Mobil

        Take US 101 to Carrillo St. Exit (not Cabrillo). Go east 2 blocks to Bath. North on Bath to 1327 (on the Left).

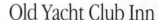

Santa Barbara

Old Yacht Club Inn

B&B

431 Corona Del Mar Drive, 93103
(805) 962-1277, Fax (805) 962-3989
Innkeepers: Nancy Donaldson & Sandy Hunt

$$/$$$

Experience turn-of-the-century charm by the sea at this Inn. Located within one block of Santa Barbara's beautiful East Beach, the Inn is known for hospitality and fine food. Opened in 1980 as Santa Barbara's first Bed & Breakfast, the Inn is housed in two vintage homes, side-by-side. All rooms have private baths, some have balconies and decks, and one has a whirlpool tub. A special highlight at the Inn is a five-course, prixe fixe dinner on Saturday evenings. Your visit includes a full breakfast, evening wine hour, bikes, beach chairs, and towels.

Approved by: AAA

From Highway 101, take Cabrillo Blvd. Exit, Route 225. Turn west on Cabrillo. Travel 1 mile to Corona Del Mar Drive and turn right.

Santa Barbara

Olive House Inn

B&B

1604 Olive Street, 93101
(805) 962-4902, Fax (805) 899-2754
Innkeeper: Lois Gregg

$$/$$$

You will enjoy the quiet comfort and gracious hospitality of this lovingly restored, 1904 Craftsman-style home located in a residential neighborhood near the Mission and Downtown. Sip a fine wine in the terraced garden, on the large sundeck, or in the living room replete with bay windows, redwood paneling, fireplace, and studio grand piano. You will relish the ocean and mountain views, private decks, and hot tubs. A delicious, full breakfast is served in the large, sunny dining room. A tea table is set for your pleasure and evening sherry and exquisite chocolates await you as well.

Approved by: AAA

From the south, exit at Milpas and go 1.8 miles. Turn right onto Olive St. From the north, exit at Mission and go left for nine blocks. Turn right onto Laguna. Go east on Arrellaga and turn left into the first long driveway.

California

7R 2S

Santa Barbara

B&B   1323 De la Vina Street, 93101
(805) 963-2283, Fax (805) 962-0994
Innkeepers: Goldie Brusby & Carol MacDonald

$/
$$$$

Tiffany Inn

Classic antiques and period furnishings welcome you throughout this beautifully restored, 1898 Victorian home. Guest rooms all have garden or mountain views and most have fireplaces. The two suites feature whirlpool spas. The Inn is a short walk from exclusive, downtown shops, restaurants, galleries, theaters, and museums. A sumptuous breakfast is served on the garden veranda and you will enjoy wine and cheese in front of the main fireplace in the afternoon. After a relaxing evening on the town, homebaked cookies await you before a restful evening.

Approved by: AAA, Mobil

From 101(N), take Arrellaga to De la Vina and turn right. From 101(S), take Mission. Follow to De la Vina and turn right.

12R

Santa Cruz

B&B
♿

1025 Laurel Street, 95060
(800) 866-1131, Fax (408) 427-2457
Innkeeper: Helen King

$$-
$$$$

Babbling Brook Inn

Cascading waterfalls, an historic waterwheel, a meandering creek, and a romantic gazebo grace an acre of gardens, pines, and redwoods surrounding this wonderful Inn. All 12 rooms are decorated in Country-French style, and most offer a cozy fireplace and private deck. Some rooms provide deep-soaking jet bath tubs. You will enjoy a large, country breakfast and afternoon wine and cheese during your visit. Helen's prize-winning cookies alone are worth the trip! The location is perfect for walking to the beach, shopping, or tennis. Over 200 restaurants are within an easy drive.

Approved by: AAA, ABBA, IIA, Mobil

Highway 17 to Highway 1 (N) towards Half Moon Bay. Exit 1 (Mission Street) on Laurel Street. Left 1 1/2 blocks.

Santa Paula

B&B

715 E. Santa Paula Street, 93060

(805) 933-3041

$$

Innkeepers: R. L. "Bob" & Ellen Smith

Step back in time and discover the elegance of yesteryear at this Inn nestled in the picturesque, historic district of Santa Paula. The majestic, 1894 Queen Anne Victorian is beautifully restored with the romantic spirit of a past era. You will experience warmth, hospitality, and country charm in the rooms, each decorated with exquisite antique furnishings and unique designer touches. Breakfast each morning is a delight with homemade specialties, fine china, crystal, silver, fresh flowers, and candlelight. If you are lucky, they will be serving Macadamia Nut Belgium Waffles!

Approved by: AAA

White Gables Inn

Take I-5(N) to 126(W) into Santa Paula. Take 10th Street exit, go north on 10th Street to Santa Paula Street. Go west to the Inn. Or, 101(N) to 126(E) into Santa Paula. Take 10th Street to Santa Paula Street. Go west to the Inn.

Santa Rosa

B&B

4257 Petaluma Hill Road, 95404

(707) 585-7777, Fax (707) 584-5634

$$-
$$$$

Innkeepers: Mike & Judy Ogne

This grand Victorian Inn proudly serves on the National Historic Homes Register. Sitting on three and one half acres in the countryside south of Santa Rosa, the Inn is in the middle of the Sonoma County Wine Country. Its location is perfect for touring the craggy north coast or the giant redwood forest in the Russian River area. Rooms are spacious with lovely Victorian country decor. Goose down comforters, fresh flowers, and a literary selection invite guests to snuggle in. The Inn pleases the senses and stimulates the soul.

Approved by: Mobil

The Gables Inn

From 101, Exit Rohnert Park Expressway. Turn east 2 1/2 miles to dead end. Turn left (north) to Inn. 4 miles north on Petaluma Hill Road.

Seal Beach

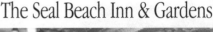
The Seal Beach Inn & Gardens

B&B

212 5th Street, 90740
(310) 493-2416, Fax (310) 799-0483
Innkeepers: Marjorie Bettenhausen & Harty Schmaehl

$$$/
$$$$

Southern California's original Bed & Breakfast Inn, is a beautifully restored historic Country Inn, one block from the Pacific Ocean. Located just south of Long Beach, the Inn artfully expresses this area's colorful history. It is French-Mediterranean in appearance, with fountains, antique street lights, an ornate iron gate, lush gardens, and exquisite furnishings. A layered patina of beauty has been achieved through years of loving attention. Honeymoon/Anniversary packages and corporate services are available.

Approved by: AAA, ABBA, IIA, Mobil

Left on Seal Beach Blvd. off 405 Freeway. Right on Pacific Coast Highway. Left on 5th Street.

St. Helena (Napa Valley)

Chestelson House

B&B

1417 Kearney Street, 94574
(707) 963-2238, (800) 959-4505
Innkeeper: Jackie Sweet

$$/
$$$$

This might have been your grandmother's house that you visited as a child. Cookies are baked every day, and there's lemonade and iced tea in summer or cocoa and hot tea in winter. A scrumptious, full breakfast is served with an ever-changing variety of dishes. You have an opportunity to chat about your travel adventures at breakfast or during the social hour. Jackie delights in helping to plan your days according to your interests. Maybe it's a wine tasting or a production tour, architectural walk, or gallery and museum visits.

Approved by: Mobil

Photo: geoffrey fulton

North from Napa on Highway 29 to St. Helena. Left at Adams (signal light) and 2 blocks to Kearney. Turn right. Second house on the left.

Summerland

2520 Lillie Avenue, 93067
(800) 845-5566, Fax (805) 969-9998
Innkeeper: Verlinda Richardson

B&B

$$$$-
$$$$$

Inn on Summer Hill

This California Craftsman styled Inn is in a seaside village just five minutes south of Santa Barbara. Built in 1989, the Inn's mini-suites offer ocean views, fireplaces, Jacuzzi® tubs, canopy beds, VCP's, stereo cassette players, and fine antiques. You will enjoy sumptuous, gourmet breakfasts, hors d'oeuvres, wine, fresh-baked cookies, and dessert served in the candlelit dining room featuring a "Teapot Collection", a pine farm table with barnyard animal chairs ,and a glowing fireplace. This combines to create an elegant European-English Country ambiance that is the perfect setting for love and romance.

Approved by: AAA, ABBA

The Inn is on the north side of U.S. 101. Driving northbound or southbound, take the Summerland exit.

Temecula

33350 La Serena Way, 92591
(909) 676-7047
Innkeepers: Betty & Dick Ryan

B&B

$/
$$$

Loma Vista

This is a California Mission style home, designed and built by the Innkeepers as a Bed and Breakfast. Temecula was named by the Indians, and the name means "mist rising from the ground." The town was on the Butterfield Stage Route from San Francisco to Missouri...hence the reason behind the many antique stores and the old west flavor of the town. The area's unique, micro-climate favors the growing of fine wine grapes.

Approved by: AAA

Exit off "15" on Rancho California Road. Go East 4 1/2 miles. Take the first dirt road, on left, past Callaway Winery.

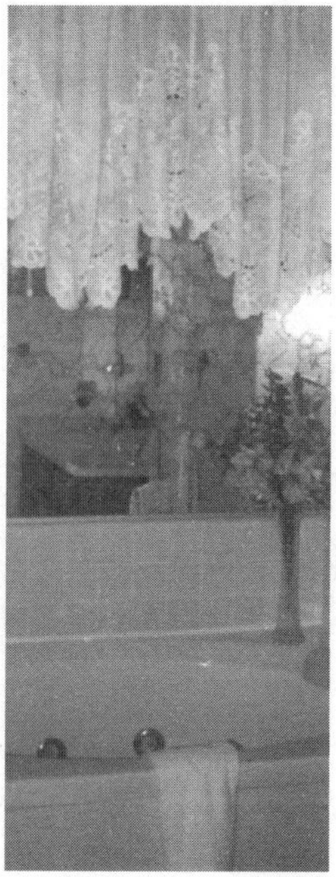

Twentynine Palms, CA

74153 Two Mile Road, 92277

(619) 367-0030

Innkeeper: Jerri Hagman - Judy Harness, Manager

B&B

$/ $$$

Homestead Inn

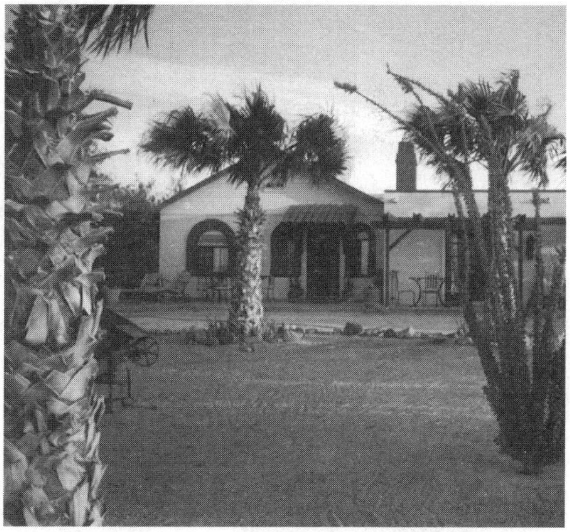

Upon entering this 15 acre property, built in 1930, you'll be impressed with the art and antique furnishings. The common room library has information on the history of the area, including Joshua Tree National Park which is less than 2 miles away. The large flagstone fireplace adds warmth and atmosphere while you share wine and hors d'oeuvres with other guests. During your stay, breakfast is served on the patios, weather permitting, allowing a full panoramic view of the mountains. Hospitality abounds at the Inn with great attention paid to details and comfort.

Approved by: AAA

From I-10 travelling Highway 62 east, turn left on Adobe Road and proceed north to Two Mile Road. Turn right, proceed about 1/2 mile. You will see a large sign and driveway on the right side of road.

2R 1S

25

V,M

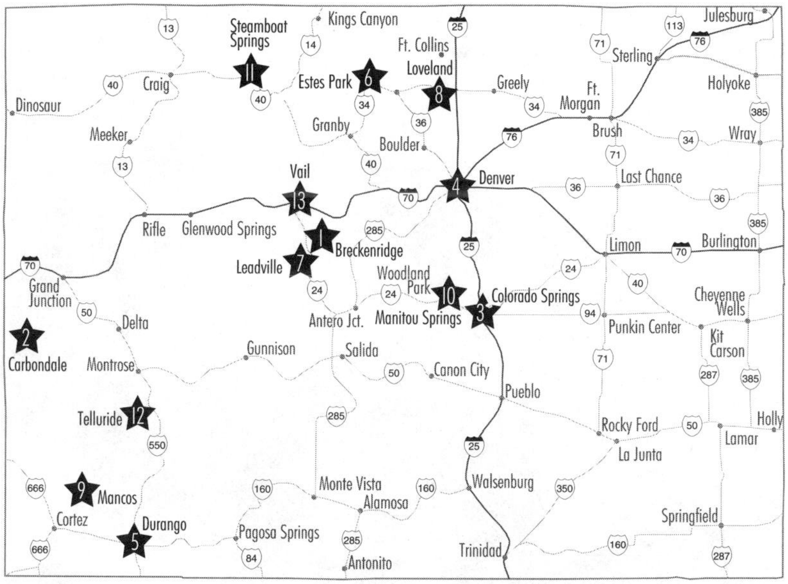

Colorado

Relay Numbers: TTY (800) 659-2656, VCE (800) 659-3656

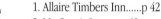

Breckenridge

Allaire Timbers Inn

B&B

9511 Highway 9/So. Main Street, 80424
(303) 453-7530, Fax (303) 453-8699
Innkeepers: Jack & Kathy Gumph

$$$/
$$$$

Nestled in the trees, at the end of historic Main Street, this log and stone B&B was designed and built in 1991 using Colorado Lodgepole pine. Rooms are individually decorated and named after Colorado Mountain passes. Two elegant suites boast private hot tubs and river-rock fireplaces. Relax by a crackling fire in the Great Room, spend quiet time together in the sun room or loft, or unwind in the outdoor spa with spectacular views of Breckenridge and the Ten Mile Range. Hearty mountain breakfasts, afternoon treats, and personalized hospitality are found year-round.

Approved by: AAA, ABBA, BBIC

1-70 to Exit 203, Frisco (87 miles west of Denver). Take Highway 9 south to Breckenridge and Main Street. Continue through town past Boreas Pass Road to sign on west side.

Carbondale

Mt. Sopris Inn

B&B

0165 Mt. Sopris Ranch Road, Box 126, 81623
(800) 437-8675
Innkeeper: Ellen Koch

$$/
$$$$$

Located on 14 acres, this was the home of a famed, Aspen Ski Corporation president. Seven hundred and seventy-five feet of the Crystal River flows at the base of a 40-foot high bluff. Docile llamas graze in the pastures and gentle breezes whistle through the pine trees as you relax by the pool and outdoor Jacuzzi®. You will be inspired by the magnificent panorama of the Crystal Valley to Mount Sopris, McClure Pass, and Chair Mountain. This is a relaxing, joyous setting for any occasion.

Approved by: BBIC

Three miles SW of intersection of Highways 82 & 133. Turn right on Mt. Sopris Ranch Road, then right up the drive.

6R 4S

BYOB

**V,M,X
DN,DV**

Colorado Springs

B&B
1102 W. Pikes Peak Avenue, 80904
(719) 471-3980
Innkeepers: Sallie & Welling Clark

$/
$$

Holden House 1902 B&B

This 1902 storybook Victorian Inn is centrally located in a residential area near historic "Old Colorado City." The Inn is filled with antiques and family treasures. Guest rooms are decorated with period furnishings and three romantic suites boast "tubs for two," fireplaces, mountain views, and more! Gourmet breakfasts might include blueberry-corn muffins and Sallie's famous Southwestern Eggs Fiesta. Complimentary coffee and tea, fresh baked cookies, and turn-down service are just some of the special touches offered. Friendly resident cats "Mingtoy" and "Muffin" will greet you.

Approved by: AAA, BBIC, Mobil

I-25 to Highway 24, Manitou Springs Exit (141). Turn left on 24 westbound and make the first right on 8th St. Turn left on W. Colorado Avenue. Go 2 1/2 blocks to 11th St., turn right, and continue down 1 block. Holden House is located on the corner of 11th and W. Pikes Peak.

7R 2S

10

**V,M,X
DN,DV**

Denver

B&B
1572 Race Street, 80206
(800) 92-MARNE, Fax (303) 331-0623
Innkeepers: The Peiker Family

$$-
$$$$$

Castle Marne

You will fall under the spell of one of Denver's grandest historic mansions. Your stay combines old world elegance and Victorian charm with modern day convenience and comfort. Each guest room is luxurious and some offer whirlpool tubs for two or private hot tubs. Enjoy Afternoon Tea in the Parlor and a full breakfast in the original, cherry-paneled, formal dining room. The Inn is a certified Denver Landmark building, listed on the National Register of Historic Structures, and is in the heart of Denver's newly designated Wyman Historic District.

Approved by: AAA, ABBA, BBIC, IIA, Mobil

From Colfax Avenue, turn north onto Race Street. The Inn will be on the right.

10R 4S

15
V,M,X
DN,DV

Denver

Queen Anne Bed & Breakfast Inn

B&B
2147 Tremont Place, 80205
(303) 296-6666, or (800) 432-inns (-4667)
Innkeeper: Tom King

$/
$$$

The Inn's two side-by-side historic Victorian mansions face a quiet park in downtown Denver. The Inn caters to business travellers during the week and almost one third of them are business women. The reasons include the downtown location, warm hospitality, and distinctive accommodations. All rooms have period antiques, fresh flowers, chamber music, private baths, phones, and desks. Free parking is available. The Inn is also a well-known romantic getaway. The suites are galleries as well for the paintings of Audubon, Calder, Remington, and Rockwell.

Approved by: AAA, ABBA, BBIC, Mobil

I-25 (north or south) and I-70 (from west) turn east on Sixth Street or Colfax. Left on Logan to deadend at Benedict Park; then left and immediate right onto Tremont Place. From Denver Int. Airport take I-70 toward city. Turn left on Colorado Blvd., right on 17th Ave. and right on Logan.

10R 6S

BYOB

20
V,M

Durango

The Leland House

B&B
721 E. Second Avenue, 81301
(800) 664-1920, Fax (303) 385-1967
Innkeepers: Kirk, Diane & Kara Komick

$/
$$$$

You'll stay in one of ten, charming rooms in a lovingly restored, two-story, brick apartment building built in 1927. Each room is named after an historic figure associated with The Leland House. The interior decor is accented with photos, memorabilia, and framed biographies of these important figures. All rooms have private baths, some with kitchens. Enjoy a full gourmet breakfast at Lola's Place, their Victorian "painted lady" restaurant next door. Breakfast can also be delivered to your door, prepared to go, or enjoyed in the lobby.

Approved by: BBIC

Turn east off U.S. 550 onto 6th Street. Proceed 3 blocks. Turn north on Second Avenue. Proceed 2 blocks. Turn west into parking lot just north of the Inn.

Durango

B&B

999 Country Road 207, 81301
(303) 259-1226, Fax (303) 259-0732
Innkeepers: Julie & Richard Houston

$$/
$$$

Lightner Creek Inn

The 20 acre pastoral setting of this Inn is nestled among rugged peaks, shimmering streams, and grazing llamas and horses. This 1903 French Countryside home has been exquisitely renovated using the charm of Victorian detail with antique furnishings and cozy fireplaces. While only four miles from Durango, (home of the Durango-Silverton Narrow Gauge train), and an easy ride to Mesa Verde, Purgatory, Telluride, and Wolf Creek, the Inn offers excellent mountain trails, trout fishing, and spectacular vistas. Gourmet breakfast served.

Approved by: AAA, BBIC

Three miles west on Highway 160 (from downtown Durango). 1.1 mile north on County Road 207.

Leadville

B&B

127 East Eighth Street, 80461
(800) 748-2354, or (719) 486-2354
Innkeepers: Sid & Judy Clemmer

$/
$$$

The Leadville Country Inn

At day's end spend your relaxing moments at this Inn. A gracious, cheery "Welcome to Leadville, The Cloud City", awaits you. Country Victorian elegance abounds in this lovingly restored Queen Anne. Be pampered in style. Luxuries include home-made cookies, king-size beds, whirlpool tub for two, or an antique copper tub. Breakfast is a gourmet's delight. Relax in the evening soaking in the courtyard hot tub surrounded by lush gardens or new fallen snow. The Inn is located in historic downtown Leadville, close to skiing, mountains, and museums.

Approved by: BBIC, Mobil

Photos: Jessie Walker

I-70 (W) to Copper Mountain Leadville Exit (Colorado Highway 91). The main street in Harrison is also Highway 91. Turn left on 8th Street. Inn is located on the left.

Leadville

Wood Haven Manor

B&B

807 Spruce, 80461
(800) 748-2570
Innkeeper: Jolene Wood

$/
$$

You will step back to an era of Victorian charm. Beautifully restored and furnished with antiques, these turn-of-the-century houses on Leadville's Bankers Row encourage you to indulge yourself. Relax in front of the fireplace with a cup of tea, curl up in bed with a good book, or take a long soak in your tub. The accommodations include an under-the-eaves retreat, cozy mid-size rooms, and romantic suites with sitting rooms offering a whirlpool or antebellum four poster bed. The Inn is just a short stroll from historic downtown.

Approved by: BBIC, Mobil

Photos by Ron Anderson Photography

Exit I-70 at Exit 195 - Copper/Mountain/Leadville. Go south on Colorado 91 for 23 miles to Leadville. Turn right on West 8th, go 2 blocks to Spruce, turn right. The Inn is on the left.

Loveland

Lovelander Bed & Breakfast Inn

B&B

217 West Fourth Street, 80537
(303) 669-0798, Fax (303) 669-0797
Innkeepers: Marilyn & Bob Wiltgen

$$/
$$$

Combining the essence of Victorian style with contemporary convenience, the Inn lies nestled in the Rocky Mountain foothills, a short drive from breathtaking Rocky Mountain National Park. The Inn has beautifully appointed guest rooms, all with private baths. A hearty gourmet breakfast is served daily around the handsome Empire dining table or during the summer, on the wraparound porch or in the garden. The Meeting & Reception Center, located directly across the street, offers catering, consulting, and facilities for weddings, receptions, private parties, and meetings.

Approved by: AAA, IIA, Mobil

From I-25 take Exit 257B. Follow U.S. Hwy. 34(W) for five miles to Garfield Ave. Turn left and go ten blocks to 4th Street. Turn right. Inn is 2nd house on the right.

Mancos

B&B

15472 County Road 35.3, 81328

(800) 992-1098

Innkeepers: Beth Newman, Ken Nickson

$

Lost Canyon Lake Lodge

This is a contemporary two-story log home nestled in the pines overlooking Lost Canyon Lake at an elevation of 7300 feet. The lodge guest rooms each have private bath. Two rooms have lofts. The common room features a moss rock fireplace and lots of wood and glass. You may wander over 20 forested acres, relax on the deck, or sit and read by the fireplace. Lost Canyon Lake Lodge offers the promise of warm hospitality and the kind of pampering that will make your visit feel like a holiday.

Approved by: BBIC

At the intesection of Highways 160 & 184, turn right and go 10.1 miles northwest of Mancos on Highway 184. Turn right on Country Road 35.3. Follow signs .8 mile to lodge.

Manitou Springs

B&B

Ten Otoe Place, 80829

(719) 685-9684

Innkeepers: Sharon Smith & Wendy Goldstein

$/
$$

Two Sisters Inn

This gracious, rose-colored Victorian Bungalow, 1993 Business of the Year Award Recipient, was built in 1919 as a boardinghouse for school teachers. The back garden honeymoon cottage invites you to tumble into its feather bed and shower under the stars. Sunny rooms adorned with family antiques and photographs feature fresh flowers and evening treats. Breakfasts are sensory culinary experiences created by resident chefs. With Pikes Peak as a backdrop, Manitou's Historic District abounds with galleries, antique shops, and its mineral springs.

Approved by: BBIC

Photos: Richard Edie, Photos & Associates

Exit 141 off I-25. Four miles west on Highway 24 to Manitou Avenue Exit. Right off the exit ramp. 1.1 miles to Otoe Place (left at the town clock).

Manitou Springs

B&B

202 Ruxton Avenue, 80829
(800) 905-KEEP, or (719) 685-5354
Innkeepers: Marvin & Vicki Keith

$-
$$$

Victoria's Keep: A B & B Inn

Built in 1892, this is a fully restored Queen Anne Victorian home complete with two fireplaces, nine stained glass windows, period wall coverings and wainscotting, a wrap-around porch, and a turret. The Inn is decorated with period antiques throughout. The guest rooms are spacious, beautifully decorated, and thoughtfully appointed. You will enjoy the daily appetizer table and complimentary wine as well as the availability of beverages at any time, use of the outdoor spa, video library, and mountain bikes. Enjoy a gourmet breakfast before your day of activity or complete relaxation.

Approved by: BBIC

I-25 connects with Hwy. 24 in Colorado Springs. Go west on Hwy. 24 to the Manitou Springs Exit. Follow Manitou Ave. west to Ruxton Ave. Turn left onto Ruxton. Follow for two blocks to the Inn.

Telluride

B&B

440 W. Colorado Avenue, 81435
(800) 707-3344, Fax (303) 728-3424
Innkeepers: Denise & John Weaver

$/
$$$

Alpine Inn Bed & Breakfast

This charming Victorian is located in the historic district, within walking distance of the ski gondola and hiking trails. Each room captures a Victorian serenity with antiques and handmade quilts. The suite features a whirlpool tub, private terrace and breathtaking views. Enjoy breakfast in the sunroom or on the sundeck and share fabulous views of the surrounding peaks. Relax on the porch with scents and colors of the wildflower garden, read a good book by the fire, or enjoy views from the hot tub. Visitors to Telluride are pleased by its lack of crowds and ecotourism focus.

Approved by: ABBA, BBIC

Take Route 145 into Telluride. From the National Historic District sign at the beginning of town, the Inn is located 1/2 mile further on the right.

10R

BYOB

V,M

Telluride

B&B

221 E. Colorado Avenue, 81435
(800) 338-7064, Fax (303) 728-3636
Innkeepers: Colleen & Tom Whiteman

$$-
$$$

This European-style Inn overlooks Telluride's historic main street, putting you just steps from dining, shopping, Town Park, summer festivals, hiking trails, and ski lifts. You will enjoy the relaxed, friendly atmosphere whether sitting in front of a cozy fire, soaking in the steam room and sauna, or lounging on the roof top deck that offers stunning views of Telluride and the surrounding mountains. The wonderfully comfortable beds, quality linens, and cleanliness are a real treat. The deluxe rooms have a sitting area and feature the spectacular "wall of windows". There is an Apres Ski in winter.

Approved by: AAA, ABBA, BBIC, Mobil

Bear Creek Bed & Breakfast

$$-
$$$

Take the Hwy. 145 spur into Telluride. The Inn is on the corner of Willow and Colorado Ave. (Main St.).

3R

BYOB

V,M

Vail

B&B

P. O. Box 1407, 81658
(303) 476-1122, Fax (303) 476-8515
Innkeeper: Pat Funk

$/
$$$$

You will enjoy a genuine mountain experience at this Austrian-style Chalet in an exclusive Vail neighborhood. If you love the outdoor life, a single stay here will provide a lifetime of memories. Depending on the season, you will experience exhilarating white water, blankets of wildflowers, flaming gold aspens, or glistening white snow. You'll awaken each morning to a wonderful breakfast. After a day outside, luxuriate in the outdoor hot tub, wrap yourself in a Chalet bathrobe, and sit by the fire in winter or enjoy the expansive views from the balcony in summer.

Approved by: BBIC

Columbine Chalet B & B

Guests must call for directions.

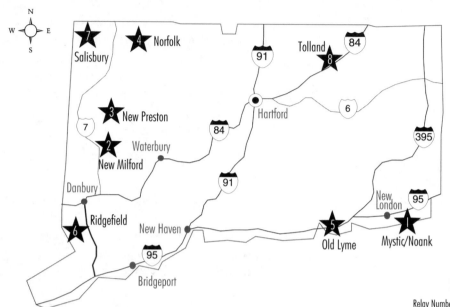

Relay Number: (800) 842-9710

Palmer Inn

Mystic-Noank

B&B

25 Church Street, 06340
(203) 572-9000
Innkeeper: Patricia White

$$$/
$$$$

This gracious, seaside mansion is just two miles from Mystic and only one block from the water. Located in the National Register Historic District of Noank, the Inn was built in 1907. Fine woods, stained glass windows, fireplaces, and original light fixtures and wall coverings enhance the beauty of this impressive building. The Inn is decorated with period furnishings and family heirlooms and you will enjoy the personalized attention in the friendly, comfortable atmosphere. After a hectic day of sight-seeing and shopping, the quiet beauty of this New England fishing village brings respite and calm.

Approved by: AAA, Mobil

From I-95 take Exit 89 to Rt. 215 (Noank Rd). Go two miles to Noank Village. Take the first left off Main Street in Noank.

14R

New Milford

B&B

5 Elm Street, 06776
(203) 354-4080, Fax (203) 354-7046
Innkeepers: Rolf & Peggy Hammer

$/
$$

The Homestead Inn

The Inn is a large, Victorian house built in 1853 as a private home. It was purchased in 1985 by the present Innkeepers, who established it as a Bed and Breakfast with an emphasis on hospitality. The guest rooms in the main house are furnished with a combination of antiques and reproductions. The adjacent Treadwell House has rooms which have been redecorated and refurnished with a look similar to the main house. Located in a residential area just off the Village Green, there are restaurants, shops, galleries, churches, and a movie theater all within walking distance.

Approved by: AAA, Mobil

From Intersection of Routes 7, 67 and 202, follow 202 (E) for 3 lights. Turn left onto Village Green (Main Street). Go to end of Village Green (3 blocks), and turn right onto Elm Street. Inn is located on the left.

17R 2S

New Preston

MAP
B&B

Rt 45 Lakeshore Drive, 06777
(203) 868-0541, Fax (203) 868-1925
Innkeepers: Kees & Ulla Adema

$$$-
$$$$$

The Boulders

Nestled in the Litchfield Hills of northwest Connecticut, this Victorian Inn is architecturally unique, combining mansion-like elegance with the warmth of the country. Set at the foot of Pinnacle Mountain, you can view breathtaking sunsets over Lake Waramaug, while enjoying the renowned cuisine in the glass-enclosed Lake Room, on outdoor terraces, or while relaxing by a fire. Private beach, boats, tennis court, bicycles, and private hiking trail are for use by guests only. Dutch-born Kees and his German wife, Ulla, run the Inn with relaxed European flair.

Approved by: IIA

Photos: George Gardner

From NY: Hutchinson River Parkway to 684 North. Then 84 East to Exit 7 to Route 7 to New Milford. Route 202 to New Preston. Left on Route 45 to Inn.

Photo: Randy O'Rourke

7R 1S
BYOB
15
V,M,X

Norfolk

B&B

69 Maple Avenue, 06058
(203) 542-5690
Innkeepers: Diane & Hank Tremblay

$$$

Manor House

Photo: Robert Neville

One of Connecticut's most romantic hideaways! The antique-decorated guest rooms, all with private baths, have special amenities such as fireplaces, private balconies, soaking tubs, and whirlpools. The common rooms, adorned with Tiffany windows, are perfect for relaxing. Enjoy the living room with a baronial fireplace, a library, and a sunporch. A full breakfast, offering a choice among several items, is served daily. Complimentary beverages are also available. You have the option of choosing from a wide range of year-round recreational and cultural activities.

Approved by: AAA, ABBA

From Route 8 in Winsted, Ct. take Route 44 (W) for 9 1/2 miles to Norfolk. At junction of Route 44 and 272 (at town green), turn right onto Maple Ave.

13R
V,M,X
DN,DV

Old Lyme

B&B

85 Lyme Street, 06371
(203) 434-2600, Fax (203) 434-5352
Innkeeper: Diana Field Atwood

$$-
$$$

Old Lyme Inn

The warm exterior of a fine 19th Century home, typifying New England's charming, colonial residences, welcomes travellers and diners alike to this elegant Inn. Guest rooms, providing all the modern conveniences, are artfully furnished with handsome Empire and Victorian antique pieces. Witch Hazel from nearby Essex and mints on your pillow reflect the Innkeeper's personal touch. White table clothes and polished silver complement an innovative and exciting dinner menu. A changing, lighter supper menu is available in the classic Victorian Bar.

Approved by: AAA

I-95 (S) to Exit 70. Right at bottom of the ramp. I-95 (N) to Exit 70. Left to first right, 1/2 mile to Lyme Street make left.

Connecticut

Ridgefield

West Lane Inn

B&B

22 West Lane, 06877
(203) 438-7323, Fax (203) 438-7325
Innkeeper: Maureen Mayer

$$$

This is a grand, nineteenth century manor home surrounded by acres of expansive lawn, flowering shrubbery, and majestic maples. All guest rooms are over-sized and individually decorated for your comfort. There are queen-size, four poster beds, cable television, 24 hour telephone service, and some rooms have fireplaces. History, with all of the conveniences of today, blend for an atmosphere of polished refinement. Fine dining, boutiques, and wonderful antique shops are within an easy walking distance.

Approved by: AAA, IIA

From NYC and the Westside Hwy., follow the Sawmill River Pkwy.(N) and take Exit 43. Turn right onto Rt. 35(E). Follow for 10 miles to Ridgefield. Inn is on the left. From I-84 take Exit 3 to Rt. 7(S) to Rt. 35 to Ridgefield.

Salisbury

Under Mountain Inn

MAP

482 Undermountain Road, 06068
(203) 435-0242, Fax (203) 435-2379
Innkeepers: Peter & Marged Higginson

$$$/
$$$$

Picture yourselves rocking under trees which predate George III. The Union Jack is flapping above. Read the Manchester Guardian, Royalty, and books on things British. Sip a proper cup of tea or Samuel Smith ale. Be transported to merrie olde England for a full English Breakfast. Indulge in bangers and mash or steak and kidney pie. Tempt your palette with shortbread and English trifle. Dream of horse-drawn sleigh rides, cranking home-made ice cream, hiking the Appalachian Trail, and boating. Experience the country getaway of your imagination!

Approved by: IIA

Taconic Parkway to Poughkeepsie/Millbrook Exit. East on Route 44 to Salisbury. North on Route 41 for 4 miles.

Relay Numbers: TTY (800) 955-8771, VCE (800) 955-8770

Amelia Island

B&B

98 South Fletcher Avenue, 32034
(904) 277-4851, Fax (904) 277-6500
Innkeepers: David & Susan Caples

Elizabeth Pointe Lodge

$$/
$$$$

This is what old Florida must have been like. Sitting prominently on the Atlantic Ocean, the Inn is only steps from the often-deserted beaches of a barrier island called Amelia. There are wonderful rooms with private baths with oversized soaking tubs (some with whirlpools). Each day enjoy complimentary full breakfast overlooking the ocean, fresh flowers, and the newspaper. Light food and dessert service is available all day. Horseback riding, tennis, golf, and sailing are nearby, and it is a short bike ride to the historic Seaport of Fernandina.

Approved by: AAA, ABBA

From I-95, take Exit 129, Route A1A. Go east 15 miles to Amelia Island. Stay on A1A to 98 South Fletcher. Inn is located on oceanside of road.

6R 4S

10

V,M,X
DV

Amelia Island

B&B

227 South Seventh Street, 32034
(800) 261-4838, Fax (904) 277-3103
Innkeepers: Nelson & Mary Smelker

$$/
$$$

The Fairbanks House

An Italianate villa, built in 1885, the Inn is listed on the National Register of Historic Places. You will enjoy the piazzas, the swimming pool, and the beautiful gardens as well as the gourmet continental breakfast and the afternoon refreshments served in the garden or the formal dining room. The Inn has just been completely restored and is furnished with period pieces, antiques, and oriental carpets which complement its extraordinary architecture. With an acre of land, you feel peacefully secluded, yet you are close to the beach, golf, and historic tours.

Approved by: ABBA

From I-95(N), take Exit 129 onto A1A. Travel east 12 miles to Amelia Island. The Inn is 30 minutes north of Jacksonville.

10R 1S

24

V,M,X
DN

Amelia Island

B&B

22 South 3rd Street, 32034
(800) 258-3301, Fax (904) 277-3831
Innkeepers: Bob & Karen Warner

$/
$$$

Florida House Inn

Amelia Island is a barrier island where the spirit of an old Florida resort lingers on. Recently restored, this 1857 hotel is the perfect combination of historic charm and modern convenience. Each room is a comfortable blend of antiques and reproductions, vintage quilts, handmade rugs, and polished heart-pine floors. Deluxe rooms offer fireplaces, Jaccuzzis®, or original claw-footed tubs. A full breakfast is served each morning in the sunny breakfast room. The cozy English-style pub, original boarding house restaurant, and brick courtyard are all part of the experience.

Approved by: AAA, Mobil

Photo: Ed Mathews

From I-95, take Exit 129. East on Highway A1A. Go over large bridge, and at the 5th traffic light (B.P. Station) turn left. Go 5 blocks, turn left onto south 3rd Street.

Bay Harbor Islands

Bay Harbor Inn

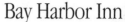

B&B

9660 E. Bay Harbor Drive, 33154
(305) 868-4141, Fax (305) 868-4141 ext. 602
Innkeeper: Alexander Lankler

$$/
$$$

This is Miami Beach's authentic, waterfront Inn located in a tropical setting, adjacent to the Bal Harbour shops and a short walk to Atlantic Beaches. Many of the rooms have lovely antiques and king-size, four-poster, mahogany beds. The creekside building offers contemporary decor and wide balconies directly on the water. The Inn serves an elegant, full, complimentary breakfast aboard the yacht Celeste. The Inn is the home of the Miami Palm Restaurant, sister to the Palm established in New York City in 1927. The Miami Palm is known for superb steaks and giant Maine lobster.

Approved by: Mobil

From Miami International proceed north on I-95. Exit at Bal Harbour Exit (125th Street). Proceed 5 miles to Broad Causeway. After Causeway, take left at 4th traffic light.

Key West

The Watson House

B&B

525 Simonton Street, 33040
(305) 294-6712, or (800) 621-9405
Innkeepers: Joe Beres & Ed Czaplicki

$$$/
$$$$$

Circa 1860, this is a distinctively furnished, small Inn/Guest House in the historic preservation district. It received the 1987 award for excellence in rehabilitation from the Historical Florida Keys Preservation Board. There is a heated swimming pool, heated Jacuzzi®, a patio, decks, and gardens. All rooms have their own distinct-style with private baths, cable color TV, air conditioning, and telephone. The large suites even have fully-equipped kitchens. A full continental breakfast is served daily. Privacy prevails in this adult hideaway in the Keys.

Approved by: AAA, ABBA

At the end of US 1, 150 miles from Miami. On Simonton Street in Historic Key West. Just 5 blocks from Truman Avenue.

Lake Helen

Clauser's Bed and Breakfast

B&B
&

201 E. Kicklighter Road, 32744
(800) 220-0310, Fax (904) 228-2337
Innkeepers: Marge & Tom Clauser

$$/
$$$

This Country Victorian Inn is located in northern central Florida, between Orlando and Daytona Beach. There is a gentle roll to the terrain. Trees are large stately oaks, magnolias, and camphors. The Inn is surrounded on three sides by woods. As you enter the Inn, you have an almost perceptible feeling of times gone by. The property is on the National Register of Historic Places. Guests are invited to soak in the hot tub in the screened, Victorian gazebo. Afternoon refreshments are provided.

Approved by: AAA

I-4, Exit 54; turn right at traffic signal on to Country Roads 41-39. Take 41-39 through village of Cassadaga to East Kicklighter Road, turn right. Inn is 3 blocks away.

Lake Wales

Chalet Suzanne Country Inn

B&B
EP
MAP
&

3800 Chalet Suzanne Drive, 33853
(800) 433-6011, Fax (813) 676-1814
Innkeepers: Carl & Vita Hinshaw

$$-
$$$$

You experience the Chalet's charm first in the beauty of the setting... palm trees leaning with the breeze; Lake Suzanne glistening under the Florida sun; low, rambling Chalet houses with gay patios, towers, and balconies. You feel it again as each guest room greets you with cordial warmth and modern comforts. The essence of the Chalet's reputation is its superb cuisine served in quaint rooms overlooking the lake. Every corner glows with antiques, stained glass, and old lamps from faraway places. Chalet Suzanne is a subtle balm... and a lasting memory.

Approved by: AAA, ABBA, IIA, Mobil

Photos: David Woods

From Interstate 4 go south on US Highway 27 for 22 miles. Then turn left at Country Road 17A. Follow signs to the Inn 1 1/2 miles. Inn is on right.

Micanopy

B&B

402 NE Cholokka Blvd., 32667
(904) 466-3322
Innkeeper: H.C. Howard Jr.

$-
$$$

Located in historic Micanopy, the oldest inland town in Florida, Herlong is an elegant three-story, Greek-Revival, brick structure with four corinthian columns. Inside there are four suites and six rooms, all with private baths; ten fireplaces; and six types of beautiful woods. There is also a cottage nearby which provides the ultimate in privacy. The house is decorated in period antiques throughout. This is a truly wonderful respite, an ideal place to shop for antiques and to sit on the peaceful veranda and watch the grass grow.

Approved by: AAA

Herlong Mansion

At Exit 73 on I-75, turn east and go 1/2 mile to Historic Micanopy sign. Turn right and go to town where the street ends. Turn left. Inn is 1 1/2 blocks on the left.

New Smyrna Beach

B&B

512 South Riverside Drive, 32168
(904) 423-4940, Fax (904) 423-4940
Innkeepers: Martha & Chuck Nighswonger

$/
$$

Watch the pelicans, dolphins, sailboats, and yachts along the Atlantic Intracoastal Waterway from the beautiful front room, wraparound porch, or your own room. The spacious three-story, 1906 home is in the historic district of New Smyrna Beach. It has a central fireplace and intricate, natural wood in every room. An expanded Continental Breakfast is served in the dining room, and low cholesterol meals are a specialty. You could take a sunset river cruise by sailboat, go deep sea fishing, enjoy the sandy beaches, and take advantage of some wonderful restaurants.

Approved by: AAA

Night Swan Intracoastal

Four miles east on Rt. 44 from I-95 (Exit 84). Pass over first bridge, (but do not cross over river -on second bridge). Turn right on Live Oak Street. First left on Andrews, and the second right on South Riverside Drive. The Inn is one block away on the right.

9R 4S

BYOB

V,M,X
DN,DV

Palm Beach, FL

B&B

365 South County Road, 33480
(407) 832-4009, Fax (407) 832-6255
Innkeepers: Barbara & Harry Kehr

Palm Beach Historic Inn

$-
$$$$$

This historic landmark building was beautifully restored to preserve its original integrity and stately elegance. It is a comfortable retreat, completely renovated with every modern convenience. Suites and guest rooms are tastefully and individually appointed with private baths and showers, A/C, cable TV, and telephones. Relax in luxury with a deluxe continental breakfast in your room. Walk a block to a refreshing beach and world-famous Worth Avenue shopping. You'll discover the beautiful tropical paradise of Palm Beach; an island of history, tradition, and tranquility.

Approved by: ABBA

From I-95, Exit 52A; From FL Turnpike, Exit 99. East on Okeechobee Boulevard. Cross bridge to Palm Beach onto Royal Palm Way. Right turn on A1A. Drive South. The Inn is opposite Town Hall.

Georgia

N
W   E
S

Relay Numbers: TTY (800) 255-0056, VCE (800) 255-0135

8R 2S

BYOB

40

V,M,DV

Atlanta

B&B

223 Ponce de Leon Avenue, 30308
(404) 875-9449, Fax (404) 875-2882
Innkeepers: Joan & Douglas Jones

$/
$$$

Prepare yourself for Southern charm, hospitality, and a full Southern breakfast. The Woodruff is a 1906 Victorian home built by a prominent family and fully restored by the Joneses. Each room has been meticulously decorated with antiques and other memorabilia of its former owner and madam, Bessie Woodruff. Dinner is never a problem with many good restaurants very close by. Equally close are a variety of must-see tourist attractions and activities. Bicycle at Piedmont Park or attend cultural activities at the Woodruff Arts Center and the Fox Theatre.

Approved by: AAA

Woodruff Bed & Breakfast

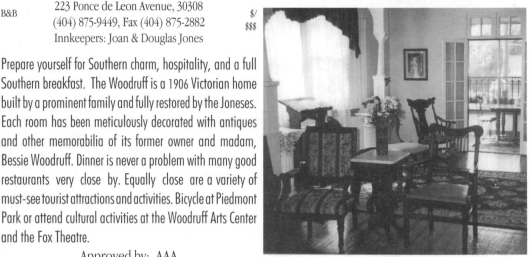

From I-75,I-85, take the 10th-14th Street Exit to 10th Street. Go east on 10th Street to Myrtle Street. Make a right on Myrtle Street, and go approximately 10 blocks to Ponce de Leon Avenue. The Inn will be on the left.

22R 7S

12

V,M,X

Savannah

B&B
&

14 East Oglethorpe Avenue, 31401
(800) 822-4553, Fax (912) 236-4626
Innkeepers: Richard F. Carlson & Timothy C. Hargus

$$/
$$$$

The Inn is a beautifully restored Victorian mansion, circa 1838, in the heart of the historic district. Twenty-two guest rooms are available in either the main Inn or the townhouse. The main Inn has a double parlor, full service bar, flower-gift shop, and landscaped courtyard. Each room is decorated with antiques, oriental rugs, and some reproductions. Some rooms have fireplaces, whirlpools, and wet bars. Cozy terrycloth robes and evening turndown with chocolates and cordials are specials touches. An elaborate continental breakfast is served, and fine dining is nearby.

Approved by: AAA, ABBA, Mobil

Ballastone Inn & Townhouse

Photos: Heather Heino

Take I-95 (S) to I-16. Go east. I-16 becomes Montgomery Street. Go to 2nd traffic light (Oglethorpe Avenue). Turn right, and go 5 blocks to Inn.

Savannah

Foley House Inn

B&B

14 West Hull Street, 31401
(800) 647-3708, Fax (912) 231-1218
Innkeepers: Mark & Inge Svensson Moore

$/
$$$$

Located on the beautiful Chippewa Square, in the heart of the Historic Landmark District, this wonderful 1896 Inn awaits its guests. The individually decorated rooms offer four poster rice beds, oriental rugs, and English antique furnishings. Most of the rooms have fireplaces, some have Jacuzzi®baths, and all have cable television. After a full day exploring the historic city of Savannah, return to the Inn for tea, cordials, and snacks. An extensive film library is available if you want to curl up and relax. If you want more activity, the Innkeepers can make arrangements for tennis and golf.

Approved by: AAA

From I-16 take the Montgomery Street Exit. Turn right onto Liberty Street, left onto Drayton, and left onto Hull Street. The Inn is the first red brick building on the right.

Senoia

The Veranda

B&B

252 Seavy Street, P. O. Box 177, 30276-0177
(404) 599-3905, Fax (404) 599-0806
Innkeepers: Jan & Bobby Boal

$$/
$$$

At the turn-of-the-century, Senoia's famous Hollberg Hotel hosted annual reunions of Georgia's Confederate Veterans and housed notables such as William Jennings Bryan. Now, beautifully restored as The Veranda, it is known for hospitality, fine cuisine, and one of the country's finest collections of kaleidoscopes. Spacious rooms have queen-size beds and luxurious private baths. One parlor has a rare, 1930 Wurlitzer player piano with organ and chimes. Rocking chairs and porch swings, fireflies and Queen Anne's Lace, pump-organ recitals and mockingbird serenades await you here.

Approved by: ABBA, IIA

From Atlanta, take I-85(S) to Exit 12. Go left on Hwy. 74 for 16.7 miles. Turn right onto Rockaway Rd. Go 3.3 miles. At the light turn left and follow one block to the Inn.

St. Simons

AP

P. O. Box 21078, 31522
(912) 638-7472, Fax (912) 634-1811
Innkeepers: Kevin & Deborah McIntyre

$$$$$

Little St. Simons Island

Located along the Georgia Coast, this is a hideaway where you can enjoy the serenity of nature, be as active as you like, relax with a book by the pool, or feel the glow of a cozy fire. Little St. Simons is a 10,000 acre, privately owned, barrier island accommodating only 24 guests at one time. The Lodge, built in 1917, is the heart of the Island where meals are served family-style and feature regional and local cuisine. Explore miles of pristine beaches, endless marshes, and ancient forests and then return to the gentle care of the attentive staff.

Approved by: IIA

Phootos: Cotten Alston

The Island is only accessible by boat. Guests may arrive in their own car at the Hampton River Club Marina on St. Simons Island and meet the 10:30 AM or 4:30 PM boat. Car rental at the Jacksonville, FL or Savannah, GA airports or van service is available.

Thomasville

B&B

725 South Hansell Street, 31792
(800) 344-4717, Fax (912) 226-0653
Innkeepers: John & Lee Puskar

$- $$$

Evans House Bed & Breakfast

Located in the Parkfront Historic District directly across from beautiful Paradise Park, the Inn welcomes honeymooners, corporate guests, travellers, history buffs, and those who simply want to enjoy the ambiance of a simpler, more gracious way of life. In winter, gas logs burn cheerfully in the public room and you are welcomed with refreshments. After-dinner liqueurs and home-made pastries or cookies are served in-room where beds are turned down and imported candies are left on the pillows. Awake refreshed and begin the day with an elegantly served breakfast.

Approved by: AAA

From U.S. Highway 84 (downtown) or U.S. 319 via old truck Route 319 (Hansell St.) across from Paradise Park. From I-75, take Valdosta Highway 84 Exit. From I-10, take Monticello FL exit to U.S. 19 (N) to old truck Route 319 (Hansell St.).

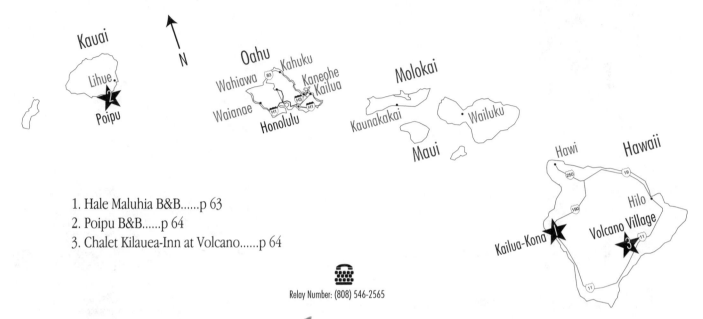

1. Hale Maluhia B&B......p 63
2. Poipu B&B......p 64
3. Chalet Kilauea-Inn at Volcano......p 64

Relay Number: (808) 546-2565

Kailua-Kona

B&B

76-770 Hualalai Road, 96740
(800) 559-6627, Fax (808) 326-5487
Innkeepers: Ken & Ann Smith

$-
$$

Hale Maluhia Bed & Breakfast

Experience Up-Country plantation living just three miles from Kailua-Kona in the heart of the Big Island Recreational Paradise. At this estate, set in Holualoa coffee country, at a cool elevation of 900', you will enjoy large guest rooms, a great room, a library and game room with a slate pool table, and three lanais. There is beach and snorkeling equipment available as well as Koi ponds, a stream, a soothing waterfall, a Chinese slate and tile Jacuzzi®, and Japanese gardens. Rest well and awaken to a full breakfast featuring fresh local fruits, juices, home-made breads, and pure Kona coffee.

Approved by: AAA, ABBA

Go south from Kailua-Kona on Hwy. 11 to Hualalai Road. Turn up-hill on Hualalai Road and go1.5 miles. Look for Inn sign and lamp-post on the right. Take a sharp right and go to the end of the concrete driveway.

Poipu Beach, Kauai

Poipu Bed & Breakfast Inn

B&B

2720 Hoonani Road, 96756
(800) 22-POIPU, Fax (808) 742-6843
Innkeeper: Dotti Cichon

$$$/
$$$$

You will experience Hawaiian hospitality and the charm and ambiance of old Kauai at this beautifully renovated, 1933 Plantation Inn. Part of the National Trust for Historic Preservation, the Inn has shaded lanais and unique whitewashed, fir interiors furnished with white wicker, pine antiques, authentic carousel horses, and restful pastels that beckon you to linger. If you choose to wander, you will discover secluded beaches, restaurants, shops, golf, and tennis a few minutes away. Enjoy exotic fruits and flowers fresh from the lush tropical gardens and soak in the spirit of Aloha.

Approved by: ABBA

From Lihue Airport, take 570(W) to 56(W) to 50(W) to 520(S) to Koloa. Turn right onto Koloa Rd. and follow one block to Poipu Rd. and turn left. Follow for 1.4 miles and turn right at the "Welcome to Poipu Beach" lava rock wall. Bear left across the bridge and take the first driveway on the left.

Volcano Village

Chalet Kilauea-The Inn at Volcano

B&B

Box 998, 96785
(800) 937-7786, Fax (808) 967-8660
Innkeepers: Lisha & Brian Crawford

$/
$$$$$

You can explore treasures from around the world while enjoying complimentary afternoon tea. Choose a superior room, each with a Jacuzzi®, inspired by an Oriental, African, or European theme. The two level TreeHouse Suite is perfect for a special occasion. Tempt your appetite with a candlelit, full gourmet breakfast. Luxuriate in the whirlpool, relax by the fireplace, peruse the library, wander in the garden, and delight in the special style here. The Inn is a lush Hawaiian haven nestled in Volcano Village. Nearby is Hawaii Volcanoes National Park, Black Sand Beach, and Hilo.

Approved by: AAA, ABBA

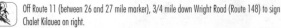

Off Route 11 (between 26 and 27 mile marker), 3/4 mile down Wright Road (Route 148) to sign Chalet Kilauea on right.

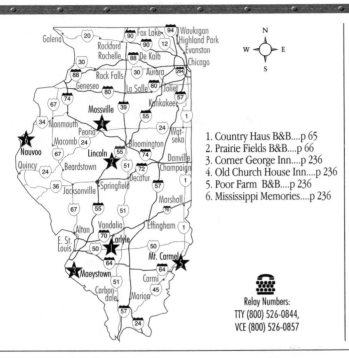

1. Country Haus B&B....p 65
2. Prairie Fields B&B....p 66
3. Corner George Inn....p 236
4. Old Church House Inn....p 236
5. Poor Farm B&B....p 236
6. Mississippi Memories....p 236

Relay Numbers:
TTY (800) 526-0844,
VCE (800) 526-0857

1. Kingsley Inn......p 74

Relay Numbers:
TTY (800) 735-2942
VCE (800) 735-2943

Carlyle, IL

B&B

1191 Franklin, 62231

(800) 279-4486

Innkeepers: Ron & Vickie Cook

$

Country Haus B&B

This is a century old home with today's comforts. Still, many of the Eastlake style charms of yesterday prevail. Each guest room is appointed with a multitude of items to make travelling easier; soft robes, hairdryers, flashlights, and even an umbrella! You'll find a comfortable country decor in both your guest room and the library. Breakfast is served to start your day off right. Carlyle Lake, a few minutes away, is the states largest inland lake and the premier sailing lake of the Midwest. Arrangements for complimentary boat parking at a local marina are available.

Approved by: IBBA

Located on the corner of Illinois Route 127 and Illinois Route 50 east in the center of Carlyle.

©State Journal-Register

B&B

Lincoln, IL
RR3, 62656
(217) 732-7696
Innkeeper: Mary Beth Sparks

Located in the heartland of the Illinois prairie, this stately 1860's manor house is on a working farm. Spacious, antique-filled guest rooms are offered in addition to several common rooms and two sun porches. Snuggle under hand-made quilts and curl up with a book by a crackling fire. Family heirlooms, plush robes, and period furniture assure you will unwind in luxury. Awaken to birdsong and an elegant breakfast featuring fresh fruit, stuffed sausage, broccoli quiche, fried apples, and freshly baked muffins and breads.

Approved by: IBBA

Prairie Fields Inn

$

©Lincoln Courier

Take Exit 126 from I55 in Lincoln. Turn east on Route 121. Follow through Lincoln. The Inn is 5 minutes out of town still on Route 121.

Indiana

Relay Numbers: (800) 743-3333

Centerville

B&B

214 Old National Road, 47330
(800) 495-2689, Fax (317) 855-2864
Innkeeper: Marcia Hoyt

$

Historic Lantz House Inn

Photos: Cliff Cox

Nestled in the heart of the Historic District, and listed on the National Register of Historic Places, is this beautifully restored, 1823 Inn. Originally built for a famous wagon maker who made the journey on the Oregon Trail, it is a comfortable refuge for relaxation. You will enjoy the soothing, yet elegant atmosphere, featuring art and shelves full of books. You will savor the gourmet breakfasts, late afternoon refreshments, and true Hoosier hospitality. The garden is the perfect spot for reading or reflection. Be sure to visit the antique shops and the world's largest antique mall which is three blocks away.

Approved by: IBBA

From I-70, take the Centerville Exit. Go south for three miles to the stop light. Turn right onto Main Street. Go 11/2 blocks to the Inn.

Chesterton

B&B

350 Indian Boundary Road, 46304
(800) 521-5127, Fax (219) 926-4845
Innkeepers: Tim Wilk & Charles Ramsey

$$-
$$$

Gray Goose Inn

Built in 1939 as a private home, this romantic Inn is Country English in style. White with dark green shutters, it is surrounded by century-old oaks and peaceful, glistening Lake Palomara. The Inn is a gracious respite from the hustle and bustle. Canada geese, ducks, and Blue Heron make the setting a virtual wildlife preserve. Wooded walking trails, a paddleboat, and rowboats add to the resort-like setting. Comfortable, well-appointed guest rooms and an uncommon breakfast complete your experience. Lake Michigan and the state and national lakeshores are only minutes away.

Approved by: IBBA

From I-94 take Exit 26A (Chesterton). Turn right at the first stoplight. Go 1/4 mile to sign, turn left. Exit I-80-90 at Exit 31. Turn left on 49 and continue to 3rd stoplight, left 1/4 mile.

Hagerstown

B&B

300 West Main Street, 47346

(800) 824-4319

Innkeepers: Jack & JoAnne Warmoth

$$

The Teetor House

"A beautiful house and gracious-as good a B&B as we ever hope to stay in", is a typical comment in the Teetor House guest book. You can stroll over 10 landscaped acres with the quiet peace of countryside, yet the Inn is near shops and restaurants. Six public golf courses, modestly priced and rarely crowded, are within 20 minutes. Antique enthusiasts enjoy browsing through local shops and nearby Centerville's giant Webb Mall. The friendly elegance of the house with its beautiful chimes, Steinway® grand piano with player, and inspiring history will bring a promise to return.

Approved by: AAA, ABBA, IBBA

Four miles north of I-70 on Road 38 in eastern Indiana. One hour drive from Indianapolis or Dayton, Ohio.

Indianapolis

B&B

7161 Edgewater Place, 46240

(317) 257-2660

Innkeeper: Joan H. Morris

$/
$$$$

The Nuthatch Bed & Breakfast

A French, country cottage surrounded by herb and scented gardens, the Nuthatch couples convenience to shopping and downtown with a quiet riverside setting. Your hosts, Bernie (a retired college professor and ham radio operator) and Joan (a librarian, now cooking instructor) enjoy sharing their home, hobbies, and the history of Indianapolis. Joan's breakfasts are special. Whether exotic or Hoosier home cooking, you're sure to enjoy the fare. If you're looking for a getaway or a spot to come "home" to after a hard day's work, this Inn offers a perfect place to let the world go by.

Approved by: IBBA

I-465 (N) to U.S. 31 (Meridian Street), south to 75th Street. East to Westfield Blvd., south to 72nd Street. East to Edgewater Place.

Main Street Bed & Breakfast

Madison

B&B

739 W. Main Street, 47250
(800) 362-6246
Innkeepers: Mark & Mary Balph

$$-
$$$

This Inn is a favorite among Madison visitors. You will rest comfortably in a beautifully-restored, 1840's Greek Revival home and wake up with coffee, tea, or hot chocolate served in your room. The hearty, continental breakfast features an assortment of pastries, homemade breads, and fruit of the season. Fully air conditioned with modern private baths, this is the ideal choice for honeymoons, anniversaries, or pampered getaway weekends. Situated within the historic district, it is only a gentle walk to gift and antique shops, superb restaurants, and the Ohio River.

Approved by: Mobil

Off I-65, take Scottsburg Exit. Continue east on Route 56 to Madison. From I-71, Carrollton Exit, go north to KY Route 36/42. West to 421 (N). Go over bridge to Madison.

Schussler House Bed & Breakfast

Madison

B&B

514 Jefferson Street, 47250
(800) 392-1931
Innkeepers: Judy & Bill Gilbert

$$

Experience the quiet elegance of a circa 1849 Federal Classic Revival home, tastefully combined with today's modern conveniences. The Inn is located in the historic district of Madison. Antique shops, restaurants, historic sites, and the Ohio River are within a pleasant walk. This recently renovated home offers spacious guest rooms decorated with antiques, reproductions, and Judy's creative handcrafted touches. Specially selected wall coverings, lace curtains, and cozy reading areas make each room unique. Breakfast is a relaxing beginning to your day.

Approved by: IBBA

One and a half blocks north of Courthouse on U.S. Highway 421.

5R 5S

BYOB

10

V,M

Michigan City

B&B
220 West 10th Street, 46360
(219) 879-1700
Innkeepers: Ben & Mary DuVal

Hutchinson Mansion

$$-
$$$

A stay here evokes the leisured elegance of a more gracious period. Built in 1876, this historic structure was restored to its former grandeur and has been furnished with antiques. Beautiful, stained glass windows, and high-beamed and decorated ceilings abound. Guests are encouraged to wander about the Mansion, to lounge in the parlor and library, to relax in the gardens, or enjoy a game of croquet on the east lawn. The Inn is located in Michigan City's historic district, just minutes from the National Lakeshore and Indiana Dunes State Park.

Approved by: IBBA

Photo: Wm. T. Swedenberg

Exit I-94 at Exit 34B. Take Route 421 north 4 miles to 10th Street. Turn left onto 10th Street. One and a half blocks to Inn on the left.

6R 1S

40

V,M,X
DN,DV

Mishawaka

AP
317 Lincolnway East, 46544
(800) 437-0131, Fax (219) 259-2622
Innkeepers: Ron Montandon & Phil Robinson

Beiger Mansion Inn

$-
$$

Listed on the National Register of Historic Places, this 22,000 square-foot Inn offers gracious accommodations. Internationally known and locally recognized for its fine dining, the restaurant serves lunch to the public and dinner on Saturday evenings. Chef Wittendorf has been recognized numerous times for her delicious and beautifully presented cuisine. The Mansion also houses "Fables Gallery," which represents over 150 fine American craftsman and artists. The Mansion is minutes from Notre Dame University, "Amish Country," and Lake Michigan beaches.

Approved by: IBBA

Two blocks east of 331 on Highway 33 in downtown Mishawaka.

Nappanee

Victorian Guest House

B&B

302 E. Market Street, 46550
(219) 773-4383
Innkeepers: Bruce & Vickie Hunsberger

$

This three story, 1887 mansion, listed on the National Register of Historical Landmarks, is highlighted by antiques, stained glass windows, and pocket doors. A warm welcome awaits you in the gracious living room that has all the ambiance of the 1800's. The Inn is located in the Amish Country where horse-drawn buggies share the road with the automobile. Close to Notre Dame and Shipshewana and only two hours from Chicago, many hours can be spent scouring the local antique shops for great finds. You will end your day with tea and very special sweets.

Approved by: IBBA

The Inn is two blocks east of the downtown junction of Hwy. 6 and Hwy. 19 (also called Market and Main Streets).

Peru

Rosewood Mansion

B&B

54 N Hood, 46970
(317) 472-7151, Fax (317) 472-5575
Innkeepers: Lynn & David Hausner

$-
$$

The Inn, built in 1872 by Elbert Shirk, is a lovely Victorian home situated in Shirk's addition near the downtown area. The Mansion has 19 rooms including eight bedrooms, each with private bath. The Inn offers the friendliness of a private home, coupled with the privacy and elegance of a fine hotel. You will enjoy the warmth of the oak panel library, the splendor of the three-story staircase with stained glass windows, the elegance of the Victorian parlor, or the comfort and charm of your beautifully decorated room.

Approved by: IBBA

Three blocks west from the intersection of Main & Broadway - north on Hood- Inn is located on the left.

South Bend

The Book Inn Bed & Breakfast

B&B   508 West Washington Street, 46601 $-
(219) 288-1990 $$$
Innkeepers: Peggy & John Livingston

Fresh flowers, antiques, 12-foot ceilings, and incredible butternut woodwork welcome you when you ring the bell here. Elegance and attention to detail are everywhere you look and there is even a quality used book store available for browsing anytime. One hundred year old Haviland china, sterling silver, Waterford crystal, candlelight, and other contented guests greet you at breakfast. As a traveller on business in this city you will feel pampered and productive as all of your needs are met. Chicago is only an hour and a half away and over 300 antique dealers are nearby.

Approved by: IBBA

From I-80-90 toll road, take Exit 77. Travel south on U.S. 31 to Washington Street and turn right. Valley American Bank, at Washington and Main Streets, is the tallest building in the city and is an easy landmark to guide you.

South Bend

Queen Anne Inn

B&B   420 W. Washington, 46601 $-
(800) 582-2379, Fax (219) 234-4324 $$
Innkeepers: Pauline & Robert Medhurst

The Queen Anne Inn, a Victorian house on the National Historic Register, displays many of the home's original features. Guests enjoy the Frank Lloyd Wright designed bookcases, the original silk wallpaper in the breakfast room, and the tiger oak staircase leading to the second floor. The Innkeepers are happy to share some tales about Mr. Good, the original owner; his daughter, Mabel; and her family. You'll want to know why the house was moved from its original location and even more about the hidden safe in one of the bedrooms. Rest, relax, and relive the past.

Approved by: AAA, IBBA

From I-80, I-90 Corridor, take U.S. 31 south to Washington Street. Turn right. Inn is just before 2nd light (Williams St.).

2R

BYOB

DV

Wabash

B&B

313 W. Hill Street, 46992

(219) 563-6901

Innkeeper: Barbara Herrold

$

Close to downtown Wabash and the new Honeywell Center Auditorium, this 1885 stately Victorian home offers a friendly and comfortable place to stay while visiting for business or pleasure. Breakfast is served in the formal dining room with a view out the unique, round bay window. Enjoy a quiet evening in front of the fire and savor the high ceilings and beautifully carved cherry and walnut woodwork. If you are musically inclined you will love the baby grand piano. For a slightly more active evening, take a walk around the city to see the many examples of Victorian architecture.

Approved by: IBBA

Around Window Inn

Follow SR 15 (Cass Street) south to one-half block past the railroad. Turn onto Hill Street, go one block. The Inn is on the southwest corner of Hill and Carroll Streets.

8R 2S

BYOB

12

V,M,X

Warsaw

B&B

503 E. Ft. Wayne Street, 46580

(800) 352-0640, Fax (219) 269-4646

Innkeepers: Bill & Debi Hambright

$$

You'll enter a time of Victorian splendor when you visit this Inn built in 1865. You will find gourmet breakfasts, spacious rooms appointed with antiques, large beds, elegant linens, and carved woodwork. The Inn is only a short walk from two of the county's 100 lakes. While exploring the lakes and the Amish country you can enjoy a picnic basket prepared by the Innkeeper. At night you will be welcomed back to your room by warm, glowing candles and homemade cookies next to your turned down bed. This is a wonderful escape where comfort meets pleasure.

Approved by: IBBA

Candlelight Inn

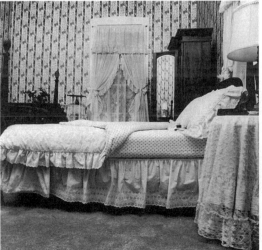

Take US 30 to State Road 15(S). Turn east onto Ft. Wayne Street. Inn is on the northeast corner of the first intersection after the railroad tracks.

14R

BYOB

V,M,X
DN,DV

Fort Madison, IA

B&B

707 Avenue H, 52627
(800) 441-2327, Fax (319) 372-7096
Innkeeper: Myrna Reinhard

$-
$$

This Victorian Inn, named after Lt. Alpha Kingsley who selected the site for Old Fort Madison in 1808, overlooks the Mighty Mississippi. A beautiful courtyard, a three-story glass atrium, a winding walnut staircase, luxury rooms appointed with period antiques, and breakfast of home-baked pastries, specially prepared granola, fresh fruit, and Gourmet, Kingsley Blend coffee await you. Alpha's on the Riverfront, a charming, upbeat restaurant next door, is open daily. You may stroll to the flood museum, antique shops, galleries, boutiques, or the riverboat casino. Historic Nauvoo is 15 minutes away.

Approved by: ABBA

Kingsley Inn

Inn is located in the heart of downtown Fort Madison.

5R

BYOB

25

V,M

Emporia, KS

B&B

628 Exchange, 66801
(316) 342-6881
Innkeeper: Barbara Stoecklein

$

Antique furnishings, beveled glass windows, and pocket doors provide turn-of-the-century elegance combined with modern conveniences. You begin your day with fresh coffee, juice, and the morning paper brought to your room, while delightful breakfast smells waft up from below. You may request room service with Breakfast-in-a-Basket. Barbara is hostess for a two-hour, tea party, which includes a visit to Grannie's Attic to dress up in long dresses, gloves, hats, purses, pearls, and high heels. It's a great way to celebrate a birthday for ladies from 5 to 95!

Approved by: KBBA

Plumb House Bed & Breakfast

Emporia is accessible by 4 major highways and is within 2 hours of Wichita, Topeka, and Kansas City. The Inn is located in downtown Emporia, 1 block north of Highway 50.

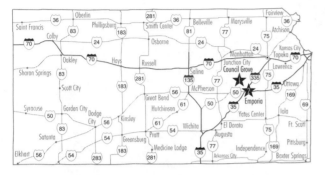

1. Cottage House......p 236
2. Plumb House Bed & Breakfast......p 74

Relay Numbers: (800) 766-3777

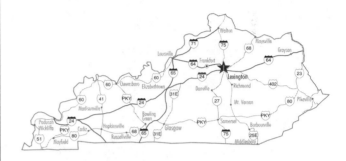

1. Bed & Breakfast at Sills Inn......p 75

Relay Numbers: TTY (800) 253-0744, VCE (800) 648-6057

Lexington, KY

B&B

270 Mongomery, Versailles 40383
(800) 526-9801, Fax (606) 873-7099
Innkeeper: Tony Sills

$-
$$$

Bed & Breakfast at Sills Inn

This restored Victorian Inn, located in historic downtown Versailles, is just seven minutes west of the Lexington Airport and the famous Keeneland Race Course. The state capital, the beautiful, bluegrass horse farm region, and the restored Shaker Village are a few of the many area attractions. Antique shops, art studios, cafes, and quaint restaurants are within a short walk. Choose from six guest rooms, each with a private bath. Two suites have double whirlpools. There is a fully-stocked guest kitchen where you can fix a late night snack.

Approved by: AAA

Cincinnati - Go south on I-75, and take Exit 115. West on Highway 922, and west on New Circle Road to Exit 5B. Ten miles to Versailles. Louisville - I-64 to Highway 60 (E). Elizabethtown - I-65 to Blue Grass Parkway (E) to Exit 68/Highway 33.

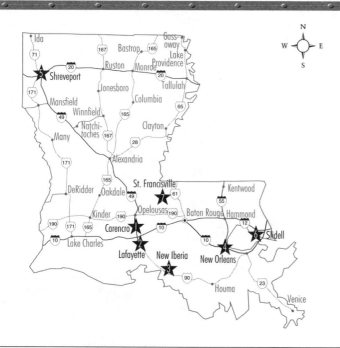

Relay Numbers: TTY (800) 846-5277, VCE (800) 947-5277

Carencro

B&B

825 Kidder Road, 70520
(318) 896-6529
Innkeepers: Joeann & Fred McLemore

$$

La Maison de Campagne, Lafayette B&B

This was the home of a prosperous, sugar cane and cotton plantation family in the early 1900's. "The Country House" has been restored to its grand style of country Victorian elegance. Each guest room has been meticulously decorated and furnished with antiques. Located in Acadiana, among live oak and pecan trees, the nine acre site has a serene country setting, 15 minutes from Lafayette and five minutes from the best Cajun restaurants. You may enjoy a leisurely stroll, swim in the pool, lie under the great live oaks, listen to the birds, and breathe in fresh, country air.

Approved by: AAA

Seven miles north of I-10 on I-49 (N); Exit 7. Right onto frontage road to right. Left on Brasseaux Road; Continue 1 3/4 mile to stop sign. Left on Kidder. Inn is located 1/4 miles on the left.

Lafayette

B&B

2631 SE Evangeline, 70508
(800) 853-7378, or (318) 264-1191
Innkeepers: Tanya & Douglas Greenwald

$/
$$

Alida's, A Bed & Breakfast

Located in the heart of "Cajun Country", this Inn reflects the gracious hospitality of its Innkeepers. After completing a three and a half year restoration of this turn-of-the-century Victorian Cottage, Tanya and Doug opened their home to the traveller. You will be comfortable and at ease here. Fresh cut flowers and wonderful aromas from the kitchen give the feeling of visiting Grandma's house. At the end of the day, you can slip into one of the huge, antique claw-foot bathtubs, sip a glass of wine in the parlor, or just relax on one of the swings on the front porch or rear patio.

Approved by: AAA

From I-10 take Exit 103A onto the Evangeline Thruway. Stay on Evangeline Thruway and Hwy. 90(E) for 5.6 miles. Turn left at the Ramada Inn intersection, turn right onto the frontage road that parallels the Thruway. The Inn is .6 miles on the left.

New Iberia

B&B

4018 Old Jeanerette Road, 70560
(800) 336-7317, Fax (318) 364-8905
Innkeeper: Emma Fox

$/
$$

Pourtos House

This large estate, beside the historic Bayou Teche, is in the heart of the Cajun country. The main house is created in the style of the Acadian plantation and is a wonderful illustration of elegance combined with comfortable livability. The mansion is located on 3 acres of lush, tree-lined grounds. Exotic birds including India Blue Peacocks, Australian Black Swans, Mute White Swans, and Mallards stroll the lawn and grace the centerpiece pond. A swimming pool, steam room, billiard table, and lighted tennis court are all available on-site and nearby are many terrific Cajun restaurants.

Approved by: AAA

Highway I-90 to New Iberia. At Lewis St. light turn north onto Lewis and continue to Parkview, turn right. Continue to Inn sign. Inn is on the right.

Shreveport

B&B

2439 Fairfield Avenue, 71104
(318) 424-2424, Fax (318) 424-3658
Innkeepers: Jimmy & Vicki Harris

$$-
$$$

Step into this Inn and relive past lives in Victorian splendor with collected treasures of the era. The Innkeepers have thoughtfully provided all of the modern amenities in their restoration of the 1905 Victorian mansion. Corporate travellers and honeymooners alike enjoy relaxing in the antique-filled rooms complete with cable television, in-room telephones, and private baths with whirlpool tubs. Nearby are antique shops, Victorian tea rooms, and river boat casinos to entice you or take a leisurely afternoon stroll through the historic district. A proper English breakfast starts your day.

Approved by: AAA, ABBA

2439 Fairfield, A Bed & Breakfast

Take I-20(E) to Line Ave. Exit left onto Christian. Go one block to Fairfield, turn left. From I-20(W), take the Fairfield Exit, turn left.

Slidell

B&B

127 Cleveland Avenue, 70458
(800) 235-4168, Fax (504) 643-2251
Innkeepers: Homer & Sharon Fritchie

$$

This 1895 Victorian mansion is just 30 minutes from the New Orleans French Quarter and the Mississippi Gulf Coast. Built by one of the city founders, it is listed on the National Register of Historic Places. It is located on a beautiful, 4 1/2 acre city block, nestled amidst 300-year-old live oak and pecan trees. Whether relaxing on a porch swing in summer, sipping hot tea before a warm winter fire, or reading a book in a large four-poster, antique bed, you will find that comfort and relaxation is a way of life at this Inn.

Approved by: Mobil

Salmen-Fritchie House

Take the 2nd Slidell exit (#263) off of I-10. Go west approximately .2 miles to Hwy 11. Turn right, go to 2nd light (Front Street) and turn right. Go 1 block to Cleveland Ave. and turn right.

Photo: Chuck Farrier

St. Francisville, LA

Barrow House Inn

B&B

524 Royal, P.O. Box 700, 70775
(504) 635-4791
Innkeeper: Shirley Dittloff

$$/
$$$

This Inn is comprised of two distinctive guest houses, circa 1780 and 1809, and sits in the heart of a magical historic district. Located in Audubon's beloved English plantation country, rooms and suites have period antiques, including armoires, canopy beds, and clawfoot tubs. Shirley offers you a choice of a continental or full breakfast as well as gourmet dinner by candlelight. Both meals are served on fine china with sterling silver. Take a unique cassette walking tour, visit a "mini-space museum", walk among huge live oaks and camellias, visit the shops, or just sit on the porch.

Approved by: Mobil

St. Francisville is located one mile off Hwy. 61, 30 miles north of Baton Rouge and 60 miles south of Natchez. Watch for the signs. Inn is located behind the court house in the center of town.

Bar Harbor, ME

Breakwater 1904

B&B

45 Hancock Street, 04609
(207) 288-2313, or (800) 238-6309
Innkeepers: Margot & Russell Snyder

$$$/
$$$$$

In 1904, John Innes Kane, great grandson of John Jacob Astor, sought an architect to design an English tudor estate located on the shores of Frenchman Bay. He hired the renowned talent, Fred Savage. The estate boasts eleven foot ceilings, leaded glass windows and French doors, and an 1800 sq. foot "great living hall" with a minstrel's gallery above the six foot wide staircase. Breathtaking sunrises over the Porcupine Islands greet guests each morning, while 4 1/2 acres of lawns, gardens, and natural woods ensure complete privacy for an intimate stay by the sea.

Approved by: ABBA

Photos: Brian Vandenbrink

Follow Route 3 into Bar Harbor, take left at stop sign, and go to end of street. Take right onto Main, and the 3rd left onto Hancock. Go to end of street and turn right.

N
W · E
S

Ft .Kent Van Buren
1
Presqueisle
11
Houlton
95
Sherman
Millinocket
Jackman
West Forks
1
Rangeley
201
Calais
Stratton
16
Skow-
hegan
Bangor
9
Rumford
2
95
1
Belfast Blue Hill
Augusta
3
Castine Bar Harbor
Bethel
Lincolnville
9
Deer Isle
Lewiston
Newcastle
10
1
4
495
Camden
Portland
11
Bath New Harbor
Kenne-
bunk
8
Kenne-
bunkport
95

Relay Numbers: TTY (800) 437-1220, VCE (800) 457-1220

10R 2S

BYOB

V,M

Bar Harbor

B&B

40 Holland Avenue, 04609-1432

(207) 288-3044

Innkeepers: Joe & Judy Losquadro

$$/ $$$

Graycote Inn

For a truly romantic getaway, this painstakingly restored 1881 Victorian on a peaceful one-acre village lot has extra large rooms or suites; all with private baths, some with fireplaces, sun porches or balconies. Sleep beneath a cloud of lace and cutwork canopy in king or queen beds. Mornings welcome you to the sun-soaked breakfast porch and a sumptuous full breakfast. Relax on the tapestried love seat in the refined but welcoming parlor watching the firelight glow on the Inn's fine collection of cranberry glass, Lladro porcelain and Hummel figurines.

Approved by: AAA, Mobil

I-95 to Bangor; I-395 to 1A toward Ellsworth. Route 3(E) to Bar Harbor. Two miles past Acadia National Park, left onto Cottage. Go 2 blocks, right onto Holland. The Inn is on the left.

3R 2S

CC

Bar Harbor

B&B

P.O. Box 216, Hulls Cove, 04609

(207) 288-9511

Innkeepers: Don Johnson & Esther Cavagnaro

$- $$$$$

Inn at Canoe Point

Follow the driveway through two acres of pines to the ocean's edge and this Inn built in 1889. The secluded location is just two miles from Bar Harbor and only 1/4 mile from the entrance to Acadia National Park. Stroll among the trees and along the rocky coast or sit at the point and watch the boats sail by. Inside, relax in front of the granite fireplace and enjoy the view of the bay and the mountains beyond. You will be lulled to sleep by the sounds of the surf in your ocean-view room. Enjoy a full breakfast served in the Ocean Room or on the deck overlooking the water.

Approved by: IIA

From Ellsworth, follow Rt. 3 for 15 miles towards Bar Harbor. Just beyond the village of Hull Cove you will see the Acadia National Park entrance on the right. 1/4 mile further on the left will be the Inn sign and the driveway to the Inn.

9R 5S

BYOB

20

V,M,X

Bar Harbor

B&B

106 West Street, 04609
(800) 437-0088
Innkeeper: Mac Noyes

$/
$$$

Manor House Inn

Elegant accommodations and turn-of-the-century ambiance greet you in this 1887 Victorian mansion. The Inn is listed on the National Register of Historic Places. Enjoy your privacy while staying within walking distance of Bar Harbor's fine shops, restaurants, whale watching, Schooner rides, and bike rentals. All of the charming guest rooms and spacious suites are furnished with fine antiques, period accessories, and gracious touches. Some have working fireplaces, garden views, and king beds. All have private baths. Afternoon tea is a special treat.

Approved by: AAA, ABBA, Mobil

From Bangor take Route 1A to Ellsworth, then Route 3 to Bar Harbor. As you come to Bar Harbor, West Street is on your left. The Inn is 1/4 mile down on your right.

6R 1S

BYOB

12

V,M,DV

Bar Harbor

B&B

16 Roberts Avenue, 04609
(207) 288-3443
Innkeeper: Susan Sinclair

$/
$$$

The Maples Inn

Built in 1903, The Maples Inn originally housed wealthy summer visitors to Mount Desert Island. This Victorian structure is located on a quiet street, within walking distance to shops, restaurants, and the sea. For a romantic getaway, reserve the White Birch Suite, complete with a cobalt and white tiled, working fireplace. Your palate will be treated to gourmet delights at breakfast. A special favorite is Blueberry Stuffed French Toast. Visit soon and let the Innkeepers pamper you with their genuine and personalized hospitality.

Approved by: AAA, Mobil

Follow Route 3 from Ellsworth to Bar Harbor approximately 15 miles. In Bar Harbor, turn left onto Cottage Street. Go 4 blocks to Roberts Avenue and make a right. (Watch for Mobil sign). The Inn is on the left side.

12R 3S

V,M,X
DV,EN

Bar Harbor

B&B

69 Mt. Desert, 04609
(800) 553-5109, Fax (207) 288-3115
Innkeeper: Marian Burns

$$-
$$$$

This is a 1864 Bar Harbor estate graced by porches, balconies, bay windows, library, formal dining room, twelve guest rooms, and three suites. Antiques, Victorian period furnishings, private baths, remote cable TV's, A/C, and nine fireplaces can be found here as well as a friendly, helpful staff. There is a full breakfast buffet and afternoon refreshments. The Inn is located in the heart of the historic district on two quiet acres featuring exquisite gardens. It is an easy walk to shops, restaurants, and the waterfront and only five minutes to the National Park.

Approved by: Mobil

Mira Monte Inn

Route 3 - historic corridor- 42 miles from 395 Exit to Route 14.

12R

BYOB

30

V,M,X
DV

Belfast

B&B
MAP

90 N. Port Avenue, 04915
(800) 335-2377, Fax (207) 338-5715
Innkeepers: John & Patty Lebowitz

$/
$$$

This is a turn-of-the-century, shingled, 4000 square foot "cottage" sitting on five and a half bay front acres in a scenic old harbor town. The Inn is decorated with antiques, original art, and oriental rugs. All rooms offer queen or king size beds, bay, forest, or meadow views, and private baths. Patty prepares meals from scratch and is a wonderful cook. You will love her scrambled eggs with lobster and sweet peppers and still-warm muffins. The town offers numerous antique shops, good restaurants, and a harbor full of boats in the summer.

Approved by: AAA, Mobil

Belfast Bay Meadows Inn

Take I-95 to Augusta, ME. Follow SR 3 to Rt. 1 in Belfast. Go south on Rt. 1 for two miles to the Inn on the left.

Blue Hill

Blue Hill Inn

MAP
B&B

Union Street, Rte 177, 04614

(800) 826-7415, or (207) 374-2844

Innkeepers: Don & Mary Hartley

$$$/
$$$$

The circa 1830, federally-styled Inn with its fireplaces, original woodwork, and antique furnishings is ideally located in the heart of this coastal village's historic district. Special amenities include nightly turn-down service, an hors d'oeuvres hour, candlelight dining, an extensive wine list, wine dinners, and schooner overnights. Galleries, Blue Hill Bay, and concerts are within walking distance. The Inn is centrally located for exploring Acadia National Park and the relatively undiscovered East Penobscot Bay area.

Approved by: Mobil

Photos: George W. Gardner

From Route 1 take 15 south to Blue Hill Inn signs to Route 177 east to Inn.

Camden

Blue Harbor House

MAP
B&B

67 Elm Street, 04843

(800) 248-3196, Fax (207) 236-6523

Innkeepers: Jody Schmoll & Dennis Hayden

$$-
$$$

You are invited to relax in this restored, 1810 Cape where yesterday's charms blend perfectly with today's comforts. The beautiful town of Camden, renowned for its spectacular setting where the mountains meet the sea, is just outside the door. The Inn's inviting guest rooms are bright with country antiques and hand-fashioned quilts. Breakfast features such specialties as lobster quiche, cheese souffle, and blueberry pancakes with blueberry butter. Dinner, available to guests by reservation, can be a romantic candle-lit affair or an old-fashioned, Down East lobster feed.

Approved by: AAA, ABBA, Mobil

From Portland , Maine Airport, take Highway 95 (N) to Exit 22, Coastal Route 1. Follow 1 into Camden. The Inn is located on the left side of Route 1, as you enter the village.

Photo: Benjamin Magro

Camden

P.O. Box 1344, 04843
(800) 43 LOBSTER
Innkeepers: Nancy & John True

B&B

$$$/
$$$$$

Inn at Sunrise Point

This new, award-winning oceanfront Inn near Camden is far from the busy highway. Three rooms and four cottages all have ocean views and the private beach is just feet away. Set on four secluded acres in a residential area, the Inn offers guests gourmet breakfast in the glass conservatory. Afternoon appetizers are served in the cherry paneled library. Extremely quiet and serene, spacious rooms offer woodburning fireplaces, TV, VCR, phones, and robes. Cottages also have whirlpools; large, separate tile showers, wet bars, and decks.

Approved by: AAA

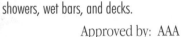

4 1/4 miles north of Camden on Highway 1. Turn right at sign of Inn. Go all the way to water.

Camden

22 High Street, 04843
(207) 236-9636
Innkeepers: Peter & Donny Smith & Diana Robson

B&B

$/
$$$

Maine Stay

A comfortable bed, a hearty breakfast, interesting antiques, and three friendly Innkeepers can be found at the Maine Stay. The Inn is situated in the High Street Historic District only two blocks from the harbor and village center. Built in 1802, the Inn is also an outstanding example of the progressive farm buildings common to 19th century Maine. With a pleasant grove to the south, the Camden Hills State Park to the west, and charming old homes (all listed in the National Register of Historic Places) to the north and east, the Inn projects the essence of New England hospitality.

Approved by: ABBA

On US Route 1.

Kennebunk

48 Beach Avenue, 04043
(207) 967-3850
Innkeepers: Laurence & Patricia Kenny

B&B

$/
$$$

Sundial Inn

The Inn has developed from an early Maine summer cottage into its present state as a Victorian Inn. Each room has its own full bath, telephone, television, thermostat, and air conditioner. The rooms have a cozy atmosphere and are decorated with designer linens and country Victorian antiques. The spacious living room, overlooking the ocean, has a cheery fireplace, wicker chairs, and chintz covered sofas. A generous continental breakfast is served in the oceanview dining room. The Inn is only a few minutes from antique shops, art galleries, and excellent restaurants.

Approved by: AAA, ABBA

Exit 3 off Maine Turnpike east on Route 35 to intersection of Route 9. Continue on Route 35, 1.7 miles (straight thru intersection to Inn.)

Kennebunkport

6 Pleasant Street, PO Box 500A-PI, 04046
(207) 967-3141,
Innkeepers: Bev Davis & Rick Litchfield

B&B

$$/
$$$$

The Captain Lord Mansion

This intimate, luxury Country Inn, sits at the top of a sweeping lawn, and overlooks the Kennebunk River. The guest rooms are decorated with fine quality antiques, rich fabrics, fine art, and queen or king four-posted beds. The warm hospitality of the Innkeepers and staff complement the inviting decor. Also enjoy a full breakfast and afternoon tea and sweets. Visit and experience the quiet elegance of this classic Inn.

Approved by: AAA, IIA, Mobil

Photos: Warren Jagger

I-95 (N), Maine Turnpike, Exit 3. Left onto Route 35 for 5 1/2 miles to Route 9 (E). Turn left and go over bridge. Take 1st right onto Ocean Avenue. Take 5th left (only 3 tenths of a mile) off Ocean Avenue. Mansion is on the left.

Photo: Kelly & King

Kennebunkport

B&B

41 Pier Road, RR 2 Box 1180, 04046
(207) 967-5564, Fax (207) 967-8776
Innkeepers: Joan & Dave Sutter

The Inn at Harbor Head

$$/
$$$$$

Visit a waterside hideaway removed from the bustling pace of Kennebunkport, on the quiet side of town. Delightful perennial gardens surround the Inn which is directly on the waterfront in Cape Porpoise Harbor...an authentic, fishing village that "time forgot." The Inn features incredibly delicious breakfasts and five divinely comfortable bedchambers! While here, relax in the sitting room or in the fireplaced library with its fantastic view of the harbor and ocean. You will enjoy an intimate atmosphere with sunshine, starshine, raindrops, fog, and the cry of the gulls.

Approved by: ABBA, Mobil

Two miles east of Kennebunkport Village, leave Route 9 at Citgo Station and proceed straight ahead 1/4 mile. Inn will be on the right.

Kennebunkport

B&B

34 Maine Street, PO Box 500A-PI, 04046
(800) 950-2117, Fax (207) 967-8757
Innkeepers: Lindsay & Carol Copeland

Maine Stay Inn

$$/
$$$

This is an elegant, yet comfortable B&B located in Kennebunkport's historic district. The main house, built in 1860, is a hip-roof Italianate with Queen Anne colonial features, including a suspended spiral staircase, crystal windows, and ornately carved mantels and mouldings. The house also boasts an inviting wraparound porch and a cupola. All the rooms in the main house are corner rooms with high ceilings, decorated in Victorian style. The Maine Stay Inn also offers cozy cottage rooms in separate buildings that encircle the two-acre property.

Approved by: AAA, ABBA, Mobil

From Main Turnpike (I-95), Exit 3 to Route 35 south 6 miles to Junction of Routes 9 & 35. Left on Route 9 through village to stop sign. Turn right at stop sign and go approximately 4 blocks.

Kennebunkport

Old Fort Inn

B&B

8 Old Fort Avenue, 04046
(800) 828-3678, Fax (207) 967-4547
Innkeepers: David & Sheila Aldrich

$$/
$$$$$

This is one of Kennebunkport's exceptional Country Inns and secret treasures. The unique combination of yesterday's charm and today's conveniences entice many guests to return yearly. The elegant guest rooms are located in a turn-of-the-century carriage house built of red brick and local stone. The rooms are furnished with a meticulous eye for detail, including canopy and four poster beds. A tempting buffet breakfast is served each morning in the Lodge Room decorated with antiques complementing the exposed beams, weathered pine walls, and massive brick fireplace.

Approved by: AAA, IIA

I-95 Exit 3, turn left on Route 35 for 5 1/2 miles. Left at light at Sunoco station for 3/10 miles to Ocean Avenue. Go 9/10 miles to Colony Hotel, then left and follow signs 3/10 miles to Inn.

Lincolnville (Camden)

The Victorian B & B

B&B

The Other Road, P. O. Box 258, 04849
(800) 382-9817, or (207) 236-3785
Innkeepers: Ray & Marie Donner

$/
$$$

Only 300 feet from the sea is this century-old Victorian home that has been restored to its original charm. Spacious rooms with queen-size beds, private baths, and fireplaces are decorated in period decor and provide a quiet atmosphere in a unique country setting. You may relax on the beautiful wraparound porch and enjoy the spectacular views of the gardens and Penobscot Bay. A full country breakfast starts your day off just right. Stroll the shoreline, explore the antique capital of Maine a few miles away, sail, shop, and then return for afternoon goodies in front of the fire.

Approved by: AAA

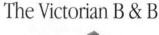

Follow Rt. 1(N) from Camden for 4 miles. Turn right through the Waters Edge Motel. The Inn is 1/4 mile off Rt. 1.

16R 3S

30
V,M,X

New Harbor

AP
MAP
&

361 Pemaquid Point, 04554
(207) 677-2105, Fax (207) 677-3367
Innkeepers: Chuck & Merry Robinson

Bradley Inn

$$/
$$$

The Inn is just a moment's walk from the historic Pemaquid Point Lighthouse. Bradley Inn is renowned for its restaurant and cozy pub. There is also boating, fishing, tennis, and golf nearby. The lovely sand and clear waters of Pemaquid Beach invite a breathtaking swim, and you will delight in exploring the tidal pools of the Rachel Carson Salt Pond. Day trips from nearby New Harbor to fascinating Monhegan Island allow you to view seals and puffins along the way. If you enjoy scouting about, there are countless museums, historical sites, antique shops, and galleries.

Approved by: AAA

Route 95 (Maine Turnpike) to Coastal Route 1 in Brunswick. Continue on Route 1 to Route 129/130 in Damariscotta (27 miles). Follow Route 130 to Pemaquid Point and the Inn.

15R

20
V,M

Newcastle

MAP
B&B

R.R. 2, Box 24, River Road, 04553
(800) 832-8669, Fax (207) 563-1390
Innkeepers: Ted & Chris Sprague

The Newcastle Inn

$/
$$$$

Come to The Newcastle Inn and you will find more than a welcome...you will find a welcome home. The Innkeepers make you feel as though they want nothing more than for you to enjoy their small Inn and to share in their tradition of genuine hospitality. At the end of your day an exceptional dinner and pampering atmosphere await you. Dream of the gourmet breakfast to come. This quiet corner of Maine's Midcoast is where you'll have the pleasure of discovering your own special hideaways. Your memories will be filled with lighthouse-crowned ocean points and seaside villages.

Approved by: AAA, IIA

Maine Turnpike to Exit 9; I-95 north to Brunswick, Exit 22, Route 1 North ; 6 miles north of Wiscasset. Take right on River Road. Continue 1/2 mile. Inn is on the right.

50R 1S

V,M,X
DV

Rangeley, ME

EP
B&B
MAP

Main Street, 04970
(800) 666-3687, Fax (207) 864-3634
Innkeepers: Ed & Fay Carpenter

Rangeley Inn

$/
$$

At the turn-of-the-century, Rangeley was a boom-town resort that catered to summer visitors from Boston and areas as far south as Philadelphia. They arrived by train and reached their hotel by steamboats that plied the lakes. Later, chauffeurs brought cars and limousines over the dirt roads into Rangeley. The Inn was built in 1907 and joined the others in hosting and providing the creature comforts of the time...all for $2 a day. The Inn stands today ready to serve guests in comfort and old-fashioned hospitality.

Approved by: AAA, IIA, Mobil

From Route 4(S), or from Route 16 (W) to Rangeley.

Maryland

N
W ◇ E
S

 Relay Number: (800) 735-2258

Baltimore

B&B

1714 Thames Street, 21231
(800) 432-0184, Fax (410) 522-2324
Innkeeper: Celie Ives

$$-$$$$

Celie's Waterfront B&B

Photos: Curtis Martin

Ever dream of a relaxed, informal but elegant, Country Inn with a roof-deck overlooking the waterfront in the city? Located in historic Fell's Point with its excellent restaurants and speciality shops, you are only a water taxi ride away from harbor attractions and the Oriole ballpark at Camden Yards. You will be pampered with whirlpools, balconies, and gardens. For travelling on business, Celie's provides for all your needs, with phones, desks, fax, and free parking. The Inn offers warm attentive surroundings only minutes away from the business district or convention center.

Approved by: AAA, MBBA

Minutes from Route 83, I-70 and I-95 (N&S). About 1 mile southeast of Harbor Place and the downtown business district.

Baltimore

B&B

1601 Bolton Street, 21217
(410) 728-1179, Fax (410) 728-3379
Innkeepers: Collin Clarke & Paul Bragaw

$$-$$$

Mr. Mole Bed & Breakfast

This 1870 Inn is on historic Bolton Hill, close to downtown, Inner Harbor, Orioles Park, the symphony, opera, antique row, Johns Hopkins, and University of Maryland. Collin has decorated the house in a comfortable English style, complete with 18th and 19th century antiques. All five suites are spacious and include private full baths and private phones. The London Suite and Print Room both include a private sitting room and two bedrooms. Garage parking (with automatic garage door opener) is included, as is a generous, Dutch-style breakfast.

Approved by: AAA, MBBA, Mobil

I-95 to I-395 to Martin Luther King Blvd. Two miles on MLK Blvd.; left on Eutaw Street. 4th stop light turn right on McMechen Street. One block to Bolton Street.

Cascade (Frederick/Gettysburg)

B&B

14700 Eyler Avenue, 21719
(800) 362-9526
Innkeeper: Eda Smith-Eley

$$-
$$$

This is an elegant 1900 manor house on the Mason Dixon Line. Cool breezes, gracious, old-fashioned porches, huge trees, the sound of train whistles, a warming fireplace, and spacious rooms welcome you. If luxury and beauty are what you are looking for, you will love this Inn. If you delight in white linens and lace, fluffy pillows and comforters, French doors and antique armoires, white wicker and cozy rocking chairs, oriental rugs and original art work, you will feel at home here. Three suites feature private whirlpool baths, and two have working fireplaces.

Approved by: MBBA

Bluebird on the Mountain

Take Route 15 to Thormont. Then take 550(N) for 8 miles, to Eyler Avenue and turn right.

Cumberland

AP
MAP
EP
B&B

120 Greene Street, 21502
(800) 286-9718, or (301) 777-0003
Innkeeper: Sharon Ennis Kazary

$-
$$$

The 1815 Cowden House and the 1890 Dent House make up this gracious Inn. Furnished in antique and period reproductions, the Inn is impressive, yet comfortable, within walking distance of the C & O Canal Towpath, the Cumberland Theatre, the Historic District, and the Scenic Railroad. Mountain bicycle rentals are available. The Haystack Mountain Art Workshops are conducted at the Inn June through November. The Inn's Oxford House Restaurant features traditional and gourmet fare. Browse in Eliza's Closet, the Inn's unique gift shop.

Approved by: AAA, MBBA, Mobil

Inn at Walnut Bottom

Travelling east on I-68, take exit 43-A. Turn left at stoplight. Travelling west on I-68, take exit 43-A. Bear right; turn right at stoplight.

The Wayside Inn

Ellicott City

B&B

4344 Columbia Road, 21042
(410) 461-4636
Innkeepers: Margo & John Osantowski

$-
$$

This stately, Federal-period, stone farmhouse sits on two acres. Built between 1800 and 1850, the Inn continues the tradition of a lighted candle in each window indicating room availability. Common Room fireplaces invite guests to read and relax. The other side of the center hall is the dining room where breakfast is served by candlelight as the fireplace glows. The original kitchen now has TV, darts, soft drinks, games, and spring water for guests. In summer, the comfortable, screened porch affords a view of the pond and the occasional heron or duck.

Approved by: MBBA

From Washington DC: I-95 (N) to Route 175 (W) to Route 29 (N) to Route 108 (W). Then go right on Columbia Road. From Baltimore: I-695 to I-70 (W) to Route 29 (S). Exit (St. Johns Lane), take a left on Columbia Road.

Middle Plantation Inn

Frederick

B&B

9549 Liberty Road, 21701
(301) 898-7128
Innkeepers: Shirley & Dwight Mullican

$$

Nestled on 26 acres, several miles east of Frederick, this charming stone and log home offers guests a peaceful weekend retreat. You'll wake each morning to nature in all its glory. Furnished with antiques collected during the Innkeepers' many travels, each guest room offers delightful 19th century ambiance combined with modern conveniences. A massive stone fireplace, stained glass window, and skylights highlight the Keeping Room where guests may read, relax, and socialize. A delightful continental breakfast is served.

Approved by: MBBA

From 270, 70, 340, and 40, take 15 north, and turn on Route 26. Go until you get to Mt. Pleasant, (this is around 5 miles on Route 26). The Inn is on the right.

Photo: George W. Gardner

Frederick

B&B

7945 Worman's Mill Road, 21701
(800) 400-4667, or (301) 694-0440
Innkeepers: Beverly & Ray Compton

$-
$$

"Spring Bank"

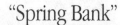

In 1882, George Houck's mansion was described in a local history book as having "all the modern improvements that judiciously expended wealth could obtain or refined taste suggest." Since 1980, the Comptons have welcomed overnight guests to their 16-room brick, country home with expansive lawn, towering trees, original architectural features, and vintage furnishings. Tenant farming continues on the adjoining 8 acres as it has for years. The Inn is near Frederick's Historic District; Monocacy, Antietam, and Gettysburg Civil War sites; Baltimore's Inner Harbor and the Nation's Capitol.

Approved by: MBBA

Photo: H. Wise

Located on Route 355, Worman's Mill Road, 1/4 mile from Route 15, just 2 1/2 miles north of downtown Frederick.

Hagerstown

B&B

20432 Beaver Creek Road, 21740
(301) 797-4764
Innkeepers: Donald & Shirley Day

$

Beaver Creek House B&B

Beaver Creek House is a turn-of-the-century, country Victorian home, located in the historic village of Beaver Creek. Guests may relax in comfort on the quiet wraparound porch where breakfast is served. They may sit in the courtyard by the fountain, stroll through the country garden, or rest by the fishpond and look into the Mountains. Nearby are the National Historic Parks of Antietam, Harpers Ferry, the C&O Canal, and the Appalachian Trail. Guests are invited to step back to a slower, gentler time in the warmth of Beaver Creek House, where the hosts offer comfort and cordiality.

Approved by: AAA, ABBA, MBBA

I-70 Exit 35, south on Route 66 .9 miles to Beaver Creek Road. Turn right and go .8 miles. The Inn is on the right.

Little Orleans

B&B

Little Orleans, 21766
(301) 478-2794
Innkeepers: Flo & Dick Essers

$

In the mountains of western Maryland you will find the peace and quiet of the "beauty spot of Maryland." Leave the interstate and follow the "Black-eyed Susan Route" up the mountainside to the Inn. As the first tourist hotel of Maryland, the Inn retains a touch of history on the Old National Pike. Here you can soak up the atmosphere of the 20's and relax on the porches overlooking the valleys to the east and west. Visit the nearby steam train, the C & O Canal, or the fascinating Geological Center. Dinner is available and there are facilities for groups.

Approved by: MBBA

Town Hill Hotel Bed & Breakfast

From I-68, take Exit 68(N) onto Orleans Rd.. Go 1/4 mile to U.S. Scenic 40(W) to the top of the mountain.

Lutherville

B&B

308 Morris Avenue, 21093
(800) 635-0370, Fax (410) 560-2161
Innkeepers: Gwen & Bob Vaughan

$$/
$$$

Framed by twin gates, the curved driveway of this historic home opens its arms to greet new guests. Inside, the gracious Victorian is quiet and peaceful...a respite from today's hectic world. With whimsical touches throughout, the Inn is furnished with crafts and comfortable antiques. Twin Gates abounds with cozy nooks to relax in...the living rooms with fireplaces, the wide front porch, the lovely gazebo and flower gardens, or the third floor library. It is convenient to the state-of-the-art, high-speed trolley, which will whisk you directly to all of Baltimore's attractions.

Approved by: AAA, IIA, MBBA

Twin Gates Bed & Breakfast Inn

On the northside of Baltimore, near I-83 & Beltway I-695. From Beltway Exit 25 north, take Bellona Avenue for 3 blocks. Turn left onto Morris Avenue. Two blocks to the Inn.

4R 1S
BYOB
V,M

New Market

National Pike Inn

B&B   9 West Main Street, 21774 $$$
(301) 865-5055
Innkeepers: Tom & Terry Rimel

Beautifully restored in the 1960's, this is considered one of New Market's finest examples of Federal architecture. Original locks and wood floors remain, as well as the original cooking crane in the kitchen's walk-in fireplace. Photos in the entrance hall dating back to the mid 1800's are intriguing. Retreat outdoors and enjoy the elaborate azalea gardens which surround a sculptured bird bath and restored 1830's Smoke House. Walking through town you will pass over 30 antique shops, an old-fashioned general store, and Mealey's Restaurant known for fine dining.

Approved by: MBBA

From Washington, 495 to 270 (N). Take Urbana Exit. At stop sign, go left, and go 1 block. Turn right onto Route 355. Go 2 blocks, and turn left onto Route 80. Go 5 or 6 miles, and turn left onto Route 75. Follow to light, and take a left onto Route 144 up hill on right.

6R

Tilghman Island

Chesapeake Wood Duck Inn

B&B   Gibsontown Road, 21671 $$$
(800) 956-2070, Fax (410) 886-2263
Innkeepers: Stephanie & Dave Feith

"Southern Hospitality on the Chesapeake Bay" is not merely a marketing theme, but a way of life here. Enjoy the feeling the moment you step on the front porch through your last bite of scrumptious breakfast. This is an 1890 Victorian overlooking Dogwood Harbor, home of the last fleet of antique, Skipjack sailing vessels in North America. The Inn is appointed with period furnishings, stunning oriental rugs, and original art. You are within walking distance of restaurants, shops and water activities. Tilghman Island is a quaint fishing village offering spectacular scenery and serenity.

Approved by: MBBA

Located 138 miles south of Philadelphia, PA or 94 miles east of Washington, DC. Connect with Route 50 East, take Route 322 to Route 33. Follow Route 33 through St. Michaels, MD to Tilghman Island.

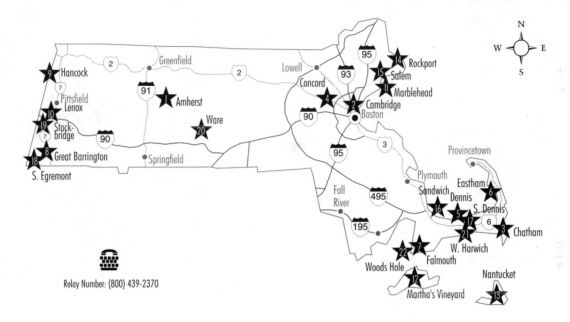

Relay Number: (800) 439-2370

Amherst

Allen House Victorian Inn

B&B
599 Main Street, 01002
(413) 253-5000
Innkeeper: Alan Zieminski

$/
$$

This 1886 Queen Anne Stick style house was the winner of the Amherst Historical Commission's Preservation Award. The cherry fireplace mantels are catalogued by the Metropolitan Museum of Art in New York. "Aesthetic Movement" decor, antiques, art, and art wallcoverings of period designers Charles Eastlake, Walter Crane, and William Morris are historically and artistically featured. Located in the Five College area, the Inn is within walking distance of the Emily Dickinson Homestead and within a 30 minute drive to Historic Deerfield and Sturbridge Village.

Approved by: AAA, ABBA, Mobil

Take Exit 19 on I-91. Follow Route 9 east for 5 miles to Amherst center. Five blocks east on Main Street from town commons.

Cambridge

A Cambridge House

B&B
2218 Massachusetts Avenue, 02140-1836
(800) 232-9989, Fax (617) 868-2848
Innkeepers: Ellen Riley & Tony Femmino

$-
$$$$$

An example of New England history, this 1892 Colonial Revival Inn is unique for its attention to detail and personalized service. You are treated to full, fancy breakfasts, fresh baked goods, fruit available throughout the day, and, in the winter, wine, cheese, and hot hors d'oeuvres served by a fire. Rooms are elegant and luxurious, featuring antiques, canopied beds, down comforters, and modern baths. The Inn is a tranquil hideaway located minutes from the hustle and bustle of downtown Boston and Cambridge. It also has easy access to the historical areas of Lexington and Concord.

Approved by: AAA, ABBA, Mobil

         Call for directions.

6R

BYOB

12

V,M,DN DV

Chatham

B&B

22 Old Harbor Road, 02633
(800) 942-4434, Fax (508) 945-2492
Innkeepers: Tom & Sharon Ferguson

$$$-
$$$$

The Old Harbor Inn

This English Country Inn provides a relaxed and harmonious atmosphere for the discriminating traveller. The aroma of home-baked muffins and scones wafts through the Inn as a buffet breakfast is served in the airy sunroom. Sip gourmet coffee and tea on the outside deck surrounded by geraniums, hydrangea, and antique roses. Galleries, theaters, and a wildlife refuge are all just steps from the front door. Visit the Coast Guard lighthouse and Chatham fish pier or dance by moonlight to the selections of the Chatham Band.

Approved by: AAA, ABBA, Mobil

Route 6 (E) to Exit 11. Turn left on Route 137 (S). Proceed to end and turn left on Route 28. Proceed 3.4 miles to Chatham Rotary. Go left, staying on Route 28 (Old Harbor Road). The Inn is located on the right.

7R

BYOB

10

V,M,X DV

Concord

B&B

462 Lexington Road, 01742
(508) 369-5610
Innkeepers: Marilyn Mudry & Gregory Burch

$$/
$$$

Hawthorne Inn

Along the path that the Minute Men took to first face the British Regulars rests this most colorful Inn where history and literature gracefully entwine. On earth once claimed by Emerson, Hawthorne, and the Alcotts, the Inn beckons the traveller to refresh the spirit in a winsome atmosphere abounding with antique furnishings. Explore rooms festooned with hand-made quilts, original artworks, and archaic artifacts. With a copy of Walden or Little Women in hand, bask near the fire or be led by the resident dog and cat to the garden for a spot of tea.

Approved by: AAA, ABBA, IIA

From Routes 128 and 95, take Exit 30 B. Follow Route 2A (W) for 3 miles. Bear right at fork (follow sign to Concord); go 1 mile. Inn is located on the left.

Dennis

B&B   P.O. Box 1007, 152 Whig Street, 02638 $$
(800) 736-0160, Fax (508) 385-5879
Innkeeper: Marie Brophy

The Inn provides country ambiance and hospitality in the heart of Cape Cod. Located on a quiet, historic street, this lovely 1857 farmhouse is a leisurely walk to the beach or village with its restaurants, shops, playhouse, and art museum. After exploring the Cape from this ideal, central location, relax in the beautiful gardens, in the parlor surrounded by antiques and orientals, or in the Carriage House great room with its white wicker furniture and knotty pine walls. The guest rooms are decorated with country antiques; most have private baths and a few have balconies.

Approved by: AAA, ABBA, Mobil

Isaiah Hall B & B Inn

Route 6 to Exit 8. Left 1.2 miles to Route 6A, then right 3.4 miles. Left on Hope Lane (opposite Gazebo); at end, right on Whig Street. Inn is located on the left.

Eastham

B&B   220 Bridge Road, 02642 $/
(508) 255-0617, Fax (508) 240-0017 $$$$
Innkeepers: Carolyn & Richard Smith

The owners of this Inn promise you an unspoiled environment at outer Cape Cod, one of the country's most beautiful areas. This 1830's home has been authentically restored and decorated with handsome antiques. The site consists of three acres, located on a back road, only minutes by car or bike to beaches, bike trails, or Orleans Village. The seven guest rooms all have private baths and there are five large suites with kitchens. Breakfast is wonderful; afternoon hor d'oeuvres divine!

Approved by: AAA, ABBA, IIA

Whalewalk Inn

By air fly to Boston (Logan) Airport, then it's a 2 hour drive to the Inn.

Eastham

4885 County Road, Route 6, 02651

B&B
(800) 554-1751, or (508) 255-6632
Innkeepers: William & Margaret Keith

$$/
$$$

Penny House

Tucked away behind a high hedge, set on two acres of lawn and trees, surrounded by bicycle paths and nature trails, you will discover this Inn. The main house, circa 1700, features the dining room as well as several of the guest rooms. The more recent additions to the house, 1751 and 1994, are where you will find the sun room, great room with large fireplace, and additional bedrooms. The rooms are all named after classic penny themes such as "Penny Serenade" and "Penny for your thoughts". One of the Innkeepers hails from Australia and will start your day with a great breakfast!

Approved by: AAA

Follow the signs for Cape Cod over the Sagamore Bridge. Go past Exit 12 and around the rotary at Orleans going toward Provincetown. The Inn is five miles beyond the rotary on the left by the Nauset Marsh Nursery.

Falmouth

B&B

261 Grand Avenue South, 02540
(800) 642-4069, Fax (508) 540-1861
Innkeepers: Liz & Rudy Cvitan

$$/
$$$

Grafton Inn

Views from guest rooms and the enclosed porch of this ocean-front, Victorian include miles of beautiful beach, breath-taking views of Martha's Vineyard, and glorious sunsets. The Inn is furnished throughout with period antiques and original artwork. Overhead paddle fans gently stir the ocean air and home-made chocolates, late afternoon wine and cheese, and fresh flowers from the English gardens enhance the atmosphere of leisure and indulgence. The Inn is on the bike path and offers complimentary bicycles as well as sand chairs and towels for the beach. A short walk leads to the Island Ferry.

Approved by: AAA, Mobil

Take Rt. 28(S) from Bourne Bridge to first traffic light at Jones Road. Turn left onto Jones Road. Continue through two more sets of lights. You are then on Worcester Court. Follow this to the blinking light where the road divides and go right onto Grand Avenue and follow to Inn.

13R

20
X

Great Barrington

MAP
684 South Egremont Road, 01230
(800) 992-1993, or (413) 528-2720
$$$-$$$$$

Innkeepers: Claudia & John Ryan/ Barbara & Gerry Liebert

This Mansion is set on 10 landscaped and wooded acres with perennial gardens surrounding the house and swimming pool. There are two comfortable living rooms. While enjoying the fire, play the piano or a game or just relax with a good book or congenial friends and your favorite drink from the well-stocked bar. The bedrooms are individually decorated with designer sheets and comforters and lots of pillows. Dinner is a treat. Claudia is known for the best duck in the Berkshires. The wine list is well priced and complements the menu.

Approved by: Mobil

Windflower Inn

From Taconic Parkway, take Route 23 (E) 14.5 miles. From Mass Pike, take Exit 2 to Route 102 (W) to Route 7(S) to 23 (W). Continue 3 miles to Inn.

...
12R 5S
BYOB
V,M,X

Hancock

B&B
P.O. Box 1079, Route 43, 01237
(413) 738-5348, Fax (518) 733-6025
$$/$$$

Innkeepers: Frank & Ronnie Tallet

This unique Inn was originally McVeigh's Saw Mill. Its Central European architecture and ambiance will make you feel you have taken a journey to the Old World. It's friendly, warm and attentive. Breakfast and afternoon tea are served on the outside patio or the Europa dining room. The common area with large fireplace can be a gathering place or a quiet corner. For those special times, there are several suites, some with fireplaces. The grounds have paths, sitting areas, and a pool. The Inn is located within a short distance of Berkshire attractions and sports.

Approved by: AAA, Mobil

Mill House Inn

From NYC, Taconic Parkway (N), take Route 295. Right to Route 22, left to Route 43 for 1 1/4 miles. From Boston, Mass. Turnpike (I-90), take Exit B3, Route 22(N) to Route 43 on NY/MA border.

Photos: Art Marasco

Lenox

EP
&

16 Church Street, P. O. Box 1810, 01240
(800) 253-0917, Fax (413) 637-9756
Innkeepers: Clifford Rudisill & Ray Wilson

$$/
$$$$

The Village Inn

In the historic district, this 1771 Colonial Inn is near shops, galleries, beautiful parks and wooded trails, Tanglewood and summer theater and dance festivals, winter skiing, fall foliage and spring flower excursions, and year-round museums such as the Norman Rockwell, Clark, Grandma Moses, and Hancock Shaker Village. A full, country breakfast menu, afternoon English Tea with scones and Devonshire-style clotted cream, and savory candlelight dinners are served in the intimate dining rooms. Light fare and potables are served late in the downstairs tavern. Winter and Spring packages.

Approved by: AAA, IIA, Mobil

From I-90 take Exit 2. Follow Rt. 20(W) through the town of Lee to the traffic light at the intersection of Rt. 20 and Rt. 183. Turn left onto Rt. 183(S). Continue 1 mile to Church Street and turn right. The Inn is 2nd drive on the right. From Rt. 7A, follow to Lenox and turn onto Church.

Marblehead

B&B

25 Spray Avenue, 01945
(800) 626-1530, or (617) 631-6789
Innkeepers: Roger & Sally Plauche

$$$/
$$$$

Spray Cliff on the Ocean

Enjoy this marvelous, English Tudor mansion, set high above the Atlantic with views extending forever. The airy, spacious bedrooms feature colorful chintzes, wicker, and flowers. The cozy, relaxed atmosphere of the fireplaced living and dining area is a perfect spot from which to gaze at the sea and bask in the surrounding beauty of the ever-changing panorama. The brick, seaside terrace, nestled in lush flower gardens, invites romance, dreams, and solitude. The setting is beautiful in all seasons and in all weather.

Approved by: AAA

From Boston, take Route 1A (N) to Route 129. Right on Clifton to end. From Route 95 take Route 114 (E) until it ends in Marblehead. Take Route 129 (W) to Clifton Avenue (at light). Left on Clifton to end.

Martha's Vineyard Island

Thorncroft Inn

B&B
278 Main Street, 02568
(800) 332-1236, Fax (508) 693-5419
Innkeepers: Karl & Lynn Buder

$$-
$$$$$

This Inn is secluded, first class, and couples oriented. All rooms have private baths, air conditioning, antique appointments, color cable TV, and phone service. Most of the rooms have working fireplaces and canopied beds. Some, in addition, have private entrances, balconies, whirlpools, or private hot tubs. Your visit includes a full country breakfast, afternoon tea, evening turndown service, and the Boston Globe newspaper delivered to your door every morning. The Inn is nestled on 3 1/2 acres of quiet, treed grounds.

Approved by: AAA, Mobil

Follow major highways to Cape Cod. Take Steamship Authority Ferry from Woods Hole.

Nantucket

Cobblestone Inn

B&B
5 Ash Street, 02554
(508) 228-1987, Fax (508) 228-6698
Innkeepers: Robin Hammer Yankow & Keith Yankow

$/
$$$

Built in 1725, the Inn is just two blocks from the boat yard on a cobbled street in the historic district. Original, preserved features are wide floorboards, a working living room fireplace, and curved-corner-support posts from the frame of a ship. Most of the guest rooms have period decorations and queen-canopy beds, and all have private baths. There is a bike rack in the fenced-in yard, a brick patio overlooking the garden, an airy sun porch with white wicker furniture, and a large living room with cable TV, telephone, and a closet full of games.

Approved by: Mobil

From Hyannis, take steamship to Nantucket. Walk straight from wharf, and take second right onto North Water Street. Your second left is cobblestoned Ash Street (not the paved Ash Lane).

Seven Sea Street Inn

Nantucket

B&B

7 Sea Street, 02554
(508) 228-3577
Innkeepers: Matthew & Mary Parker

$$/
$$$$

When visiting Nantucket, you want your time there to be special. At this Inn, you will experience attentive service and elegant accommodations that will make your stay memorable. Seven Sea Street is a beautiful oak post and beam Inn, located on a side street in Nantucket Village. Each guest room has a queen-sized canopied bed, cable TV, air conditioning, phone, and refrigerator. You will be served an elegant continental breakfast each morning. In the evening, watch the harbor sunset from the widows-walk deck or relax in the whirlpool.

Approved by: AAA, Mobil

From Steamboat Wharf, it's a 3 minute walk. Take the first right onto South Beach Street, then second left onto Sea Street. The Inn is on the left.

Yankee Clipper Inn

Rockport

MAP
B&B

96 Granite Street, 01966
(800) 545-3699, Fax (508) 546-9730
Innkeepers: Bob & Barbara Ellis

$$$/
$$$$$

Situated on a peninsula jutting into the Atlantic, the Inn offers gracious accommodations in three converted residences. The neo-classic building designed by Bulfinch, in 1840, was formerly a "gentleman farmer's" home. The main building was built in 1929 and is an eclectic combination of Georgian and Art Deco design with beautiful ocean views. It is surrounded by carefully tended gardens. The third building, features floor-to-ceiling picture windows facing directly on the ocean. Enjoy the heated, salt-water pool, and a menu featuring New England cuisine.

Approved by: ABBA, IIA, Mobil

Photos: Fredrik D. Bodin

Route 128 (N) to Cape Ann to first set of lights. Left on Route 127 to Rockport. Left at 5 corner intersection. Stay on 127. Two miles to Inn.

17R 5S

The Salem Inn

Salem

B&B 7 Summer Street (Route 114), 01970
(508) 741-0680, Fax (508) 744-8924
Innkeepers: Richard & Diane Pabich

$$/
$$$

Built in 1834 by sea captain Nathaniel West, this lovely, Federal-style Inn blends the warmth and charm of yesteryear with the comfort and convenience of today. Accommodations include spacious, comfortable, and individually decorated guest rooms featuring antiques, period detail, and homey touches. Guest suites, complete with equipped kitchens, are ideal for families. All rooms have a queen or dual-king bed, air-conditioning, direct-dial telephone, color cable TV, and private bath. Many have working fireplaces, and two have whirlpool baths.

Approved by: AAA

Photos: Marc Teatum Photography

Route 95, take 114 (E) into downtown Salem to Inn. From Boston, take Route 1A (N) to Salem, and then Route 114 (W) to Salem Inn.

6R 1S

Captain Ezra Nye House

Sandwich

B&B 152 Main Street, 02563
(800) 388-CAPT, Fax (508) 833-2897
Innkeepers: Elaine & Harry Dickson

$/
$$

A sense of history fills this 1829 federal home built by clipper-ship captain Ezra Nye, who was described as "one of the finest of them all... a great figure even among the lordly aristocrats of the transatlantic packet trade." The rooms, decorated with antiques, include canopied, four-poster, and sleigh beds. Within walking distance of the ocean, the boardwalk, marina, museums, shops, fine dining, and Shawme Pond, the Inn stands proud in the center of Sandwich Village.

Approved by: AAA, ABBA, Mobil

After crossing Sagamore Bridge, stay on Mid-Cape Highway (Route 6) to Exit 2. Turn left onto Rt. 130. Go 1 1/4 miles. Turn right at church onto Main Street. The Inn will be on the right.

S. Dennis

B&B
MAP

333 Main Street, 02660
(800) 282-1619, or (508) 398-5966
Innkeepers: Pat & Dave York

$/
$$

Captain Nickerson Inn

This delightful, Victorian, Sea Captain's home was built in 1828 and changed to the present Queen Anne style in 1879. The comfortable front porch is lined with white wicker rockers and the living room and dining room, each with a fireplace, are lovely with stained glass windows. The Inn sits on a bike path and is only one-half mile from the Cape Cod Bike Rail Trail. Bicycles are available to overnight guests for a small fee. Nearby are world-class beaches, craft and antique shops, and a small church with the oldest working pipe organ in the country. The full breakfast is not to be missed.

Approved by: AAA, ABBA

Call for directions.

Stockbridge

B&B

P. O. Box 618, 01262
(413) 298-3337, Fax (413) 298-3406
Innkeepers: Lee & Don Weitz

$$/
$$$$$

The Inn at Stockbridge

Consummate hospitality and outstanding breakfasts distinguish your visit to this turn-of-the-century, Georgian Colonial estate set on 12 secluded acres in the heart of the Berkshires. Whether you are dining on the sunny patio overlooking the flower gardens and fountain, or seated with other guests by candlelight at a formal polished mahogany table, the tone is set for a special stay. The Inn has a gracious, English country house feeling. A visit here will put you close to the Norman Rockwell Museum, Tanglewood, summer theater, Hancock Shaker Village, and four-season recreation.

Approved by: IIA, Mobil

From the Massachusetts Turnpike, take Exit 2. Go west on Rt. 102 for approximately 5 miles to Rt. 7. Take Rt. 7(N) for 1.2 miles. The Inn is on the right. From NYC take the Taconic Pkwy. to Rt. 23(E) and Rt. 7(N) past Stockbridge 1.2 miles.

Ware

B&B

121 Church Street, 01082

(413) 967-7798

Innkeepers: Fraidell Fenster & Richard Watson

$

A beautiful, maple-canopied street brings you to the door of this Inn. The wraparound porch of the 1880 Victorian home beckons you to relax while the two acres of grounds invites you to explore. You are in the country here but close to Old Sturbridge Village, Old Deerfield, and the Springfield area attractions. After a day of adventures return to the comfort of American Primitive decor with heirloom quilts and an extensive early cradle collection. In winter, enjoy the fire with hot, mulled cider; in summer, lounge in the hammock with lemonade. Be prepared for the "no lunch" breakfast!

Approved by: AAA

Wildwood Inn Bed & Breakfast

Take Exit 8 from I-90 and turn left onto Rt. 32N. Follow to the junction of Rt. 32N and Rt. 9E. Turn right in front of the theater. Turn left onto Church Street at the 2nd set of traffic lights. The Inn is on the right, 3/4 of a mile up the hill.

West Harwich

B&B

77 Main Street, 02671-0667

(508) 432-9628, Fax (508) 432-9628

Innkeepers: Jack & Eileen Connell

$$/
$$$

This Inn is reminiscent of a small, Irish hotel and is decorated in comfortable antiques, oriental rugs, and lace doilies. There are private suites set in the pines for the romantic, all with sitting rooms or areas, color cable T.V., air conditioners, and small refrigerators. Relax in the large comfortable living room by the fireside or in the spa on a wraparound porch overlooking the swimming pool and gardens. Full, family- style Irish breakfast is featured by candlelight. The Claddagh Tavern is a delightfully Irish, intimate pub serving homemade meals.

Approved by: AAA

Cape Cod Sunny Pines

Once on Cape Cod by either bridge take Route 6 (Mid Cape Highway) to Exit 9. Go right on to Route 134. Take 3rd traffic light make left to Rt 28. Then 1/2 mile on right you will see signs.

5R 1S

BYOB

12

V,M

Woods Hole, MA

B&B

Box 238, 320 Woods Hole Road, 02543
(800) 320-2322, Fax (508) 457-7519
Innkeeper: Diana Smith

$/
$$$

This is a faithful reproduction of an Old Cape Cod home, focusing on warmth, hospitality, and an eye for detail that will delight you. Handsome quilts and other needlework create a country feeling. Senses are teased by fragrances from the kitchen each morning, and one need not wait until breakfast for that wonderful first cup of coffee. Scented ironed sheets, flowers at bedside, and thick, oversized towels warm the soul as well as the body. Your breakfast by candlelight in the parlour with a roaring fire or poolside, depending on the weather, will be remembered.

Approved by: AAA

The Marlborough

Expressway south (Route 3) from Boston. At Cape Cod Canal, take Route 28 (S) to Falmouth. At Route 28 (S)/Rt 28 (N) junction, take right to Woods Hole. Inn is located 1 1/2 miles on left.

Michigan

N
W · E
S

1. Urban Retreat B & B......p 110
2. Chicago Street Inn......p 236
3. Chicago Pike Inn......p 110
4. Hidden Pond B & B......p 236
5. Dutch Colonial Inn......p 236
6. Mendon Country Inn......p 111
7. Sans Souci Euro Inn & Resort......p 111
   Inn at Union Pier......p 114
8. Historic Nickerson Inn......p 112
9. Bayside Inn......p 236
   Maplewood Hotel......p 112
   Park House......p 236
   Red Dog B & B......p 113
   Sherwood Forest B & B......p 113

Relay Number: (800) 649-3777

Ann Arbor

B&B

2759 Canterbury Road, 48104
(313) 971-8110
Innkeepers: Andre Rosalik & Gloria Krys

$

The Urban Retreat B&B

The B&B has been providing lodging by reservation only for business and pleasure travellers since 1986. Located in a quiet, suburban neighborhood, the ranch home combines all the conveniences of modern living with quality furnishings from the past. Two guests rooms are available. Curl up in the living room with a lap cat and a good book, or grab the binoculars and watch the bird feeders from the year-round porch. Stretch your legs in the adjacent 127 acre wildlife preserve. A delicious breakfast is served overlooking the garden.

Approved by: Lake to Lake

US 23 to Exit 37B. West on Washtenaw 3 lights. South on Huron Parkway 1/3 mile. West on Canterbury. The B&B is on the right.

Coldwater

B&B

215 E. Chicago Street, 49036
(517) 279-8744
Innkeeper: Rebecca Schultz

$$/
$$$$

Chicago Pike Inn

This Colonial Reform mansion, built in 1903, has been renovated to its grand Victorian splendor. The beautifully restored rooms are individually decorated for pleasure and comfort and have many thoughtful touches. Set in an historic neighborhood, the Inn's original parquet floors, gas chandeliers, stained glass window, and stunning cherry staircase are complemented by period antiques and collectables. Becky and her staff have a knack for making your stay memorable. They serve breakfast and seasonal refreshments with warmth and hospitality.

Approved by: AAA, Lake to Lake, Mobil

Photos: Tom Bagley

Located 100 miles west of Detroit, 120 miles east of Chicago, 35 miles southeast of Battle Creek. The Inn is on US 12 (Chicago Street), one mile west of the Coldwater Exit (#13) of I-69.

Mendon

Mendon Country Inn

B&B

440 W. Main, 49072
(616) 496-8132, Fax (616) 496-8403
Innkeepers: Dick & Dolly Buerkle

$
$$$

The Inn was originally built in 1843, and the brick structure of today was rebuilt in 1873. The interior was designed in the grand style of the Post Civil War era. The Innkeepers have added two other buildings on their 14 acres. There are now nine rooms with private baths and nine whirlpool suites. Activities are offered throughout the year such as quilting retreats, an Old Tyme Thanksgiving, and a country Christmas. In the summer, you can enjoy canoeing off the dock or use the bicycles built for two. On Saturday nights, there are free back porch concerts.

Approved by: Lake to Lake

Photos: David Owens

South of Kalamazoo (30 minutes) or north of Indiana/Ohio Turnpike on 131 to Three Rivers then east 12 miles on Highway 60 to Inn.

New Buffalo

Sans Souci Euro Inn & Resort

B&B

19265 S. Lakeside Road, 49117
(616) 756-3141, Fax (616) 756-5511
Innkeeper: Angelika Siewert

$$$$

Fifty acres of spring-fed lakes, wildflower meadows, and whispering pines stretch behind the gates of this Inn, opening sweeping views of Lake Michigan's pastoral countryside. Accommodations are crafted into barns, complete with modern amenities in European decor. You may choose a suite in solitude, a family vacation home, or an English cottage for two at private Lake Sans Souci. Only 70 miles from Chicago, you are close to many restaurants, antique malls, vineyards, and galleries. Swim, fish, skate, and ski on-site. Angie will welcome you to her hidden treasure.

Approved by: Lake to Lake

Exit 1 from I-94 in Michigan. Go south for 3/10 mile towards LaPorte. Go east on Wilson Rd. and continue to the end of the road.

Pentwater

Historic Nickerson Inn

B&B

262 W. Lowell, PO Box 986, 49449
(616) 869-6731, Fax (616) 869-6151
Innkeepers: Harry & Gretchen Shiparski

$/
$$$$

In 1913, Charles Nickerson started construction on the Inn on a bluff overlooking Lake Michigan. He used many handmade blocks made from the sand from the dune on which it is built. The Inn was opened on July 1, 1914. From that day forward, the Inn has been known for its warmth, gracious hospitality, and fine dining. Nickerson Inn has been completely renovated over the past three years, and the traditional atmosphere of grace, elegance, beauty, and casual charm has been maintained. Great emphasis is placed on the "personal touch."

Approved by: Lake to Lake

Highway 31 (N) to Pentwater Exit. Left on Monroe to Hancock to Lowell (Dairy Creme on S.W. corner). Left on Lowell. Inn is located 2 blocks on right.

Saugatuck

Maplewood Hotel

B&B

428 Butler Street, 49453
(616) 857-1771, Fax (616) 857-1773
Innkeepers: Catherine L. Simon & Sam Burnell

$/
$$$

Built in 1860, the Maplewood Hotel has operated as a resort hotel for the past century. This Greek-Revival structure, with its 25 foot pillars, boasts a traditional charm of yesteryear. All 15 rooms provide a private bath, TV, AC, and phone. Five suites offer a whirlpool and a sitting area or fireplace. Breakfast is served in the formal dining room or on the screened-in-porch adjacent to the deck and pool area. The public also has an opportunity to enjoy fine dining at lunch. The Hotel is centrally located in downtown Saugatuck.

Approved by: Lake to Lake

     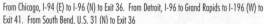
From Chicago, I-94 (E) to I-96 (N) to Exit 36. From Detroit, I-96 to Grand Rapids to I-196 (W) to Exit 41. From South Bend, U.S. 31 (N) to Exit 36

The Red Dog Bed & Breakfast

Saugatuck

132 Mason Street, 49453

(616) 857-8851

B&B $

Innkeepers: Daniel Indurante, Kristine Clark & Gary Kott

Built in 1879, this Bed & Breakfast is located in downtown Saugatuck, a quaint, harbor village nestled in the sand dunes near Lake Michigan. You are steps away from the unique shops, fine restaurants, and interesting art galleries that have made this year-round resort town and artists' colony "The Cape Cod of the Midwest." Furnished in a mix of contemporary furnishings and antiques, the Red Dog offers a comfortable place to relax in the heart of Saugatuck. There's never a minimum stay required, and children are always welcome.

Approved by: Lake to Lake

Located in downtown Saugatuck. Use Exits 36 or 41 off of I-196.

Sherwood Forest Bed & Breakfast

Saugatuck

938 Center Street, 49453

(800) 838-1246, Fax (616) 857-1996

B&B $/ $$$

Innkeepers: Keith & Susan Charak

Surrounded by woods, this beautiful Victorian-style home with a large wraparound porch was built in the 1890's. The guest rooms are traditionally furnished with antiques, cozy wing chairs, and plush area rugs. Outside, there is a heated, in-ground swimming pool with a mural of dolphins. Lake Michigan and a public beach are 1/2 block away. The area's wide, white sandy beaches are the perfect place for strolling, swimming, or watching spectacular sunsets. Whatever the season, there is always something special going on at "The Forest."

Approved by: AAA, ABBA, Lake to Lake

I-96 North to Exit 36 (Saugatuck-Douglas). North on Blue Star Highway to the stop light at Center Street. Left 1 mile. The Inn is on the right.

16R 2S

V,M,DV

Union Pier, MI

9708 Berrien, 49129

(616) 469-4700, Fax (616) 469-4720

Innkeepers: Joyce Erickson Pitts & Mark Pitts

B&B

$$/$$$

The Inn at Union Pier

Just 200 steps from the beach, the Inn caters to weekend getaways and weekday corporate retreats. Spacious rooms offer a mix of Scandinavian Country and Lakeside Cottage styles. Many rooms feature Swedish fireplaces, porches, or balconies. Unwind in the sauna and hot tub or relax and enjoy Michigan wines and popcorn served every evening. A bountiful breakfast and afternoon snack are included. Corporate meeting amenities include: phones, fax, copier, 46" television with VCR, A/V equipment and conference room.

Approved by: Lake to Lake

         Take I-94 to Michigan's Exit 6 (Union Pier). Go west 1 mile to flashing light. Turn right onto Red Arrow Highway. Go 1/2 mile to Berrien and turn left. The Inn is 1 1/2 blocks on the left.

Minnesota

N
W E
S

Relay Number: (800) 657-3529

9R 1S

B&B

Brooklyn Center, MN
6150 Summit Drive N., 55430
(800) 428-8382, Fax (612) 569-6320
Innkeeper: Steve Barrett

$$$

Inn on the Farm

The Inn is located at the Earle Brown Heritage Center and offers a bed and breakfast experience that you will not soon forget. Housed in a cluster of historic farm buildings, the Inn is on the grounds of a beautifully restored Victorian gentleman's country estate, just 10 minutes from the heart of downtown Minneapolis. As a guest, you may choose from the exquisitely furnished and beautifully decorated rooms, each with a private whirlpool tub, luxurious queen-size bed, and period furniture. Breakfast is served in the dining room and afternoon tea in the Parlor.

Approved by: AAA

From I-94 exit onto Shingle Creek Parkway. Take the Summit Drive Exit and turn left to the Inn.

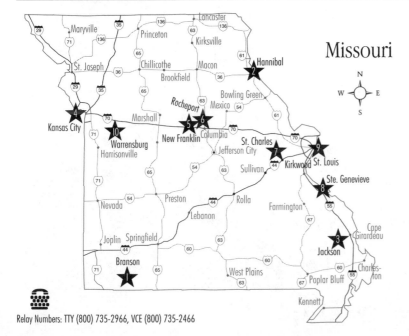

Missouri

Relay Numbers: TTY (800) 735-2966, VCE (800) 735-2466

Fifth Street Mansion B & B Inn

Hannibal

B&B

213 South Fifth Street, 63401
(800) 874-5661 or (314) 221-0445
Innkeepers: Donalene & Michael Andreotti

$

Listed on the National Register of Historic Places, this 1858 mansion offers a blend of warm, Victorian charm and comfortable amenities. Antique furnishings and decor complement the stained glass, distinctive fireplaces, and original gas light fixtures. You will enjoy a bountiful breakfast under the chandelier that lighted the dinner hosting Mark Twain on his last visit to Hannibal. Whether sightseeing, antiquing, rocking on the porch, or reading by the fire you will find whatever you are seeking...recreation, rest, or romance. Above all you will find old-fashioned hospitality.

Approved by: AAA, Mobil

From Hwy. 79(N) turn left onto Church. Turn left onto Fifth Street. The Inn will be on the right.

Garth Woodside Mansion

Hannibal

B&B

RR 1, 63401
(314) 221-2789
Innkeepers: Irv & Diane Feinberg

$-
$$

This 1871 Victorian Mansion is unchanged outside, and original furnishings span over 150 years. The romance of the Inn will capture you with its clawfoot tubs, canopy beds, and nightshirts for your use. Enjoy fireside chats with new-found friends. You are invited to mingle, browse, and share Victorian delights. Your spacious bedchambers are a careful selection of fabrics, laces, and textures chosen to blend with one of the finest, private, 19th century furniture collections. It feels like home with its easy intimacy. There are 39 magnificent acres...to share a magical experience.

Approved by: AAA, Mobil

100 miles north of St. Louis just off Highway 61. Take Warren Barret Road. Make the first right turn. Follow this country lane 1/2 mile with the Mansion on your right.

12R

BYOB

14

V,M,X

Kansas City

B&B
♿

116 East 46th Street, 64112
(816) 531-7979, Fax (816) 531-2407
Innkeepers: Susan Moehl & Penni Johnson

$$/ $$$

Southmoreland on the Plaza

This 1913 Colonial is in the heart of Kansas City's cultural, shopping, entertainment, and financial districts. Just 1 1/2 blocks from the renowned Country Club Plaza and Nelson-Atkins Museum of Art, Southmoreland is suited for both business travellers and vacationers. Amenities include afternoon wine and cheese, fresh flowers and fruit in the rooms as well as private decks, fireplaces, or double Jacuzzi® baths, parking, A/C, antique furnishings, common areas with fireplaces, TV/VCR, and a film library. Sports and dining privileges at an historic private club.

Approved by: ABBA, BBIM, IIA, Mobil

Located within 2 blocks of Country Club Plaza.

9R

BYOB

Rocheport

B&B

504 Third Street, 65279
(314) 698-2022
Innkeepers: Vicki & John Ott

$/ $$$

School House B&B

 (icons continue)

This Inn, once a school building, is "head of the class" in comfort and charm. Original blackboards, an antique school bell, and large, framed prints of pages from grade school reading books are set among Victorian antiques, clawfoot tubs, and Waverly prints. The "Show 'n Tell Room" even has a heart-shaped whirlpool. In the beautifully, landscaped gardens there's an adult-size swing set, fountains, and benches. The Katy Trail, the longest hiking and biking trail in the country, is 2 blocks from the Inn. School was never so memorable!

Approved by: BBIM

85

V,M

I-70 Exit 115 which is Route BB. North 2 miles, on right (Route BB becomes Third St.) at the corner of Third and Clark.

Ste. Genevieve

B&B

339 St. Mary's Road, 63670
(800) 275-6041, or (314) 883-7171
Innkeepers: Royce & Margaret Wilhauk

$/
$$$

This French Creole-style house sits on two and a half acres in the Historic District and was designed for romance. Warm hospitality and tranquility await in the traditionally furnished guest rooms featuring queen-size beds, fireplaces, Jacuzzi® baths, and cable television. The first and second floor sitting rooms each have a fireplace, library, and table games. Sit on the wraparound porch and enjoy the pastoral setting or walk to a variety of restaurants, shops, and historic sites. During the evening social hour, ask your hosts about the adjacent restoration of the circa 1785 Bequette-Ribault House.

Approved by: BBIM

Creole House

Take Exit 150 off Hwy. 55 and follow Hwy. 32 for 5 miles to Hwy. 61(S). Drive one mile and turn left onto St. Mary's Rd. Inn will be on the left.

Photo: J.M.C. Photo Service

Ste. Genevieve

B&B

146 South Third Street, 63670
(800) 275-1412, or (312) 883-3493
Innkeepers: Mike & Barbara Hankins

$$/
$$$

To visit here is to step gently into the time when riverboats plied the mighty Mississippi and weary travellers looked forward to the hospitality of this famous hotel. At this two hundred year old landmark, the graciousness of the past is carefully blended with modern comforts to make your stay a very special experience. The 1790's, Federal-style building has operated as a hotel since 1805 and was known for the finest accommodations between Natchez and St. Louis. Today, each of the romantic guest rooms contains a collection of country, Victorian antiques and delightful whimsies.

Approved by: BBIM

The Southern Hotel

Take I-55 to Hwy. 32(E). Follow for 1/2 mile to the center of the Historic District. Turn right at 4th and Market Streets.

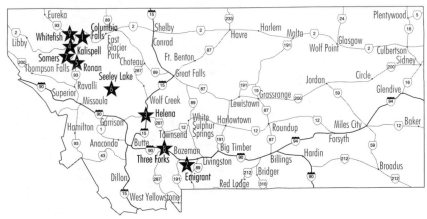

VCE (800) 735-2466

Emigrant

Box 84, 59027

(406) 333-4063

Innkeepers: Pete & Carol Reed

B&B

$$

This gateway to Yellowstone is nestled in the majestic Rocky Mountains, just minutes away from the scenic National Park. The spacious country home sits on the banks of the pristine Yellowstone River, a noted blue-ribbon trout stream. The Norwegian Montanan Innkeepers will greet you with "Velkommen" as they invite you to share their piece of heaven on earth in Paradise Valley. Leisure, Leather and Lattes can all be enjoyed where a river runs through it. The Inn promises a good night sleep, a delicious home-cooked breakfast, and Montana friendship.

Approved by: MBBA

Paradise Gateway

25 1/2 miles south of Livingston, near the north entrance to Yellowstone Park. Halfway between mile markers 26 & 27 on Highway 89 south.

Helena

B&B

328 N. Ewing, 59601
(406) 442-3309
Innkeepers: Bobbi Uecker & Rock Ringling

$$

The Sanders-Helena's B&B

This three-story, Queen Anne mansion offers elegant accommodations steeped in Helena's historic past. The Inn was built in 1875 by Harriet and Wilbur Sanders. Wilbur, one of Montana's first US senators, founded the State Historical Society. The sitting room still has its original wainscotting, paintings, and parquet floor. The dining room has its original stained glass window and built-in oak buffet. Each guest room contains more original furnishings as well as private bath, TV, and phone. Listed on the National Historic Register.

Approved by: AAA, MBBA

Photos: John Reddy

From I-15, take the Capitol Area Exit leading west. At Montana Avenue, turn left (south) to 6th. At 6th, turn right (west) to Ewing. At Ewing, turn right to 7th. Inn is located at the corner.

Ronan

B&B

1184 Timberlane Road, 59864
(800) 775-4373, or (406) 676-4373
Innkeepers: Doris & Leonard McCravey

$$

The Timbers Bed & Breakfast

This stunning Inn, with a magnificent view of the Rocky Mountain Mission Range, is secluded on 21 acres just minutes from Flathead Lake. Cathedral ceilings, hand-hewn beams, and barnwood dining area create a sophisticated, yet warm, country atmosphere. The house is glassed-in and has a wraparound deck that provides unparalleled views of the mountains. Enjoy one of Doris's cinnamon country breakfasts while listening to stories of Leonard's 27 years on the Pro-Rodeo circuit. Ski or hike on trails accessible from the grounds, or plan a day trip to nearby Glacier National Park.

Approved by: MBBA

From Missoula, take 93 north to mile marker 46. Turn right (Timberlane Road). Go 2 miles to Inn.

Seeley Lake

B&B

P. O. Box 350, 59868
(800) 977-4639, or (406) 677-3474
Innkeeper: Marilyn Shope Peterson

$$-
$$$

The Emily A B & B

This Inn, built in the center of the Circle Arrow Ranch, commands a sunny valley tucked between ranges of the Rocky Mountains at the headwaters of the Columbia River. Wide porches overlook the wilderness while picture windows frame views of an eight acre lake, wildflower-filled meadows, the Clearwater River, and rugged mountains. Inside, the Lodge is comfortable and furnishings include a world-class collection of sports memorabilia and fine pieces of Western art. Wake up to the songs of the meadowlarks, enjoy a western breakfast, and experience the beauty of Montana.

Approved by: AAA, MBBA

Photos: Roger Wade Studio

The Lodge is located on the 20 mile marker, five miles north of Seeley Lake on Hwy. 83.

Whitefish

B&B

537 Wisconsin Avenue, 59937
(406) 862-5488, Fax (406) 826-5489
Innkeepers: Susan Moffitt & Christopher Ridder

$/
$$

Good Medicine Lodge

Spacious rooms, most with balconies and mountain views, have vaulted wood ceilings and lodgepole beds. Flexible accommodations, featuring queen and twin beds, can sleep up to five guests. The lodge is built of cedar timbers and has a rustic, informal atmosphere. Decorated in a Western motif, the roomy interiors are punctuated by roaring fireplaces and solid wood furnishings with fabrics influenced by Native American textiles. The Inn has a guest laundry, ski room with boot and glove dryers, and a shuttle service. The grandeur of Glacier Park awaits nearby.

Approved by: AAA, MBBA

From I-90 or US-2, take US-93 north to Whitefish, then follow the signs to the Big Mountain. The Inn is 1/2 mile north of town.

RELAY NUMBERS: TTY (800) 326-6868, VCE (800) 326-6888

East Ely

220 East 11th Street, 89315-1110
(702) 289-8687, June - September
Innkeepers: Jane & Norman Lindley

B&B

$

Steptoe Valley Inn

Open June through September, this is an oasis in America's Great Basin outback. The Inn is a 1907 grocery store reconstructed in casual elegance with Victorian-cottage decor. Rooms have private balconies that overlook the mountains, railroad museum, or rose garden. Guests are pampered as they begin their days with the likes of oven-baked, Dutch Baby pancakes, apple-cinnamon sausage, and information about the area's hiking, 4-wheel-drive trails (Jeep rentals are available), train rides, ghost towns, garnet prospecting, and wildlife viewing.

Approved by: AAA

October - May please call (702) 435-1196. In Ely, 70 miles from Great Basin National Park. From the intersection of Highways 50 and 93, go 4 blocks east on 93 (N) and then 4 blocks north on "East 11th Street."

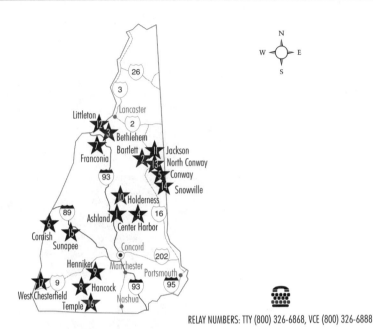

RELAY NUMBERS: TTY (800) 326-6868, VCE (800) 326-6888

7R 2S

BYOB

12

V,M

Ashland

B&B

43 Highland Street, 03217
(800) 637-9599, or (603) 968-3775
Innkeepers: Karol & Betsy Paterman

Glynn House Victorian Inn

$$/
$$$

Enjoy the gracious elegance of the 1890's in this beautifully restored Victorian tucked away in the heart of the White Mountains. You will marvel at the cupola towers, the wraparound porch, the carved oak woodwork and the pocket doors. The Inn is tastefully decorated with Queen Anne pieces and each guest room is unique with period furnishings and modern amenities. A gourmet breakfast in the sunny dining room starts you off on a day of outdoor activity, antiquing, or merely enjoying the Victorian era as preserved by your hosts.

Approved by: AAA

From I-93(N) or (S), take Exit 24. Turn right at the bottom of the ramp onto Rt. 25 and Rt. 3. Travel 7/10 mile into Ashland and turn left onto Highland Street.

17R

Photo: George Bouret

Bartlett

Route 302, 03812
(800) 292-2353, Fax (603) 374-2547
Innkeeper: Mark Dindorf

B&B

$/
$$

Country Inn At Bartlett

Discover a Bed & Breakfast Inn that welcomes hikers, skiers, families, and friends in all seasons. Relax on a porch rocker, sit by the fireside, or soak in the outdoor hot tub. Cross-country ski or mountain-bike out the back door! Set in a stand of tall pine and surrounded by National Forest, this Inn offers a great location for exploring the White Mountains and the spectacular waterfalls of Crawford Notch State Park. Hearty breakfasts, the Inn, Cottage Rooms, and expert trail advice make this a comfortable, casual, mountain retreat.

Approved by: ABBA

Located on Route 302 at the west end of Bartlett Village. From I -93, take Route 3 (N)(Exit 35) to Route 302. Turn right on Route 302 (E). Inn is 25 miles on right.

8R 1S

Bethlehem

Old Littleton Road, 03574
(800) 441-2606, Fax (603) 444-4823
Innkeepers: Nancy, Pat & Hardy Banfield

B&B

$$$/
$$$$

Adair - A Country Inn

This is a country estate built on 200 acres offering quiet elegance in the heart of the White Mountains. It was built in 1927 by Washington attorney, Frank Hogan, as a wedding gift for his daughter. Over the years, Adair has hosted many distinguished guests including actress Helen Hayes and former Presidents Dwight Eisenhower and Richard Nixon. It is Georgian Colonial Revival in design and offers extensive gardens, dramatic views, a tennis court, terrific breakfasts, and excellent nearby golf, walking, hiking, and skiing. Evening dining is available in season.

Approved by: AAA

When travelling on I-93, Exit 40 will bring you right to Adair's driveway. From Route 302, Adair is 3 miles west of the center of Bethlehem Village.

Centre Harbor

B&B

RFD #1, Box 99M, 03226
(800) 5-REDHIL, Fax (603) 279-7003
Innkeepers: Rick Miller & Don Leavitt

Red Hill Inn

$$-
$$$

This is a restored mansion set on 60 acres overlooking Squam Lake and the mountains. The main building is brick Colonial Revival and was built in 1903. There are four other buildings on the property which date back to 1850 and all contain guest rooms. Individually decorated rooms, all with private baths and telephones, are furnished with an eclectic blend of antiques. Many rooms have fireplaces and some have Jacuzzis®. There are cozy dining rooms as well as the Runabout Lounge. All food is made from scratch. Chef Elmer is famous for his desserts so leave plenty of room!

Approved by: AAA, Mobil

Take Rt. 93(N) to Exit 23. Turn right onto Rt. 104 and go towards Meredith. When Rt. 104 ends at the traffic light, turn left onto Rt. 3. Drive 4 miles and turn right onto Rt. 25B. The Inn is 1/4 mile on the right.

Cornish

B&B

Route 12A, 03745
(800) 401-9455, Fax (603) 675-5010
Innkeepers: Barbara & Bill Lewis

The Chase House

$$$

The Inn, a National Historic Landmark, is situated on the bank of the beautiful Connecticut River and offers outstanding views of Mount Ascutney and the scenic Upper Valley. Maintaining the style and elegance of the past, the Inn offers beautifully appointed guest rooms. The large gathering room has exposed, hand-hewn posts and beams and pit-sawn boards. A fieldstone, raised-hearth fireplace and minstrel loft make this spacious room both intimate and unique. A full breakfast featuring seasonal fruits and homemade specialties is served in the dining room or on the adjoining terrace.

Approved by: AAA, ABBA

Photos: George Gardner

From I-89(N) or (S), take Exit 20. Follow Rt. 12A(S) for 17 miles. From I-91(N), take Exit 8. Follow Rt. 131(E) across the Connecticut River. Follow Rt. 12A(N) 4 miles. From I-91(S) take Exit 9. Follow Rt. 5(S) to Rt. 44. Go east over Bridge, then 12A(S) for 1.3 miles.

Franconia

B&B

Easton Valley Road, Box 15, 03580
(603) 823-7775, Fax (603) 444-0100
Innkeepers: Kate Kerivan & Lee Strimbeck

Bungay Jar B & B

$$

Built from an 18th century barn, this post and beam house is nestled on 15 wooded acres bounded by river, forest, and spectacular mountain views. You are greeted by a crackling fire and the aroma of mulled cider in a two-story living room reminiscent of a hayloft. Antique country furnishings encourage a relaxed mountain house feeling. The guest suites are lavish and there is a sauna for tired hikers and cold skiers. Enjoy blueberry pancakes, popovers, and fresh fruit salads while mountain gazing in the morning sun from the table overlooking decks and gardens or from the many porches.

Approved by: AAA

Exit 38 from I-93. Follow Rt. 116(S) for just under 6 miles. Driveway and sign on the left. From I-91, Exit Woodsville. Take 302(E) to 112(S) to 116(N). Go 1/2 mile past the Town Hall and Fire Station, driveway is on the right.

Franconia

EP
MAP
B&B

1300 Easton Road, 03580
(800) 473 -5299, Fax (603) 823-8078
Innkeepers: The Morris Family

Franconia Inn

$

Not just a winter ski lodge! As the snow melts, four red clay tennis courts pop up and a large, sunny pool appears. Cross-country skis, boots, and poles disappear to be replaced by horses, saddles, and stirrups. Where snowbanks once reigned, gardens flourish. The snow-covered airfield becomes an active glider port. Finally, the snowcapped White Mountains shed their blanket of snow and become a hiker's paradise. The Inn's dining room, living room, library, verandas, and Rathskeller lounge all invite relaxation and are a part of your home away from home.

Approved by: AAA, ABBA

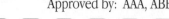

Exit 38 off of I -93, then take Route I-116(S), 2.5 miles.

Franconia

MAP

Route 18, 03580
(800) 356-3802, or (603) 823-7761
Innkeepers: JoAnna & Lee Wogulis

$$$

Lovett's Inn by Lafayette Brook

Just a few miles outside the village sits this enchanting Inn, listed on the National Register of Historic Places. Surrounded by the magnificent White Mountains, this is a place that helps restore the body as well as the soul. Seasonal activities abound or relax and enjoy the serenity of the Inn. A variety of rooms are available in the historic main building or in warm cottages. Favorite New England dishes are uniquely presented by the creative chef. Romantic dining, spirits at the unusual marble bar, and the soft glow of the fireplace are all part of the memory that will bring you back.

Approved by: AAA

Follow I-93 to Rt. 18. Travel approximately two miles to the Inn.

Photo: George Gardner

Henniker

B&B

The Oaks, 03242
(800) 531-0330, or (603) 428-3281
Innkeepers: Ellie, John & Laurel Day

$$-
$$$$

Colby Hill Inn

Congenial Inn dogs, Bertha and Delilah, greet you with handshakes. The cookie jar beckons at this rambling, 1795 Inn, a complex of farmhouse, barns, and carriage house on five village acres. Choose from one of the 16 antique-filled guest rooms. Some have a working fireplace, and all provide private baths and phones. Enjoy a before-dinner beverage in the gazebo or by the parlor fire. The food is memorable from the bountiful breakfasts to the acclaimed, candlelit-dinners. Classic New England scenery abounds around this village on the river.

Approved by: AAA, IIA, Mobil

Seventeen miles west of Concord off Route 202/9. South 1/2 mile on Route 114 to blinking light and pharmacy. Turn right. Inn is 1/2 mile on the right.

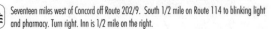

27R

34
V,M,X

Holderness

MAP
B&B

Route 3 & Shepard Hill Road, 03245
(800) 545-2141, Fax (603) 968-2116
Innkeepers: David & Bambi Arnold

$$$$/
$$$$$

The Manor On Golden Pond

This is a beautiful English Country House nestled among tall pines atop Shepards Hill. This wonderful location provides the property with a spectacular vista of Squam Lake and the mountains beyond. The elegant Manor and its rustic cottages are situated on 14 manicured acres, with the lakefront portion providing a private beach and dock. Acclaimed for its elegant lodging, fine dining, and cozy pub, the Manor and the surrounding area also provide a rich setting for year-round enjoyment.

Approved by: AAA, Mobil

From Boston (Logan Airport), take I-93 (N) to New Hampshire Exit 24 (Ashland-Holderness). Bear right off the exit onto Route 3 (S) and proceed for 4.7 miles. Driving time is less than 2 hours.

16R 3S

20
V,M,X
DN

Jackson

B&B
MAP

Thorn Hill Road, Box A, 03846
(800) 289-8990, Fax (603) 383-8062
Innkeepers: Jim & Ibby Cooper

$$$-
$$$$$

Inn At Thorn Hill

A favorite of romantics and adventure travellers, this 1895 Stanford White Inn overlooks Jackson Village and Mt. Washington. The Inn is perfect for relaxing, escaping from daily stresses, and for pampering after a day of hiking or skiing. The main Inn features Victorian decor with antique-filled rooms, a drawing room with a soapstone woodstove and baby grand piano, a wood-paneled pub, and a dining room with a fireplace. There is a carriage house and cottages as well. The full-service pub features an extensive wine list to complement the four-course seasonal dinner menu.

Approved by: AAA, Mobil

Take I-91 or I-93 to Rt. 302(E) to Rt. 16(N) to Jackson. In Jackson Village take Rt. 16A through the covered bridge to Thorn Hill Rd. Turn right and drive up the hill to the Inn.

North Conway

Buttonwood Inn

B&B
MAP
P. O. Box 1817, Mt. Surprise Road, 03860
(800) 258-2625, Fax (603) 356-3140
Innkeepers: Peter & Claudia Needham

$/
$$$

This 1820's cape tucked away on Mt. Surprise, only two miles from the village, offers wonderful New England hospitality. From a full breakfast to the four-course, candlelight dinner in winter, the offerings here will satisfy any palate. In the summer stroll the grounds, enjoy the gardens, and find the foundation of a long ago barn that is the backdrop for the swimming pool. During the winter go out the back door and ski on 65 kilometers of groomed, cross-country trails. The individually decorated rooms, the generous amount of common space, and the warm welcome make you feel at home.

Approved by: AAA, ABBA, Mobil

Follow I-95 to Portsmouth, NH. Take the Spaulding Turnpike(N) to the end and take Rt. 16(N) to North Conway. At the traffic light in the center of the village turn right onto Kearsarge Street. Continue to the top of the hill, bear left. At stop sign go straight and bear left in 1/2 mile to Inn.

Littleton

The Beal House Inn

B&B
EP
247 West Main Street, 03561
(603) 444-2661
Innkeepers: Catherine & Jean-Marie (John) Fisher-Motheu

$

A special place to celebrate the good things in life! The Beal House, an Inn since 1938, allows you to enjoy the charm of 1833 while visiting this lively White Mountain Village. Antique treasures, canopy beds, and down comforters, create welcoming guest rooms designed for comfort. Breakfast gatherings by fireside feature Belgian Waffles by the Belgian host, in addition to a hearty first course. Fresh, authentic French cuisine is served at dinner in an old world atmosphere, with a wine list offering over 300 choices of wines. Local artwork is available for sale.

Approved by: AAA

Exit 41 or 42 off of I-93, at Junction of US Route 302 & NH Route 18. Three hours north of Boston, 3 hours from Montreal, PQ, Canada.

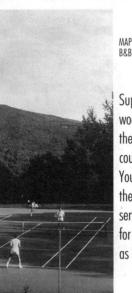

Sunapee

MAP
B&B

Stagecoach Road, 03782
(800) 232-5571
Innkeepers: Michael & Holly Durfor

Dexter's Inn

$$$/
$$$$

Superbly groomed lawns, flowering gardens, meadows, and woods surround the Inn which offers inspiring views of the countryside. You may relax at the pool, stroll along country lanes, and enjoy croquet, horseshoes, or shuffleboard. You could even take a lesson from the resident pro on one of the three all-weather tennis courts. Breakfast and dinner are served daily, and there is a select wine list. Perfectly located for day trips, you are close to excellent summer theater as well as Dartmouth College and Colby-Sawyer College.

Approved by: AAA, IIA, Mobil

I-89(N) Exit 12 and Route 11(W) for 5.5 miles to Left on Winn Hill Road. Continue 1.5 miles. I-91(N) Exit 8. Take Route 11/103(E) for 18 miles to Route 103. Continue 1 mile to left on Young Hill Road.

Temple

B&B

Route 45, 03084
(603) 878-3285
Innkeepers: Judy & Bill Wolfe

Birchwood Inn

$

Rufus Porter murals grace the small, candlelit dining room of this family-run Inn resting by the common of a quiet colonial village. On the National Register of Historic Places, the Inn features guest and common rooms filled with interesting antiques. Serving meals is a special pleasure here. The blackboard menu changes daily and is designed to please every taste. The freshest foods are prepared to order and carefully presented by the Innkeepers. Whether your choice is hiking or hay rides, antiquing or summer theatre, you will enjoy the warmth of this original Inn.

Approved by: AAA

Temple is on Rt. 45, 1.5 miles south of Rt. 101 and 10 minutes east of Peterborough.

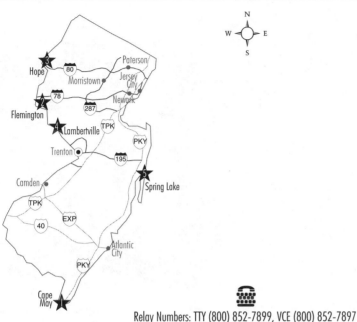

Relay Numbers: TTY (800) 852-7899, VCE (800) 852-7897

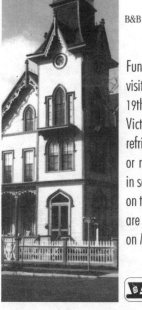

Cape May

B&B

34 Gurney Street, 08204
(609) 884-4506
Innkeepers: Marianne & Jay Schatz

$$/
$$$$

The Abbey Bed & Breakfast

Fun and laughter in a spectacular setting are hallmarks of a visit to The Abbey. Fourteen rooms in two adjacent, restored, 19th century homes are furnished throughout with high-style Victorian antiques. All rooms have private baths and refrigerators, and some have air conditioners. There is on-site or remote parking. Beach chairs and passes are provided in season. Your stay includes a full breakfast each morning, on the veranda or served in the dining room. Tea and tidbits are offered at 4:30 pm. The public is invited to tour and tea on Monday, Wednesday, and Friday at 4pm.

Approved by: AAA, Mobil

Photo: SeaView Color

Garden State Parkway to "0" Exit into Cape May. The Abbey is in the heart of the historic district.

Cape May

Carroll Villa Hotel-Mad Batter Restaurant

B&B

19 Jackson Street, 08204
(609) 884-9619, Fax (609) 884-0264
Innkeepers: Mark Kulkowitz & Pam Huber

$/
$$$

A national landmark building (circa 1882), the Carroll Villa is located in the heart of Cape May's historic district, just a half-block from both the ocean and the charming Victorian shopping mall. Home of the nationally acclaimed Mad Batter Restaurant, you can enjoy breakfast, lunch, or dinner on the European Porch, in the sky lit dining room or secluded garden terrace. Twenty-one individually decorated, air conditioned guest rooms are complete with antique furnishings, Victorian period wallpaper, lace curtains, and ceiling fans. Some offer ocean views.

Approved by: AAA, Mobil

Photos: George W. Gardner

Garden State Parkway to "O" Exit. Go over bridge, past marinas, straight onto the end of Lafayette Street. Turn left, then down two blocks.

Cape May

Inn at 22 Jackson

B&B

22 Jackson Street, 08204
(800) 452-8177, or (609) 884-2226
Innkeepers: Chip Masemore & Barbara Carmichael

$$$/
$$$$

The navy blue, purple, and white Queen Anne Victorian is an eye-catcher as you travel between the pedestrian mall and the ocean on Jackson Street. Although Victorian, the Inn is eclectic, casual, often whimsical, but always romantic. Majolica, toys, games, and Chip's "ladies" of the turn-of-the-century will bring a smile to your face as you explore the house. Each suite offers not only a color television, but also a microwave, a box refrigerator, and central air conditioning if needed. The beach is just 1/2 block away, yet Cape May is a town for relaxation in all seasons.

Approved by: ABBA

Take the Garden State Parkway south to Cape May. Go straight on Lafayette Street to the end and turn left onto Jackson. The Inn is on the right.

Photo: Library of Congress

 9R 7S

BYOB

12

V,M

Cape May

B&B
635 Columbia Avenue, 08204
(609) 884-8690
Innkeepers: Tom & Sue Carroll

$$/
$$$$

The Mainstay Inn

Built by a pair of wealthy gamblers in 1872, this former elegant, exclusive clubhouse is now one of the most well-known B&B Inns in the country. Guests enjoy 12, antique-filled guest rooms (all with private bath), three parlors, spacious gardens, and rocker-filled verandas as well as breakfast and afternoon tea. Beautiful beaches, historic attractions, biking, birding, golf, and tennis are all available in Cape May, a National Historic Landmark community. The Inn is open late March through Christmas.

Approved by: AAA, IIA, Mobil

Garden State Parkway to "0" Exit. Go over bridge, past marinas, straight onto Lafayette Street. Turn left onto Madison at light, and turn right on Columbia at water tower. Inn is 3 blocks on the right corner.

 16R 7S

BYOB

15

V,M

Cape May

B&B
102 Ocean Street, 08204
(609) 884-8702
Innkeepers: Dane & Joan Wells

$$/
$$$$

The Queen Victoria®

The Wells family welcomes you with warm hospitality and special services to their three restored houses in the center of the historic district. Relax on porches overlooking Victorian gardens. Fortify yourself with a buffet breakfast and afternoon tea for antiquing, touring, or playing at the beach. Dine nearby at several of New Jersey's finest restaurants. All rooms have air conditioning and private baths; many have whirlpool tubs. Suites are also available. The Inn and the town are noted for festive Christmas decorations and tours.

Approved by: AAA, ABBA,IIA, Mobil

Garden State Parkway to "0" Exit. Go over bridge, past marinas, straight onto Lafayette Street. Go to second light, and turn left onto Ocean Street. Go 3 blocks to Inn.

5R

BYOB

12

V,M,X

Flemington

B&B

162 Main Street, 08822
(908) 788-0247
Innkeepers: Pam Venosa & Al Scott

$$

The Inn is a Queen Anne Victorian "painted lady" circa 1891, in the historic district. Cabbage roses abound in the Victorian furnishings. Romantic, luxurious guest rooms feature queensize-canopy and four-poster beds. One room has a working fireplace; another, a clawfoot tub. A baby grand piano, wraparound front porch, parlor fireplace, and guest pantry offer relaxation and indulgence. Catering to the romantic getaway is the "Romance & Roses" Package, which includes a four-course candlelight dinner, roses, handmade chocolates, champagne, and breakfast in bed.

Approved by: AAA

The Cabbage Rose Inn

From Route 78 (W), take Route 287 (S) to Exit 13. Then follow Route 202 (S) to Flemington.

8R

BYOB

8

V,M,X

Lambertville

B&B
♿

207 Goat Hill Road, 08530
(609) 397-1516, Fax (609) 397-9353
Innkeepers: Terry Ann & Richard Anderson

$$/
$$$

This stone manor house, built in 1820, is more than a wonderful place to stay, it is an experience that appeals to all the senses. Explore the estate and discover the quaint carriage house, several farm buildings, and abundant wildlife. The colorful gardens fill the air with the essence of mother nature's marvelous fragrances. The tantalizing aroma of fresh-baked goodies from the kitchen and birds singing harmony with the romantic, classical sounds of Vivaldi or the serenity of New Age music soothe the soul and create the magic of Chimney Hill.

Approved by: ABBA

Chimney Hill Farm B & B

From Lambertville take the second left after the Bridge Street light onto Swan Street. Take Swan Street to Studdiford Street and turn right. This will change to Goat Hill Rd. Follow to the top of the hill and the Inn is on the left.

Spring Lake

Ashling Cottage

B&B

106 Sussex Avenue, 07762
(800) 237-1877, or (908) 449-3553
Innkeepers: Goodi & Jack Stewart

$/
$$$

Built in 1877 with lumber from the Philadelphia Centennial's Agricultural Hall, this carpenter Gothic cottage has been welcoming ladies and gentlemen of distinction to the exclusive, seaside resort of Spring Lake ever since. The name Ashling is derived from a Gaelic word meaning "dream." This warm and romantic Inn lives up to the title. Every room is distinctive. One has a private porch, some offer claw-footed soaking tubs, and one features a sunken bathroom. Your hosts, Goodi & Jack, welcome you with casual hospitality endeavoring to make your vacation dreams come true.

Approved by: AAA

Photo: David Greenfield

Garden State Parkway to Exit 98 to Route 34 (S). One mile to traffic circle, east on Route 524. Four miles to ocean, then turn right. Continue 12 blocks to Sussex Avenue.

Spring Lake

La Maison

B&B

404 Jersey Avenue, 07762
(800) 276-2088, Fax (908) 449-4860
Innkeeper: Barbara Furdyna

$$/
$$$$

Tucked away on a quiet, yet centrally located, tree-lined street, this Inn and gallery provide an elegant, relaxed European atmosphere. Bright and airy Louis Philippe rooms feature French sleigh beds with fluffy down comforters, as well as fresh flowers and amenities that include completely modernized private baths, air conditioning, and cable TV. With its stately mansard roof, shuttered windows, and wraparound porch, it is considered one of the town's oldest buildings. Creative and delicious breakfasts include mimosas, cappuccino, or espresso.

Approved by: AAA

Left Photo: Country Inns/Bed & Breakfast Magazine, George Kopp

Garden State Parkway to Exit 98 to Route 34 (S). One mile to traffic circle, east on Route 524. Proceed on 524 through 3 traffic lights, over RR tracks, to Fourth Avenue. Turn right and continue for 5 blocks to Jersey Avenue.

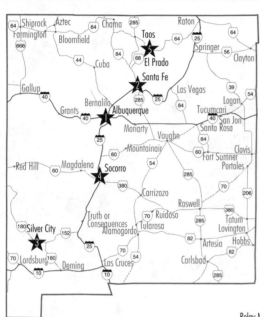

Relay Numbers: TTY (800) 477-9913, VCE (800) 272-7002

Santa Fe

Alexander's Inn

B&B

529 E. Palace Avenue, 87501
(505) 986-1431
Innkeeper: Carolyn Lee

$/
$$$

Built in 1903, this Craftsman home has been lovingly restored to provide a warm, comfortable, and romantic atmosphere. Large porches overlook bountiful gardens where you may enjoy yummy breakfasts and homemade cookies and lemonade. In keeping with the turn-of-the-century style are hardwood floors, fireplaces, antiques, laces, quilts, and stencilling throughout. While encouraged to make yourself at home, the friendly staff is always ready to assist you. Just five blocks from the Plaza, an air of peace and tranquility pervades at the Inn.

Approved by: NMBBA

Take I-25(N) and exit at Old Pecos Trail. This becomes Old Santa Fe Trail. Follow to the intersection with Paseo de Peralta. Turn right and follow to Palace Ave. Turn right onto Palace and go two and a half blocks. The Inn is on the left.

Four Kachinas Inn

Santa Fe

B&B
512 Webber Street, 87501
(505) 982-2550
Innkeepers: John Daw & Andrew Beckerman

$$

Located on a quiet street and built around its own private courtyard, the Inn is a short walk from the historic Santa Fe Plaza via the Old Santa Fe Trail. Four Kachinas offers rooms with private baths and entrances. The guest rooms are furnished with southwestern art and handiwork including antique Navajo rugs, Hopi kachina dolls, and handcrafted wooden furniture. The ground floor accomodations have individual garden patios; the upstairs room offers views of the mountains. A continental-plus breakfast is served in your room; there is afternoon tea with cookies in the guest lounge.

Approved by: AAA, NMBBA

From I-25, take the Old Pecos Trail Exit and head north toward the center of town (approx. 3 miles). Turn left at Texaco Station onto Santa Fe Avenue, then turn right onto Webber Street.

Grant Corner Inn

Santa Fe

B&B
122 Grant Avenue, 87501
(505) 983-6678
Innkeepers: Louise Stewart & Pat Walter

$$$

Steps away from Santa Fe's historic Plaza, this 1905 colonial manor home stands surrounded by lush weeping willows and white pickets. The guest rooms are appointed with antiques and quilts and offer comfort and romance to the traveller. Overnight guests as well as the public are served bountiful breakfasts and brunch on the patio or in the charming dining room. A fresh fruit and cereal board, homemade breads, pastries, and jams complement the many innovative hot dishes. You will enjoy the evening refreshment and social hour and getting to know Louise, Pat, and their staff.

Approved by: IIA, NMBBA

From I-25(N), exit St. Francis. Bear left (north) for 5 miles. Turn right onto Alameda. Turn left onto Guadalupe and turn right onto Johnson. Parking and the Inn will be on the left.

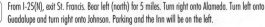

Santa Fe

Territorial Inn

B&B
215 Washington Avenue, 87501
(505) 989-7737, Fax (505) 986-1411
Innkeeper: Lela McFerrin

$$/
$$$

You'll love this 100-year-old home located one block north of Santa Fe's Historic Plaza. The area offers shopping, fine dining, and the art district. Enjoy the elegantly remodelled, Victorian style rooms and living area. There is also a lush rose garden patio perfect for relaxing. Continental breakfast of fresh berries, pastries, juice, and gourmet coffee is served in the beautiful dining area, or it may be delivered to your room. Personal service is the hallmark of the Inn.

Approved by: Mobil, NMBBA

Photos: Country Inns/Bed & Breakfast Magazine, Laurie Dickson

North on I-25, Exit 284. Go to 4th light, then make a right. Proceed to third light, and make a left on Washington Avenue.

Silver City

The Carter House

B&B
101 North Cooper Street, 88061
(505) 388-5485
Innkeeper: Lucy Dilworth

$

The Inn is located on the main floor of this Queen Anne Colonial-Revival building. There are common rooms and a wonderful large, front porch with an excellent view of the nearby mountains. Downstairs is a 20 bed dormitory-style, Hostelling International facility for budget-minded travellers of all ages. The area is one of the finest in the entire west for hiking, bicycling, rockhounding, and birdwatching. In addition to the Gila Cliff Dwellings National Monument, there are museums, ghost towns, and natural hot springs to be enjoyed.

Approved by: AAA, NMBBA

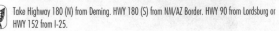

Take Highway 180 (N) from Deming. HWY 180 (S) from NM/AZ Border. HWY 90 from Lordsburg or HWY 152 from I-25.

Socorro

The Eaton House

B&B

403 Eaton Avenue, 87801
(505) 835-1067
Innkeepers: Anna Appleby & Tom Harper

$$

Built in 1881 in the exact center of New Mexico, the Inn combines history with luxury. Each room opens onto the wide, brick portal that surrounds the courtyard lawn. This common area is shared by four species of hummingbirds, orioles, swallows, kingbirds, and guests. Each morning a full breakfast of homemade specialties is served in the dining room. Basket breakfasts and box lunches are convenient when exploring the Bosque Del Apache Wildlife Refuge or backroad historic sites. The Inn is ideally located for viewing the past and experiencing the present.

Approved by: NMBBA

From I-25, take Exit 147. Turn left one block after traffic light. Go 4 blocks to end of the street and turn left. Follow Eaton House wall to driveway,; turn right and follow signs to entrance.

Taos, NM

La Posada De Taos

B&B

309 Juanita Lane, P.O. Box 1118, 87571
(800) 645-4803, or (505) 758-8164
Innkeepers: Nancy & Bill Swan

$$-
$$$

Escape to this romantic, secluded adobe Inn just 2 1/2 blocks from the Plaza in the Historic District. It was the first B & B in Taos. You can walk to galleries, museums, shops and restaurants. You will return to casual elegance here while enjoying the common area centered around a traditional New Mexican fireplace. Each guest room is filled with country pine antiques and offers a fireplace or wood-burning stove. You will savor a delicious, full breakfast. There is a wonderful separate honeymoon house.

Approved by: AAA, ABBA, NMBBA

From Taos Plaza, go west on Don Fernando. Turn south onto Manzanares, and drive 1 block. Turn west onto Juanita Lane (dead end).

4R

BYOB

V,M

Taos, NM

B&B

P. O. Box 960, El Prado, 87529
(800) 334-8467, or (505) 776-8467
Innkeepers: Kay & Charles Giddens

$$

Little Tree Bed & Breakfast

Here you will experience an authentic, all adobe house built in the old pueblo style with 16 inch walls, arches, vigas, latillas, and kiva fireplaces. Slow down and enjoy the quiet of the country; sit in the adobe-walled garden and gaze at Taos Mountain; watch the aerial acrobatics of the summer visitors, the hummingbirds. Take long walks down the sparsely travelled road to the historic village of Arroyo Hondo. In the winter, after a day skiing at nearby Taos Ski Valley, sit in the living room sipping hot drinks and watch the gentle snow falling in the courtyard. You can reach out and touch the stars.

Approved by: NMBBA

Go north from Taos Plaza on Hwy. 64(W) to the blinking light. Turn right onto Hwy.150 driving toward the Ski Valley. Turn left onto Hwy. 230 and go 1.9 miles to the intersection with Hondo-Seco Rd. Turn left onto paved road and go 2 miles. The Inn is on the left.

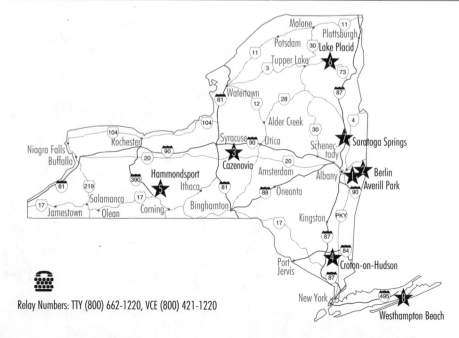

New York

Relay Numbers: TTY (800) 662-1220, VCE (800) 421-1220

Berlin

B&B

Route 22, 12022
(800) 845-4886, or (518) 658-2334
Innkeeper: Edith Evans

$-
$$

The Sedgwick Inn

Located in the beautiful Taconic Valley, on the New York side of the Berkshires, this 1791 historic colonial has been described as "the quintessential Country Inn." The Sedgwick Inn, with its well-stocked library and inviting parlor with fireplace, is a place of casual elegance and old world charm. There are five antique-filled bedrooms with private baths in the main house and six rooms, furnished colonial-style, in the annex. An old carriage barn houses gifts and crafts. The Inn is renowned for its fine food. It is convenient to the Berkshires, Southern Vermont, and the Capital District.

Approved by: AAA, IIA

From Route 295, Route 7, or I-90, connect with Route 22 to the Inn.

Cazenovia

B&B

79 Albany Street, 13035
(315) 655-3461, Fax (315) 655-5443
Innkeeper: Howard M. Kaler

$$/
$$$

Lincklaen House

A visit to this Inn is to return to an era of elegant hospitality. It is a beautiful, four-season Country Inn built as a luxurious stopover for 19th century travellers. The friendly staff will lead you through the main floor with its high ceilings, handsome classical carved moldings, painted wood panels, and three large fireplaces. Each guest room and suite is unique and has been given the amenities which 20th century travellers require, yet retains the charm preserved from its history. The well-known restaurant serves innovative American cuisine while the East Room is the setting for Afternoon Tea.

Approved by: IIA

Photo: Gene Gissin Photography

From I-81 take Exit 15 and follow Rt. 20(E) for 17 miles. Travelling east on I-90, take Exit 34A. Follow I-481(S) for 4 miles. Take Exit 3E and follow Rt. 92(E) for 13 miles to Cazenovia. Travelling west on I-90 take Exit 34. Follow Rt. 13(S) for 14 miles to Cazenovia.

Croton-on-Hudson

B&B

49 Van Wyck Street, 10520
(914) 271-6737, Fax (914) 271-3927
Innkeeper: Barbara Notarius

$$/
$$$$$

Alexander Hamilton House

This is a sprawling Victorian situated on a cliff overlooking the Hudson. On the grounds are a mini-orchard and in-ground pool. The home has many period antiques and collections. Some suites offer a fireplace, and the bridal chamber provides a king bed, Jacuzzi®, entertainment center, fireplace, and lots of skylights. A one bedroom apartment is also available. Nearby are West Point, the Sleepy Hollow Restorations, Lyndhurst, Boscobel, hiking, biking, and sailing. New York City is under an hour away by train or car.

Approved by: AAA, ABBA, Mobil

Exit Route 9 at Route 129, and go east 1 block to light. Turn left on Riverside, go right on Grand, and left on Hamilton to the end. Hamilton intersects Van Wyck in front of the Inn.

Hammondsport

B&B

11 William Street, 14840
(800) 982-8818 , or (607) 569-3402
Innkeepers: Ellen & Franklyn Laufersweiler

$$

The Blushing Rose

This wonderful B&B is located in the heart of New York State's wine country in a quaint village with many fine shops and restaurants. The Inn offers a return to the warm, cozy ambiance of 19th century America. Each of the four spacious guest rooms offers a sitting area and private bath. Keuka Lake is just steps away where you'll find great places to swim, a pleasant park, and a boat launch. If water sports are not on your agenda, there are nine boutique wineries around the lake and many places to hike or bike. You will start your day refreshed and ready for the special breakfast to come.

Approved by: AAA, ABBA

Exit 38 off of Route 17 (W) of Corning, New York. Southeast from Buffalo and Rochester off 390 to 17.

Lake Placid

MAP
B&B

15 Interlaken Avenue, 12946
(800) 428-4369
Innkeepers: Roy & Carol Johnson

$-
$$$$

Interlaken Inn

This Victorian Inn features guest rooms and a Carriage House, all individually decorated with lovely wall papers, antiques (many of which are for sale), and luxurious bed coverings. The high quality cuisine is rivaled only by the rich decor of the dining room with its walnut paneling and tin ceiling. Sports enthusiasts will enjoy the area known for its down-hill skiing at Whiteface Mountain, cross-country skiing, and ice skating in the winter. During the temperate months enjoy hiking, bicycling, fishing, and golf. Fall is especially gorgeous!

Approved by: IIA, Mobil

Photo: Nancie Battaglia

         I-87 to Route 73 to Lake Placid. Take Maine Street to Mirror Lake Drive to Interlaken Drive and Inn.

Saratoga Springs

B&B

55 Union Avenue, 12866
(800) 398-1558
Innkeepers: Jody & Tom Roohan

$$/
$$$$$

Union Gables Bed & Breakfast

After extensive renovation and restoration, this 1901 Queen Anne Victorian opened in June of 1992. Enjoy a warm and friendly atmosphere where you are welcome to play the piano, relax on the massive Saratoga Porch, or pedal the streets of town on the loaner bikes. The rooms are spacious, bright, and airy in the classic Victorian style, yet with all the comforts and conveniences of modern living (refrigerators, telephones, televisions, and central air). Located in the heart of the Downtown Historic District, it is near shops, the antique center, and restaurants.

Approved by: AAA

         From I-87 (N), take Exit14. Turn right off ramp onto Union Avenue. Less than 1 mile to Inn.

Saratoga Springs

B&B

102 Lincoln Avenue, 12866
(518) 587-7613
Innkeepers: Bob & Stephanie Melvin

$/
$$$$$

Westchester House

This enticing Victorian is festooned in a seven-color paint scheme which highlights the whimsical Queen Anne architecture. Surrender to the graceful beauty of oriental carpets on gleaming wood floors, lace curtains, high ceilings, antique clocks, and the rich luster of natural woods. You'll discover hand-crafted mouldings, comfortable parlours, an extensive library, and a baby grand piano. Firm mattresses, luxury linens, tiled baths, ceiling fans, air-conditioning, fresh flowers, and chocolates are found in the elegantly appointed rooms.

Approved by: AAA, Mobil

I-87 Exit 13 (N), puts you on Route 9 (South Broadway). Continue approximately 4 miles north to Lincoln Avenue. East on Lincoln Avenue to Inn.

Westhampton Beach

B&B

2 Seafield Lane, 11978
(516) 288-1559, Fax (516) 288-0721
Innkeeper: Elsie Collins

$$-
$$$$

1880 Seafield House

This 100-year-old B&B is the perfect place for a romantic hideaway, a weekend of privacy, or just a change of pace from city life. Only 90 minutes from Manhattan, the Inn is ideally situated. The Estate includes a swimming pool and a tennis court for your enjoyment. You can walk quickly to the ocean beach. The Hamptons offers numerous outstanding restaurants and shops in addition to opportunities for antique hunting. Indoor tennis facilities are available locally, and Guerney's International Health Spa and Montauk Point are nearby.

Approved by: ABBA

L.I. Expressway to Exit 70, turn right. At the end of Route 111 turn left onto Route 27 (E). Take Exit 63 to Westhampton Beach. Go to third light, and make a left to Mill Road. Proceed to the end. Take left onto Main, then second right to Seafield. Inn is on left.

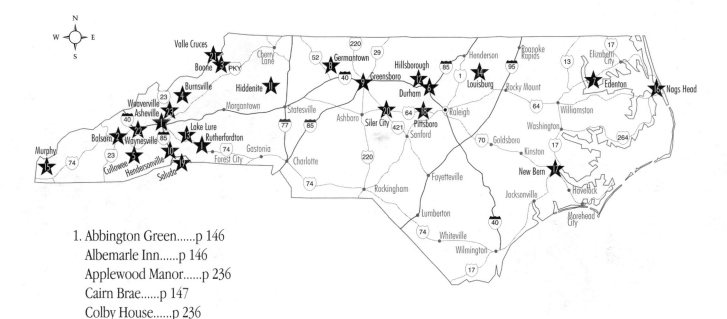

5R 1S

BYOB

12

V,M,X

Asheville

B&B

46 & 48 Cumberland Circle, 28801
(800) 251-2454, Fax (704) 251-2872
Innkeeper: Valerie Larrea

$$/
$$$

Abbington Green B & B Inn

This stunning, 1908 Colonial Revival Inn is located in the Montford Historic District and is on the National Register of Historic Places. The Inn has a distinctly elegant yet comfortable English flavor with fireplaces, antique furnishings, and fine rugs. Each of the stylishly appointed guest rooms is named for a park or garden around London and features a canopy-draped, queen size bed and air conditioning. A sumptuous, full-course breakfast is served each morning beside the dining room fireplace. This is a perfect place to celebrate a special occasion or to stay while on business.

Approved by: NCBBI

From I-40, take I-240 to Exit 4C on Montford Avenue. Go north to the traffic light at West Chestnut, turn right onto West Chestnut. Turn left onto Cumberland Avenue. Proceed two blocks and bear right onto Cumberland Circle. The Inn is on the left.

10R 1S

BYOB

V,M,DV

Asheville

B&B

86 Edgemont Road, 28801-1544
(800) 621-7435, or (704) 255-0027
Innkeepers: Kathy & Dick Hemes

$/
$$$

Albemarle Inn

This is a distinguished, Greek-Revival mansion with high ceilings, oak paneling, and an exquisite carved-oak stairway with a unique circular landing and balcony. Built in 1909, it became an Inn in 1941. Its most celebrated guest was the composer, Bela Bartok, who completed his "Asheville" concerto while residing here. The spacious guest rooms and common areas are furnished with traditional antiques and reproductions. On the National Register of Historic Places, the Inn's emphasis today is on comfortable elegance, delicious breakfasts, and unmatched hospitality.

Approved by: NCBBI

From I-240, take Exit 5B. North on Charlotte Street 0.9 miles to Edgemont Road. Right on Edgemont, and go 0.2 miles to Inn.

3R 1S

BYOB

V,M

Asheville

B&B
217 Patton Mountain Road, 28804
(704) 252-9219
Innkeepers: Milli & Ed Adams
$$

Nestled on three acres of woods above Asheville, the Inn offers a peacefully secluded, mountain retreat away from the city. A large terrace surrounded by 200-year-old oaks makes a quiet spot to sip an afternoon refreshment and watch the sun set on the Blue Ridge Mountains. Walking trails, beautiful views, a hammock for lounging, comfortable guest rooms, and a cozy living room are all here for your enjoyment. Cairn Brae is Scottish for "rocky hillside" and it is the perfect description of this private spot which seems a world away, yet is only minutes from downtown.

Approved by: AAA, Mobil, NCBBI

Cairn Brae

Take I-240 to Asheville. Exit onto Charlotte Street. Go south onto College Street one block to Town Mountain Rd. Go left 2.5 miles to Patton Mountain Rd. and turn left, then right at Water Tank for .8 mile.

4R 1S

V,M,X

Asheville

B&B
&
40 Canterbury Road, 28801
(704) 258-9725
Innkeepers: Joan & Don Tracy
$$

This rustic brown-shingled lodge houses a romantic interior. It is characterized by warm, polished, wood floors, oak-beamed ceilings, wood-burning fireplaces, French doors galore, chintz fabrics, and whimsical accessories. Enjoy beautiful views from the covered, 40-foot veranda or pool-side patio. Four large suite-sized bedrooms are made for more than sleeping; they are rooms for living in, relaxing, and dreaming. Some rooms have French doors onto balconies overlooking the pool, some have fireplaces, and some are surrounded by great trees.

Approved by: NCBBI

Dogwood Cottage Inn

Coming west on I-240, take Exit 5B, turn right on Charlotte Street. Coming east on I-240, turn left on Charlotte. Go 1/2 mile on Charlotte, then turn right on Cherokee. Make your 3rd left on Canterbury.

Asheville

B&B

296 Montford Avenue, 28801
(800) 254-9569, Fax (704) 254-9518
Innkeepers: Ripley Hotch & Owen Sullivan

$$$

The Inn on Montford

In the center of Asheville's Montford Historic District, the Inn was designed in 1900 by Biltmore supervising architect R.S. Smith as a Shingle-style interpretation of an English cottage. Decorated with a dazzling collection of English and American antiques, fine oil paintings, oriental rugs, and porcelains, the Inn has four guest rooms with fireplaces and queen-sized poster beds. The full breakfast includes such specialties as Bavarian, puffed-pancakes, stratas, very berry croissants, and homemade muffins and breads as well as fresh fruit, gourmet coffees, and teas.

Approved by: NCBBI

I-40 to I-240, Exit 4C. Go north on Montford for 2/3 of a mile. Inn is located on the left side.

Asheville

B&B

235 Pearson Drive, 28801
(800) 552-5724, Fax (704) 251-0929
Innkeepers: Carol & Art Wenczel

$$

The Wright Inn & Carriage House

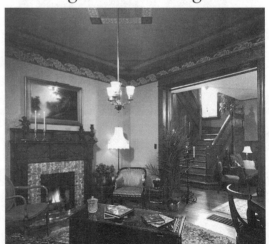

Its location on a quiet, tree-lined street and the large, old-fashioned porch are the first signs that this is a place to slow down, relax, and enjoy yourself. Inside, this Queen Anne Victorian, listed on the National Register of Historic Places, is furnished with antiques and family heirlooms that take you back to an era of comfortable luxury. Excellent breakfasts, tea time, and personal attention make each day a special one. Lovely linens, china, silver, and crystal add to the realization that here, you are a pampered guest. The Carriage House is a perfect place for family groups and reunions.

Approved by: ABBA

Photos: Carroll Morgan Photography & Good Design

From I-240 take Exit 4C (Montford Ave.). Continue on Montford Ave. for .9 mile to Watauga Street. Turn left onto Watauga and go one block. The Inn is on the left corner of Watauga Street and Pearson Drive.

Balsam

B&B

Balsam Mountain Inn Road, Box 40, 28707
(704) 456-9498
Innkeeper: Merrily Teasley

$$/$$$

Balsam Mountain Inn

You'll find this historic Inn nestled between three peaks. Built as a Victorian Railroad Inn, it was constructed in 1908 to serve the East's highest depot. Today, you can relax, rest, and rock on the sweeping 100-foot porches. Guests read from the 2000-volume library, ramble through 26 acres of forest trails and visit another era through period decor. You can relish good food and revel in the comfort of plump pillows and thick comforters. Close by are the Smoky Mountains, Blue Ridge Parkway, Biltmore Estate, and mountain crafts.

Approved by: AAA, ABBA, Mobil

Photos: B.J. Carpenter

Exit 27 off I-40. Follow U.S. 23/74 13 miles southwest. Turn left into Balsam just after the Blue Ridge Parkway overpass. Take an immediate right, cross railroad twice, and enter driveway straight ahead.

Boone

B&B

404 Old Bristol Road, 28607
(800) 849-9466
Innkeepers: Tim & Lori Shahen

$$/$$$

Lovill House Inn

Built in 1875 by Captain Edward Francis Lovill, this gracious farm house offers an authentic, country experience. There are rockers on the wraparound porches, three acres of wooded farm land, a steam, a waterfall, a shaded hammock, and mountain bikes. Spacious common and guest rooms and lots of thoughtful touches underscore the cordial informality of the Innkeepers. Enjoy the fresh flowers throughout, a hosted social hour, evening turn-down service, and an open, country kitchen where guests are welcome to finish off the cookie batter.

Approved by: AAA, NCBBI

Located on Old Bristol Road which intersects U.S. Highways 421 and 321. 7/10 mile west of downtown Boone.

Burnsville

NuWray Inn

B&B

Town Square, 28714
(704) 682-2329 or (800) 368-9729
Innkeepers: Chris & Pam Strickland

$/
$$

You will experience the feeling of days past at the oldest Country Inn in Western North Carolina. NuWray is surrounded by the beautiful Blue Ridge Mountains. Charming and comfortable accommodations are available year round. The Inn offers 26 unique guest rooms all with private baths. Common areas and parlors are accented by period antiques. Overnight guests enjoy a hearty country breakfast, and legendary, family-style dinners are available evenings and Sunday afternoon. The Inn is ideal for those wishing to explore the natural beauty of this special area.

Approved by: ABBA, Mobil

Photo: Wyatt's Photography.
From I-40 and I-26 (Asheville), follow Highway 19/23 north for 20 miles. Veer right on Highway 19, and go east 15 miles. From I-40 (Marion) or Blue Ridge Parkway, follow Highway 226 north to Highway 19. Turn left, and go west 15 miles.

Cullowhee

Cullowhee Bed & Breakfast

B&B

150 Ledbetter Road, 28723
(704) 293-5447
Innkeepers: Charles & Janet Moore

$

Located on a hillside among pines, oaks, and maples, the Inn offers mountain views and the relaxing atmosphere of an immaculate, country home. Western Carolina University, one mile away, is easily accessible for year-round sports and cultural events. The traditional, two-story home sits in the center of its five acres, with covered porches overlooking an expansive lawn and scattered flower beds. In the back, a large granite patio extends to a stone retaining wall and outdoor fireplace. Explore the Great Smoky Mountains or the Appalachian Trail.

Approved by: NCBBI

From Sylva (NC) travel 107 (S). Turn left onto SR 1002 into Cullowhee. Cross river bridge, and immediately turn right onto SR 1336 (Monteith Gap Road). Take first right onto Ledbetter Road. Inn is located on right.

6R 2S

BYOB

12

V,M,X
DN, DV

Durham

B&B

$/
$$$

106 Mason Road, 27712
(800) 528-2207, Fax (919) 477-8430
Innkeepers: Jerry, Barbara & Cathy Ryan

In 1775, as the Lipscombes were building their family home, Waxhaw and Catawba Indians passed their door on the Great Trading Path. Since 1985, when the property became the Arrowhead Inn, visitors from 50 states and many foreign countries have sampled the Inn's colonial charm and homey hospitality. With its carefully restored rooms, meticulous cleanliness, thoughtful amenities, and home-cooked full breakfasts, Arrrowhead evokes fond memories of "Grandma's house." More importantly, guests come to know the Innkeepers as genial hosts and perhaps long-time friends.

Approved by: AAA, Mobil, NCBBI

Arrowhead Inn

Take I-85 to exit marked "Duke St./Roxboro/501(N). Go north 6.9 miles to the light at Mason/Snowhill. Turn left onto Mason, and immediately turn right into the drive.

8R 1S

18

V,M

Edenton

B&B
MAP

$

202 W. Queen Street, 27932
(919) 482-8945
Innkeepers: Bill & Phyllis Pepper

Whether you are anticipating sailing with Captain Bill on the Albemarle Sound, an exciting mystery weekend looking for clues, or relaxing on the front porch of the Inn, you will love your stay here. A former caterer, Phyllis prepares a variety of the usual breakfast dishes as well as some surprising versions of guests' favorites. A continental breakfast greets you at your door and is followed by a three-course, gourmet breakfast in the Harbor Room. Afternoon refreshments are presented in the center hall and fine dining is available for four or more guests with 24 hours notice.

Approved by: NCBBI

Captain's Quarters Inn

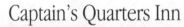

Take I-95(S) to Richmond, VA. Take 64 to Norfolk, VA. and Rt. 17(S) to Edenton. Turn left at the 5th Edenton exit. At 3.3 miles you will see the Inn sign on the left. Take I-95(N) to Rocky Mount, NC. Take 64(E) to Williamston and Rt. 17(N) to Edenton. Turn right at the 1st exit. Go 3.3 miles.

Edenton

MAP

300 North Broad Street, 27932
(800) 348-8933, Fax (919) 482-2432
Innkeepers: Arch & Jane Edwards

$$$$-
$$$$$

The Lords Proprietors' Inn

Edenton, founded in 1722, was once the colonial capital of North Carolina. The quiet, tree-lined streets of the extensive historic district are flanked by fine 18th and 19th century homes. Three of the homes comprise the Inn. The largest is a stately brick Victorian with a wraparound porch. Next door is a smaller frame house built in 1801. In the back are lodgings converted from a former tobacco pack house, boasting Edenton's longest porch. Visitors enjoy spacious parlors with fireplaces, a library, and large, graciously-appointed guest rooms. Tuesday-Saturday enjoy the four-course dinner.

Approved by: IIA

From Washington, DC or points north, take, I-95 (S) to 295. Above Richmond, VA, take 295 to 460 (E). Just below Petersburg, VA, take 460 (E) to Suffolk, VA. Take 32 (S) from Suffolk to Edenton.

Greensboro

B&B

205 N. Park Drive, 27401
(800) 535-9363, Fax (910) 274-9943
Innkeepers: Mike & Vanda Terrell

$/
$$

Greenwood Bed & Breakfast

The house, circa 1911, faces a park in Greensboro's National Historic District. There are family heirlooms, antiques, and original oil paintings displayed through out the house. Your candlelight breakfast includes homemade muffins, breads, french toast, freshly squeezed orange juice, coffee and tea. Private baths, evening turn-down service, wine, and Southern hospitality will make your stay unforgettable.

Approved by: AAA, ABBA, NCBBI

From I-40 and I-85, take S. Elm Street Exit toward downtown (Elm-Eugene Street). Continue for 3 miles, turn right on Smith and left on Elm. Make a right on N. Park Drive.

14R 1S

BYOB

V,M,X
DV

Hendersonville

B&B

783 N. Main Street, 28792
(800) 537-8195, Fax (704) 692-1010
Innkeepers: John & Diane Sheiry & Darla Olmstead

$$-
$$$

The Waverly Inn

Guests arrive as strangers, and leave as friends as a result of John, Diane, and Darla's hospitality. Colorful flags embellish the wide veranda where rocking chairs and casual, afternoon social hours put the stress of everyday life out of your mind. Within walking distance of fine restaurants, exceptional shopping, and antique stores in the historic district, this Inn has something for everyone. John's scrumptious, all-you-can-eat breakfasts are just the way to start your day off right! Located near Biltmore Estate, Flat Rock Playhouse, and the Carl Sandburg National Historic Sites.

Approved by: AAA, IIA, Mobil, NCBBI

I-26 to Exit 18B. West on Route 64, 2 miles, then right on Main Street. Inn is located 1 block up on left.

12R 1S

BYOB

24

V,M

Hiddenite

B&B
MAP
AP

Sulphur Springs Road, Box 58, 28636
(704) 632-0063, Fax (704) 632-3562
Innkeepers: Eileen Lackey Sharpe & Lynn Sharpe Hill

$-
$$$

Hidden Crystal Inn

Located in the gem-rich hamlet of Hiddenite in the Brushy Mountains, this art and antique-filled Inn is a jewel. The Inn is set among extensive gardens and you will enjoy the library featuring an exhibit of local minerals as well as books and videos. Relax by the pool, rent a bike, visit the emerald mine, take in the plays, music or exhibits at the nearby museum or shop for furniture, antiques, and crafts in the Hickory-Lenoir area. The New American cuisine features vegetables and herbs from the Inn's garden. This is altogether a tantalizing spot to "tarry awhile".

Approved by: ABBA

Photo: M.P. Cowan

The Inn is 17 miles from the Statesville junction of I-77 and I-40. From I-40(W), take Exit 150 to Taylorsville. Drive 12 miles to Hiddenite, turn right onto Sulphur Springs Rd. Inn is 1/2 mile on the left.

Hillsborough

B&B

209 E. Tryon Street, 27278
(919) 644-1600, Fax (919) 644-1600
Innkeeper: Katherine Webb

The Hillsborough House Inn

$$-
$$$$

The Inn offers its guests an incredibly luxurious atmosphere without losing any of the relaxed, comfortable feel of a small-town Inn. Enjoy the wonderful 80-foot front porch and a good book, watch a film, have a complimentary drink, or gather with friends in the library or the den. Refresh yourself in the pool or stroll through almost seven acres of woods, gardens, and ponds. The Inn overlooks St. Mary's Road, an ancient Native American trading path that ran from Virginia to South Carolina and which later formed the eastern edge of the original town of Hillsborough.

Approved by: AAA, NCBBI

Exit 164/I-85, Exit 261/I-40. Follow Hillsborough signs. Go to 6th traffic light, and then turn right onto E. Tryon Street. At 2nd stop sign, turn left into Inn drive.

Lake Lure

B&B

Route 1, Box 529A, 28746
(800) 733-2785, Fax (704) 625-4002
Innkeepers: Jack & Robin Stanier

Lodge on Lake Lure

$$-
$$$

Located on the lake and nestled in the foothills of the Blue Ridge Mountains, this large, rambling Inn offers breathtaking views. The great room is warm and inviting with vaulted ceilings, walls of wormy chestnut, hand-hewn beams, and a 20-foot tall fireplace. The library provides books, games, TV, and a video player. Rocking chairs on the veranda await you. Guest rooms exude individuality and mountain charm. You can swim and fish at the boathouse, there are chairs for sunning, and canoes. An afternoon lake cruise on the pontoon boat is a must.

Approved by: AAA, NCBBI

Off Highway 64/74 in Lake Lure, 25 miles southeast of Asheville.

Louisburg

B&B

305 North Main Street, 27549
(919) 496-6776, Fax (919) 496-1520
Innkeepers: John & Susan McKay

$

Hearthside Inn Bed & Breakfast

All of us have heard the stories of those who lived in small town America. Enjoy taking a trip back into this past era with a visit to the Hearthside Inn. Sit for a spell on the front porch or take the time to stroll around town and admire the historic family homes where several generations have resided. You can treasure the past while resting comfortably with modern convenience. Awaken to the aroma of fresh-baked muffins and begin your day with a bountiful breakfast served family style. Whether travelling for business or pleasure, you are offered a warm welcome here.

Approved by: AAA, NCBBI

From Highway 401 (N) or (S), follow Louisburg College signs. Turn left on Main Street. Inn is the third house on right. From I-85 (N), follow Route 39 to 401; I-85 (S) take Highway 56 to Highway 401.

Murphy

B&B

500 Valley River Avenue, 28906
(800) 824-6189, or (704) 837-9567
Innkeepers: Bob & Kate Delong

$/
$$

Huntington Hall Bed & Breakfast

Circa 1881, Huntington Hall has been lovingly restored to its charming, country, Victorian state. An historical record search is underway in hopes of a nomination for the National Register of Historical Places. Everyday brings a new breakfast entree, perhaps crêpes with ginger peaches and apricot sauce or french toast glazed in butterscotch and topped with real whip cream and pecans. Dietary restrictions can be accommodated. Relax on the front porch, enjoy the cool mountain breeze, and experience fine dining nearby.

Approved by: AAA, NCBBI

One block north of U.S. 64/19/129, on Business 19 at the intersection of Dillard Street.

20R 6S

Nags Head

B&B

6720 S. Virginia Dare Trail, 27959
(800) 368-9390, Fax (919) 441-9234
Innkeepers: The Lawrences

$/
$$$$

First Colony Inn™

You'll be charmed by the comfortable elegance of the Outer Banks' only historic B&B. Remote-controlled heat pumps, TV, Jacuzzis®, and wet bars blend with English antiques. The shingle-style building with its continuous double verandas is on the National Register of Historic Places. Watch the sunrise over the Atlantic, enjoy the continental buffet in the breakfast room, and then stroll down the boardwalk to the beach. Enjoy beachcombing, swimming, or fishing. Go sightseeing, birdwatching, or windsurfing before tea. End the day watching the sunset over the Sound.

Approved by: AAA, ABBA, Mobil

Enter parking lot on east side of U.S. 158, mile post 16, Nags Head.

7R

New Bern

B&B

509 Pollock Street, 28562
(800) 849-5553, or (919) 636-5553
Innkeepers: Howard & Dee Smith

$-
$$

The Aerie

Just one block from Tryon Palace in the heart of the historic district, the Aerie offers the closest accommodations to all of New Bern's historic attractions. The Victorian-style house, built in 1882, was a private residence for almost a century. Today it is furnished with fine antiques and some reproductions. The Innkeepers emphasize good food and drink. They offer complimentary wine, beer, and soft drinks throughout your stay, and fresh-baked cookies or cake in the evening. A generous breakfast consisting of three entree choices greets you each morning.

Approved by: AAA, Mobil, NCBBI

Enter the New Bern Historic District from Route 70 or Route 17, following signs for Tryon Palace. The Inn is 1 block east of the Palace.

New Bern

King's Arms Inn

B&B

212 Pollock Street, 28560
(800) 872-9306, or (919) 638-4409
Innkeepers: Richard & Patricia Gulley

$

Named for a local tavern which is said to have hosted members of the first Continental Congress, the Inn is located just a short carriage ride away from Tryon Palace and the historic district. Each spacious room has a decorative fireplace, private bath, unique decor, television, and telephone. Breakfast served to guest rooms consists of home-baked breads and muffins, fresh fruit juice, and King's Arms coffee (an exclusive blend) or tea. The morning paper accompanies this repast. The Innkeepers will arrange golf, tennis, boating, and dinner reservations.

Approved by: AAA, Mobil

From U.S. 70, exit onto E. Front-Cross over bridge. First light is Pollock; turn left onto Pollock. The Inn is the second house on the right.

Pittsboro

The Fearrington House

B&B

2000 Fearrington Village Center, 27312
(919) 542-2121, Fax (919) 542-4202
Innkeepers: R. B. & Jenny Fitch

$$$$/
$$$$$

Tucked away on farm land dating back to the 1700's, the Inn is filled with antiques, original art, and fresh flowers from the expansive formal gardens. Some rooms are clustered around a garden courtyard; others overlook a 12-acre park. A hearty breakfast sends guests off to explore the unique shops of the Fearrington Village Center. Enjoy the nearby amenities of Chapel Hill, Durham, and Raleigh or relax in the blissful garden setting. Dinner is available in the exquisite Fearrington House Restaurant, known for its regional cuisine, or in the more casual Market Cafe.

Approved by: AAA, IIA, Mobil

I-40(W) from airport, take Exit 273 B/Chapel Hill. Follow 54(W) for 3 miles. Turn right beyond overpass onto NC54(W)/US 15-501(S) Bypass. After 2.2 miles, take Sanford/Pittsboro 15-501 Exit. Turn left onto 15-501(S). After approx. 8 miles look for Fearrington Village Signs.

Saluda

Ivy Terrace Bed & Breakfast Inn

B&B
&

Highway 176, Box 639, 28773
(800) 749-9542, Fax (704) 749-2017
Innkeepers: Diane & Herbert McGuire

$$/
$$$

Surrounded by stone terraces and hidden under towering evergreens, this is the perfect escape from everyday challenges. The 1890's home has been renovated providing modern conveniences yet retaining its charm. Settle into your room, enjoy a fine dinner nearby, and return to a crackling fire before retiring on chilly evenings. Breakfast may include local cider, hazelnut oatmeal pancakes with sauteed apples, and fresh link sausages. You may dine inside or outside on the stone patios and then sightsee at the Biltmore House, hike Pearsons Falls, or tour the Blue Ridge Parkway.

Approved by: NCBBI

Take I-26 to NC Exit 28-Saluda. Proceed past the Texaco one mile to Hwy. 176 and turn right. The Inn is the first drive on the left.

Saluda

Orchard Inn

MAP
B&B

Highway 176, P.O. Box 725, 28773
(800) 581-3800, Fax (704) 749-9805
Innkeepers: Veronica & Newell Doty

$$/
$$$$

Personal service, a secluded setting, and elegant dining, all make this the perfect choice for either a quiet, weekend get-a-way or an executive-level company retreat. Sitting atop the 2500 foot Saluda Rise, the steepest standard-gauge, mainline-railroad grade in the country, the Inn invites you to experience rooms beautifully decorated with period antiques, artwork, and numerous books. After a day sightseeing or meeting in the newly-redecorated conference facility, you may dine on a four-course meal served in the eastern-facing dining porch.

Approved by: IIA

Photos: George W. Gardner

From I-26, take Exit 28 (Saluda). Go 1 mile west up hill to 176, then turn left. Inn is located 1/2 mile on right.

3R 1S

BYOB

12

V,M,X

Siler City

B&B

3188 Siler City-Snow Camp Road, 27344
(800) 742-6049, or (919) 742-6049
Innkeepers: David Simmons & Lisa Reynolds

$/
$$

Located in the heart of the state, this is a 10-year-old post and beam country home with an eclectic collection of antique and traditional furniture. The house sits on a ridge, overlooking the Rocky River and surrounded by one of the largest stands of Mountain Laurel east of the mountains. The setting is captivating with English country gardens, nature trails, and wildlife. Dave, the Innkeeper, is one of the area's most respected chefs. Your full breakfast will include the highest quality products, most of which are organic and locally grown. Gourmet vegetarian items are always available.

Approved by: NCBBI

Bed and Breakfast at Laurel Ridge

From US 64 and US 421(N). Turn onto Pearlyman Teague Rd. Go to stop sign, turn right onto Siler City-Snow Camp Road. Go 1/4 mile, Inn will be on the right.

9R 3S

BYOB

V,M

MAST FARM INN
Restaurant & Lodge

Photo: Michael Siede

Valle Crucis

MAP

PO Box 704, 28691
(704) 963-5857, Fax (704) 963-6404
Innkeepers: Francis & Sibyl Pressly

$$$/
$$$$

You can't miss this big, green farmhouse with its wraparound porches and 12 farm buildings when you come around the bend of the road on your way to the village. The Inn is on the National Register of Historic Places. Whether it's relaxing before a cheery, winter fire or rocking on the front porch enjoying the summer view of the mountain valley, life at this newly-restored Inn is pleasant and peaceful. Lodgings are in the main house and farm buildings. In season, the bountiful harvests supply produce used in preparing "country cooking with a gourmet touch".

Approved by: IIA

Mast Farm Inn

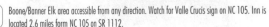

Boone/Banner Elk area accessible from any direction. Watch for Valle Crucis sign on NC 105. Inn is located 2.6 miles form NC 105 on SR 1112.

14R 2S

BYOB

Waynesville

AP
Hemphill Road, 28786
(704) 926-0430, Fax (704) 926-2036
Innkeeper: Deener Matthews

$$$$/
$$$$$

The Swag

You'll discover an elegant log lodge nestled atop a 5000 foot mountain with a mile long frontage on the Great Smoky Mountains National Park. The cool summer days, panoramic views, and wilderness setting all contribute to make this the idyllic, romantic destination you have been seeking. The Inn's vegetable garden helps assure freshness in the gourmet meals. The fourteen guest rooms are enhanced by original art, patchwork quilts, steam showers, fireplaces, wood stoves, and private balconies. This is the ultimate nature hideaway! November to May call (212) 570-2086.

Approved by: IIA, Mobil

I-40 west of Asheville, Exit 20 onto 276. Travel 2.8 miles to Hemphill Road (Creek Realty sign on road as well as Swag sign). Go up Hemphill Road 6.5 miles.

7R 1S

BYOB

Weaverville

B&B
26 Brown Street, 28787
(800) 839-3899
Innkeepers: Paul & Mary Lou Gibson

$/
$$

Dry Ridge Inn

A unique, fourth story peak tops this century-old, country farmhouse nestled near the Blue Ridge Mountains. Originally built in 1849 for a revival campground, the Inn takes its name from the surrounding area the Cherokees called Dry Ridge. An extensive library and interesting antiques provide an atmosphere of country comfort and charm. Discover original art by Mary Lou in the third floor art gallery. Shade trees and the high altitude makes relaxing on the front porch a memorable experience. Walk to restaurants or take a short drive to Asheville's many attractions.

Approved by: NCBBI

Exit at New Stock Road from Routes 19/23. Right at first light, and left at second light. Travel 2 miles on Business Route 19 (N). Turn right on Brown Street.

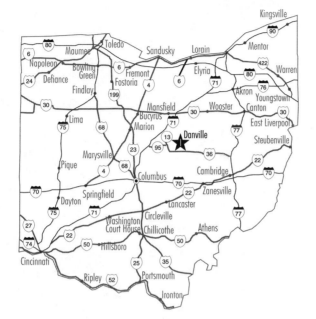

Relay Number: (800) 750-0750

1. White Oak Inn......p161

10R

BYOB

16

V,M
DV

The White Oak Inn

Danville

MAP
B&B

29683 Walhonding Road, 43014
(614) 599-6107, Fax (614) 599-9407
Innkeepers: Ian & Yvonne Martin

$/
$$$

In the rolling hills of the Walhonding Valley sits this large home, crafted by hand from red and white oak timbers. It is a scene of peace and relaxation, close to Ohio's Amish community, offering rockers and swings on the front porch and 14 acres of woodlands. The quest rooms are lovingly furnished with antiques and filled with pampering touches. The antique, square, grand piano is the focus of the common room, where you can enjoy afternoon refreshments in front of the fireplace. Hearty country breakfasts and gourmet candlelight dinners are specialties.

Approved by: AAA, IIA, Mobil

       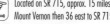

Located on SR 715, approx. 15 miles east of Mount Vernon. From I-71, take 229 east to Mount Vernon then 36 east to SR 715. From I-77, take 36 west to SR 715.

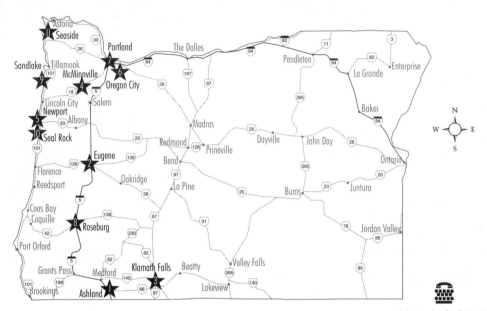

Relay Number: (800) 526-0661

5R 2S

BYOB

14

V,M

Ashland

B&B

1313 Clay Street, 97520
(503) 488-1590
Innkeeper: Dan Durant

$/
$$$$

Country Willows Bed & Breakfast

This Inn has it all, including a quiet, country-hillside setting with ducks, geese, goats, and spectacular views of the Cascade Mountains. The farm house is set on five lovely acres. When remodeling in 1983, a cabin dating back to 1896 was discovered. The original 13-stall barn now contains two suites. One deluxe suite has a fireplace, soaking tub, and its own redwood deck overlooking the lower acre. Enjoy the outside porches, redwood den with fireplace, living room, heated pool, and Jacuzzi®.

Approved by: AAA, OBBG

From South- I-5, take Exit 11, 1 1/4 mile to Clay; turn left to top. From North - I-5, take Exit 14. Turn right and go to light. Turn left and go 1 mile to Siskiyou. Turn right and go 2 blocks to Clay. Left on Clay continue to top.

Ashland

Hersey House

B&B

451 North Main Street, 97520
(503) 482-4563, Fax (503) 482-2839
Innkeepers: Gail E. Orell & K Lynn Savage

$$

This is an elegantly restored turn-of-the-century home with a pleasing blend of architectural elements from the Queen Anne and Craftsman periods. Rich greens and pale yellows accent warm tones of the original wood trim and antique oak furniture. There is a working Aeolian player piano. Enjoy sumptuous, multi-course breakfasts served on family china with silver and linens. Innovative entrees include gingerbread pancakes with lemon curd, Thundercloud plum blintzes, and Oregon blue cheese custards. It is only a short walk to downtown, and the lush Lithia Park.

Approved by: OBBG

Arriving from the north, take I-5 Exit 19, Ashland. Arriving from the south, take I-5 Exit 11. Proceed along Siskiyou and Lithia Way to North Main.

Ashland

The Morical House

B&B

668 North Main Street, 97520
(800) 208-0960, or (503) 482-2254
Innkeepers: Gary & Sandye Moore

$/
$$$

Enjoy this meticulously restored 1880's farmhouse with panoramic views of the Rogue Valley and Cascade Mountains. The room on the third floor is particularly suitable for those romantic occasions. Breakfast, with emphasis on healthful and locally-grown products, is served mornings from 8:00-9:30 in the dining room and on the sun porch. Special amenities include afternoon refreshments, two acres of grounds with spring-fed waterfalls, putting green, croquet, and rose and herb gardens. The Inn is one mile north of Oregon Shakespeare Festival.

Approved by: OBBG

From I-5, take Exit 19. Follow signs to Ashland. Inn is the fourth building on the left after entering city limits.

Ashland

Mt. Ashland Inn

B&B

550 Mt. Ashland Road, 97520
(503) 482-8707
Innkeepers: Elaine & Jerry Shanafelt

$/
$$$

This beautifully handcrafted, log Inn is surrounded by tall evergreens and commands spectacular views which include the majestic Mt. Shasta. The large, stone fireplace, oriental rugs, stained glass, colorful quilts, antiques, and finely-crafted furniture create a welcoming atmosphere. The ground floor room has a whirlpool-for-two and rock waterfall. Hike and cross-country ski from the Inn on the Pacific Crest Trail; downhill ski three miles away. Ashland and the award-winning Oregon Shakespeare Festival are only 16 miles away.

Approved by: AAA, Mobil, OBBG

Take I-5, Exit 6 (Mt. Ashland Exit). Follow signs to Mt. Ashland Ski Area. Go west 5 1/4 miles on Mt. Ashland Road. Inn is located on the right.

Ashland

Oak Hill Country Bed & Breakfast

B&B

2190 Siskiyou Blvd., 97520
(800) 888-7434, or (503) 482- 1554
Innkeepers: Tracy & Ron Bass

$/
$$

This charming 1910 farmhouse, located just minutes from the Oregon Shakespeare Festival, offers the convenience of the city with the ambiance and tranquility of the country. Each of the Inn's five bedrooms is decorated in a country motif and has a queen-size bed, private bath, and air conditioning. Extra beds and TV's are also available. The family-style, gourmet breakfast is truly the "Main Event" at the Inn. Guests eat together in the spacious, sunny dining room. The Innkeepers offer their guests the best in country cooking and friendly conversation.

Approved by: AAA, OBBG

From South, I-5, Exit 11 (Siskiyou Blvd.) to Inn. From North, I-5 to Exit 19. Follow sign to Ashland (Main Street becomes Siskiyou Blvd.). Continue to Inn.

Ashland

B&B

333 North Main Street, 97520
(800) 435-8260, Fax (503) 482-7912
Innkeepers: Francoise & Lester Roddy

$/
$$$

The Woods House Bed & Breakfast

Peaceful gardens with roses, herbs, and majestic trees surround the Inn. Located in the Historic District of Ashland, it is four blocks from the famous Oregon Shakespeare Festival, theatres, shops, and restaurants and the 100-acre Lithia Park. Guest rooms feature antique laces, canopies, hand-crafted finishes, warm woods, watercolors, oriental carpets, fine linens, special amenities, and fresh flowers from the garden. Anticipate strong coffee, good books, oven-fresh cookies, and garden breakfasts. You will enjoy warm hospitality and service with a smile.

Approved by: AAA, Mobil

Off I-5, halfway between San Francisco and Portland. Take Exit 19, and proceed 2 miles from exit, following signs to "Shakespeare Center." The Inn is located on the right.

Eugene

B&B

814 Lorane Highway, 97405
(503) 343-3234, Fax (503) 485-1219
Innkeepers: Eunice & George Kjaer

$/
$$

Kjaer's House In The Woods

Urban convenience and suburban tranquility describe this 1910 Craftsman-style home surrounded by rhododendron, azaleas, and huge fir and oak trees. This park-like setting with resident wildlife offers easy access to points of interest nearby. The common rooms are highlighted by original maple and oak floors, Oriental carpets, antiques, a rosewood grand piano, and a book and music library. A hearty breakfast is served with careful attention to special dietary needs. Specialties include fruit soups, Willamette Valley berries, baked egg dishes, and Oregon cheeses.

Approved by: OBBG

Left Photo: Multi-Image Management, Inc.

 From I-5, take Exit 189. Go west on 30th Ave. Cross Hilyard; turn left on 29th (which becomes Lorane Highway after crossing Williamette). Inn is 1 mile from Williamette.

3R 1S

BYOB

V,M

Newport

B&B

520 S.W. 2nd Street, 97365
(503) 265-9571
Innkeeper: Jan LeBrun

$$

Oar House Bed & Breakfast

This historic showplace on the central Oregon coast was built in 1900 and renovated in 1993. In addition to unique bedrooms, you will enjoy a tastefully furnished living room with a bar area for socializing. The sitting room has a fireplace and music system. The lighthouse tower, reached from the third floor by ship's ladder, offers 360 degree views of the Pacific, the picturesque village, romantic sunsets, and dramatic winter storms. After a restful evening, join other guests in the dining room for an inspired breakfast from the Innkeeper's repertoire of gourmet morning fare.

Approved by: OBBG

From the traffic signal at Hwy. 101 and Hurbert, go west to the second stop sign. The Inn is across the street.

4R

V,M,X

Portland

B&B

125 SW Hooker Street, 97201
(800) 745-4135, Fax (503) 295-6727
Innkeeper: Lori Hall

$/
$$

General Hooker's B & B

Superbly located in a quiet Historic District within walking distance of downtown, the Inn is a Victorian combining the best of two centuries: the mellow grace of family heirlooms from the Great Migration and the comfort and convenience of modern amenities. Eclectic throughout, the home features a restrained use of Victorian detail and a varied collection of Northwest art. Furniture is comfortable and tasteful and the food is vegetarian and heart-healthy. The Innkeeper is a 4th generation Portlander and readily shares her wealth of area knowledge.

Approved by: AAA, OBBG

From downtown Portland, follow 1st Ave. south from the Marriott Hotel for 3/4 mile to Hooker Street. Turn right. The Inn will be on the right.

Roseburg

House of Hunter

B&B

813 SE Kane Street, 97470
(503) 672-2335
Innkeepers: Jean & Walt Hunter

$/
$$

On a quiet, residential street with other historic homes is this Classic Italianate built in the late 1800's. In 1990 extensive renovations were made; preserving the essential character, adding new plumbing, electrical, and air conditioning and resulting in a light, airy, and expansive atmosphere. The lovely second floor rooms feature English wardrobes, hand-made quilts, and antique accents. Enjoy early morning coffee or tea and goodies left outside your room and followed by a full breakfast in the dining room. Enjoy the patio and putting green and if you stay two days there is free use of a raft.

Approved by: OBBG

From I-5 take Exit 124. Follow to Kane Street and turn right. The Inn is on the left.

Sandlake

Sandlake Country Inn

B&B

8505 Galloway Road, 97112
(503) 965-6745
Innkeepers: Margo & Charles Underwood

$$/
$$$

Sshhh...This is a secret hideaway nestled on the awesome Oregon Coast; a private, peaceful place for making memories. The 1894 shipwreck-timbered farmhouse, now on the Oregon Historic Registry, is tucked into a bower of old roses on two acres just off the Three Capes Scenic Loop. You might discover hummingbirds, chess, cookies and milk at midnight, Mozart, a three-course breakfast delivered to your door, award-winning oatmeal, an exuberant country garden, old books, a rose arbor swing for two, vintage movies, hot-spiced cider, a honeymoon cottage, and a million stars.

Approved by: ABBA, Mobil

From Tillamook, take US 101 (S) 11 miles. Turn right at Sandlake turnoff. Go 5 1/2 miles to Sandlake Grocery, then turn right onto Galloway Road. Inn is located 1/2 mile on the left.

Seal Rock, OR

B&B   6575 N.W. Pacific Coast Highway, 97376 $$
(503) 563-2259
Innkeeper: Barbara Tarter-Kyle

Blackberry Inn Bed & Breakfast

Nestled in pines, blackberry brambles, and gardens, the Inn is only a surf-sound from sandy, uncrowded beaches with tidepools, petrified shells, beachcoming, and agate hunting. Enjoy blackberry tea and snickerdoodles, rubber duckies and private baths. A Jacuzzi®, games, color TV, deck, and horseshoe pit are all available. The Inn is near the Oregon Coast Aquarium, Marine Science Center, and the Sea Lion Caves. Seclusion, Japanese food, fudge, espresso, antiques, trade beads, and wood and rock art are all reasons to visit Seal Rock

Approved by: OBBG

South of Newport, along the Central Oregon Coast, between mileposts 152 and 153 on Highway 101.

Pennsylvania

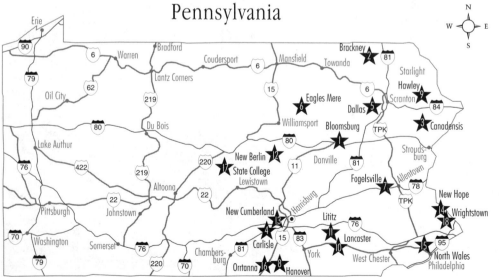

Relay Numbers: TTY (800) 654-5984, VCE (800) 654-5988

Bloomsburg

B&B
991 Central Road, 17815
(717) 387-1500, Fax (717) 784-3718
Innkeepers: Elizabeth "Babs" & Andrew Pruden

$$/
$$$$

You would probably never suspect that a moment's drive from the interstate would transport you to a world of peaceful strolls by a duck pond and personal wake-up calls. This is an oasis along the highway where continuous attention to detail is evident. It is apparent that the goal here is to make everyone feel pampered, whether you are eating a distinctive gourmet meal or spending the night in one of the country cottages surrounding the informal courtyard or in the main house, an 1839 white brick farmhouse.

Approved by: AAA

The Inn at Turkey Hill

Conveniently located at Exit 35 of I-80. The Inn is on the corner at the first traffic light, approximately .5 miles from the interstate.

Carlisle

B&B
150 Hickorytown Road, 17013
(717) 258-0717, Fax (717) 258-0717
Innkeepers: Denise Fegan & Chuck DeMarco

$/
$$

This is a two hundred year old, brick farmhouse in the quiet surroundings of the beautiful farm country of central Pennsylvania. In three of the guest rooms sleep comfortably in queen size beds or get lost in the king size bed of the fourth room. After a game of tennis or a hike on the Appalachian Trail, enjoy homemade cookies and a soft drink from the refrigerator which is provided for your use. Watch television or play a game in the family room or curl up with a book in the quiet living room. Although there are no trail rides at this time, you can board your horse overnight in the stone bank barn.

Approved by: AAA

Pheasant Field Bed & Breakfast

The Inn is located two miles east of Carlisle and six miles west of Mechanicsburg, PA.

Dallas (Wilkes-Barre)

B&B

R.R.I. Box 349, 18612
(800) 854-3286
Innkeepers: Jeanettie & Clifford Rowland

$/
$$

Ponda-Rowland Bed & Breakfast

A circa 1850 Inn, this is part of a 130-acre working farm in the Endless Mountains. The rooms all have private baths, king-size beds, ceiling fans, and are furnished with museum quality, children-proof, country antiques. The country comfort is perfect for a fun-filled family retreat or a romantic getaway. There are mountain views (binoculars furnished), play areas, farm animals, and a private wildlife sanctuary with trails, ponds, and meadows. Have refreshments during cool evenings in the Great Room by the large stone fireplace and a country breakfast by candlelight.

Approved by: AAA, ABBA

Exit 36 from NE Extension PA Turnpike (Route 9), or Exit 47B from I-81, Route 309 (N). Follow "Rowland Farm" signs at Village of Beaumont.

Eagles Mere

MAP

Mary & Sullivan Avenues, 17731
(717) 525-3273
Innkeepers: Susan & Peter Glaubitz

$$$

Eagles Mere Inn

Eagles Mere Inn rests on a mountain top in Northeastern Pennsylvania, 3 1/2 hours from New York City, Philadelphia, and Baltimore. A stay here offers the ultimate in stress relief! There is peace and quiet with a private, crystal-clear, mile-long lake with swimming, sailing, canoeing, incredible waterfalls, hiking, vistas, cross-country skiing, ice toboggan, golf, tennis, antique shops, and more! This Inn has 15 rooms with private baths, old-fashioned hospitality, and outstanding food. A full breakfast and five-course gourmet dinner are included in the rates.

Approved by: ABBA, IIA, Mobil

From Eastern Pennsylvania, take Route 80 (W) to Route 42 (N).
From Western Pennsylvania, take Route 80 (E) to Route 220 (N) to Route 42 (N).

10R 13S

Fogelsville

EP
B&B

2141 Packhouse Road, 18051
(610) 285-4723, Fax (610) 285-2862
Innkeepers: Beth & Al Granger

Glasbern

$$$-
$$$$$

Fireplaces and whirlpools embellish this German farm complex established in the mid-nineteenth century and updated as an Inn in 1985. Contemporary American cuisine is featured in the Barn's refurbished Granary and under the timbered cathedral ceiling of the Great Room. Flower and vegetable gardens now flourish for the guests' pleasure where a farm family once labored daily for basic provisions. A pastoral landscape is complemented by a meandering stream, ponds, and paths.

Approved by: AAA, ABBA, IIA, Mobil

Photos: George W. Gardner

From I-78, take Exit 14B Route 100 (N) for .2 miles. Turn left (W) at light, continue for .3 miles. Turn right (N) on Church Street for .6 miles. Turn right on Pack House Road for .8 miles to the Inn.

16R 4S

Hawley

B&B

4 Main Avenue, 18428
(800) 833-8527, Fax (717)226-1874
Innkeepers: Jeanne & Grant Genzlinger, Marcia Dunsmore

$/
$$$

Settlers Inn at Bingham Park

Chestnut wood beams, a large, native-bluestone fireplace, leaded windows, the outdoor patio, and herb gardens all add to the ambiance of this restored Tudor Manor. Guest rooms are cheerfully decorated with rose-flowered wallpapers and white wicker furniture along with antiques and quilted bedcovers. The dining room is well-known for its creative regional cuisine featuring the products of local farms and an in-house bakery. Lake Wallenpaupack and the upper Delaware River are nearby providing many recreational activities. The antique stores are wonderful.

Approved by: IIA, Mobil

Photo: Bob Jennings

Photo: George W. Gardner

I-84 to Exit 7, Route 390 (N) to 507 (N) to 6 (W). Go 2.5 miles to Inn.

Lancaster

B&B

1049 E. King Street, 17602
(800) 747-8717, Fax (717) 397-3447
Innkeepers: Karen & Jim Owens

$$-
$$$$

In the heart of historic Lancaster county, this Spanish Mission Revival Inn, unique in Amish country, offers modern comforts in a traditional, luxurious setting. It is listed on the National Register. Each inviting guest room has a king or queen-size bed, private bath, and a comfortable sitting area. Many of the baths have stained-glass windows, turn-of-the -century fixtures, and oversized tubs perfect for languorous soaks. During check-in, tea awaits in the elegant library by the fireplace. Friendly, hospitable Innkeepers arrange dinner, tours, and personalized maps of the area.

Approved by: AAA, Mobil

The King's Cottage

Exit Route 30 at Walnut Street, and turn right at end of ramp. At 2nd stop light, turn left. At 2nd stop sign, turn left onto Orange Street. Proceed 1 block, then turn right onto Cottage Avenue. Inn is last building on the right.

Lititz

B&B
&

500 Blantz Road, 17543
(800) 594-8018, Fax (717) 627-3483
Innkeepers: Werner & Debrah Mosimann

$$/
$$$

Surrounded by meadows and gardens, this is a quiet retreat in Lancaster's Amish Country with an atmosphere reminiscent of Switzerland with open beams, natural woodwork, and handcrafted furniture. It is a perfect place to relax after visiting the farmers markets, biking through the farmland or even riding the roller coaster at Hersey Park. All rooms feature patios or balconies where flowers bloom profusely. Wake up to the smell of a special blend of freshly brewed coffee and indulge in an unforgettable breakfast. The cinnamon-raisin French toast or Eggs Florentine are specialties not to miss.

Approved by: AAA, IIA

Swiss Woods B & B

From Lancaster take Rt 501 (N) through Lititz. After the 501 Motel, turn left onto Brubaker Valley Rd. Go 1 mile to the lake. Before the bridge, turn right onto Blantz Rd.

New Berlin

B&B

321 Market Street, 17855-0390
(717) 966-0321, Fax (717) 966-9557
Innkeepers: John & Nancy Showers

$/
$$

The Inn at Olde New Berlin

This elegantly appointed Victorian Inn is the perfect place for enjoying quiet pleasures. Inn memories are made from the inviting front porch swing to the baby grand piano in the step-down living room to the herb garden where the restaurant's seasonings and garnishes are selected. The superb dining opportunities at Gabriel's Restaurant, coupled with the antique-filled guest rooms, provide romance and luxurious ambiance. You will discover pampering in a rural setting and leave feeling nurtured, relaxed, inspired, and ready to return.

Approved by: AAA

Follow Rt. 80(W), to Lewisburg/Rt.15(S) Exit. Drive into Lewisburg and at the intersection of Rt. 45 and Rt. 15, turn right. Follow Rt. 45(W) for 4 miles. Turn left (south) onto Dreisbach Church Rd. Proceed 5 miles into New Berlin. At the stop sign, turn right. Inn is on the right.

New Cumberland

B&B

204 Limekiln Road, 17070
(717) 774-2683
Innkeepers: Chad & Phyllis Combs

$-
$$

Farm Fortune, A Bed & Breakfast

Forget the pace of the 20th century and come here to imagine life in the 1700's when the Inn was built. This B&B welcomes you to its foyer with a lovely staircase, interesting woodwork, wide-board floors, and rumored history of runaway slaves hiding below the floors. Its rooms are furnished with antiques. You will enjoy the crackling fire in the walk-in fireplace in the Keeping Room or breakfast by the fire in the Country Kitchen. The B&B overlooks the Yellow Breeches Creek and is near Gettysburg, Lancaster, Harrisburg, Hershey and Carlisle.

Approved by: AAA, ABBA

        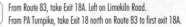

From Route 83, take Exit 18A. Left on Limekiln Road.
From PA Turnpike, take Exit 18 north on Route 83 to first exit 18A.

North Wales

Joseph Ambler Inn

B&B

1005 Horsham Road, 19454
(215) 362-7500, Fax (215) 361-5924
Innkeepers: Steve & Terry Kratz

$$/
$$$

As you make your approach up the long, winding drive you are at once struck by the peaceful, historic setting of this Country Inn. Nestled on 12 acres of picturesque lawns and gardens, the Inn sits like an oasis in busy Montgomeryville, PA. The Inn features delightful guest rooms in three authentically restored buildings as well as the Colonial Restaurant in the fieldstone barn. Be certain to try the house specialty, Rack of Lamb! The rooms are furnished with antiques and reproductions and each has air conditioning, telephone, television, and a private bathroom.

Approved by: ABBA

Photo: Carl Schwenk

The Inn is located on Horsham Road (Rt. 463) approximately one mile east of the intersection of Routes 202, 309, and 463 in Montgomeryville.

Orrtanna

Hickory Bridge Farm

B&B

96 Hickory Bridge Road, 17353
(717) 642-5261
Innkeepers: Mary Lynn Martin & Dr. & Mrs. Hammett

$$

When you are visiting Gettysburg, this is the perfect place to relax. Only eight miles west of the battlefield, the farm is nestled at the foothills of the Appalachian Mountains. You may stay in one of the four private cottages overlooking a well-stocked, trout stream or in one of the several rooms in the 1750 farmhouse that is decorated with antiques. Staying at the farm would not be complete without a fine dinner that is served on weekends in the restored Pennsylvania barn. The dining room is also beautifully decorated with antiques. You will enjoy the history, the festivals, sports, or leisure here.

Approved by: AAA, IIA, Mobil

Take Rt. 116 west from Gettysburg. Go three miles north to Orrtanna.

Pine Grove Mills (State College)

B&B

347 W. Pine Grove Road, P. O. Box 326, 16868
(800) 251-2028, or (814) 238-2028
Innkeeper: Mae McQuade

$/
$$$

Split-Pine Farmhouse B & B

Every bedchamber here emits an aura sure to delight and comfort the carefree vagabond or the pilgrim on a solemn journey. From the forested bower on the twilight side of the house with its stump tables and antlered curtain swags, to the downy-nested room where swans serenely glide, a playful empathy consoles or enchants. The morning table offers nourishment for all the senses; with color, texture, variety, and taste in both the feast and the fittings. Hospitality here is genuine and generous. This Inn is not too far from your real world, but very close to Heaven.

Approved by: ABBA

The Inn is on Rt. 45, six miles from State College. State Routes 322 and 220 and I-80 are 5 to 30 minutes away.

Wrightstown (New Hope)

B&B

677 Durham Road, 18940
(215) 598-3100
Innkeepers: Ellen & Richard Butkus

$$-
$$$

Hollileif Bed & Breakfast

Just six miles west of New Hope on 5 1/2 acres of rolling countryside, Hollileif offers romantic ambiance, fireplaces, and central air conditioning along with gracious service and attention to detail. Guest rooms are appointed with fresh flowers, antiques, and country furnishings and have private baths. You will savor a four-course breakfast, served at individual tables in the Breakfast Room, and enjoy afternoon refreshments by the fireside or on the arbor-covered patio. You may even relax in a hammock hung lazily in the meadow overlooking the stream.

Approved by: AAA, Mobil

Located on Route 413. Inn is 4/10 of a mile south of Route 232, 6 miles south of Route 32, and 5 1/2 miles south of Route 202.

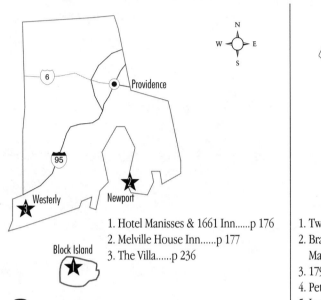

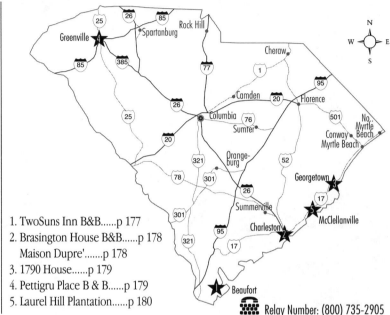

1. Hotel Manisses & 1661 Inn......p 176
2. Melville House Inn......p 177
3. The Villa......p 236

Block Island

Relay Number: (800) 745-5555

1. TwoSuns Inn B&B......p 177
2. Brasington House B&B......p 178
   Maison Dupre'......p 178
3. 1790 House......p 179
4. Pettigru Place B & B......p 179
5. Laurel Hill Plantation......p 180

Relay Number: (800) 735-2905

Block Island, RI

P.O. Box I, 02807
(401) 466-2836, Fax (401) 466-2858
Innkeepers: Joan & Justin Abrams/Rita & Steve Draper

B&B

$/
$$$$$

Hotel Manisses and 1661 Inn

The Hotel is an 1870 Victorian hotel that has been lovingly restored by the Abrams family. The guest rooms are named after famous shipwrecks and offer private baths. Some rooms have whirlpools. The award-winning dining room offers inventive cuisine drawing upon local seafood, fresh herbs, and vegetables grown in the Manisses' gardens. Part of this complex is the 1661 Inn which overlooks the Atlantic Ocean and Old Harbor. The Animal Farm, just adjacent, has become a popular point of interest on the Island.

Approved by: IIA

One hour by ferry from Point Judith, RI. Point Judith is 32 miles from Providence and 92 miles from Boston.

7R 1S

Newport, RI

Melville House Inn

B&B

39 Clarke Street, 02840
(401) 847-0640, Fax (401) 847-0956
Innkeepers: Vince DeRico & David Horan

$/
$$$

Built circa 1750, the Inn is on the National Register of Historic Places and located in the heart of Newport's Historic Hill District. It sits on a quiet street of interesting colonial buildings, just one block from Thames Street with its Brick Market, wharfs, restaurants, and shops. Trinity Church, circa 1726 and Touro Synagogue, the first in the country, are only two blocks away. The rooms are furnished in the colonial style. Breakfast is served in a sunny dining room and an afternoon tea features refreshments, homemade biscotti, and soup on cold days. Fabled Mansions and beaches are nearby.

Approved by: AAA, ABBA, Mobil

From Boston area, take Rt. 24(S) to Rt. 114(S) into Newport. From New York and Connecticut, take Rt. 95(N) to Exit 3A in Rhode Island. Follow Rt. 138(E) into Newport.

5R

Beaufort, SC

TwoSuns Inn Bed & Breakfast

B&B

1705 Bay Street, 29902
(800) 532-4244, or (803) 522-1122
Innkeepers: Carrol & Ron Kay

$$/
$$$

Visit the nationally landmarked community of Beaufort, founded in 1711. Relax in a fully restored, 1917 grand home with individually themed guest rooms, modern amenities and baths, antiques and collectibles, and the finest panoramic bay view in town. Enjoy a casual atmosphere where guests mingle during "Tea & Toddy Hour." Visit historic antebellum homes, stroll in a waterfront park, browse antique shops, and enjoy coastal dining. TwoSuns is "A Prince of an Inn in an Antibellum Brigadoon" with warm hospitality by Carrol and Ron.

Approved by: AAA, Mobil, SCBBA

Approximately 25 miles from I-95 (Southbound SC Exit 33 to US 21/Northbound SC Exit 8 to Highway 170 (E) to U.S. 21) into Historic Beaufort.

3R 1S

Charleston

B&B

328 East Bay Street, 29401
(803) 722-1274, Fax (803) 722-6785
Innkeepers: Dalton & Judy Brasington

$$

Brasington House B&B

Located in the heart of Charleston's historic district, this antebellum, Charleston home was meticulously restored in 1987 by its current proprietors. The antique furnishings blend with the Greek Revival features, Marble Victorian mantles, and decorative, plaster cornices in the living and dining room. The wide porches running the length of the house are typical of Charleston "style" single houses. Judy and Dalton help their guests with suggestions for sightseeing, restaurants, shopping, and other area activities.

Approved by: AAA, SCBBA

At eastern terminus of I-26, take Meeting Street south to George Street. Turn left 2 blocks to East Bay Street. Turn right, then immediately turn left into parking lot.

12R 3S

Charleston

B&B

317 East Bay Street, 29401
(800) 844-INNS, Fax (803) 723-3722
Innkeepers: Bob & Lucille Mulholland & Mark Mulholland

$$-
$$$$$

Maison Dupre'

Built in 1804, this Inn is comprised of three "single houses" and two carriage houses. All have been restored with the style and grace of a "Country French" Inn. Upon entering the wrought-iron gates, you are in a beautiful, brick courtyard with flowing fountains and landscaped "Charleston" gardens. Your stay includes turndown service with chocolates, continental breakfast with French pastries, and a "Low Country" tea party each afternoon. The Inn displays the original, French impressionist style paintings of the owner, Lucille Mulholland.

Approved by: AAA, SCBBA

Enter Charleston on I-26 or Route 17. Proceed downtown on Meeting Street. Turn left on George Street. Proceed to Inn at corner of East Bay Street.

Georgetown

B&B

630 Highmarket Street, 29440
(803) 546-4821
Innkeepers: Patricia & John Wiley

$/
$$$

1790 House-Bed & Breakfast Inn

You will love this meticulously restored, 200-year-old, West Indies colonial plantation style Inn, located in the heart of historic Georgetown. Enjoy lovely gardens, luxurious rooms all with private baths, full breakfast, and afternoon tea or wine. You may stay in the "Rice Planters" room, the "Indigo" room, the beautiful honeymoon cottage with Jacuzzis®, or one of the other lovely rooms. Walk to shops, restaurants, and historic sights. Close by are Brookgreen Gardens, Pawleys Island, Grand Strand (a golfer's paradise), Myrtle Beach, and Charleston.

Approved by: AAA, ABBA, Mobil, SCBBA

Highway 17 or 521 into town.

Greenville

B&B

302 Pettigru Street, 29601
(803) 242-4529, Fax (803) 242-1231
Innkeepers: Gloria Hendershot & Janice Beatty

$/
$$$

Pettigru Place B & B

Quietly located on a beautiful, historic, tree-lined street in the heart of downtown, the Inn is convenient for business and leisure travellers. Stroll through the garden and relax in this restored, Georgian-Federalist design home built in the early 1920's. Choose a room to suit your mood. There is an "out of Africa" look; a touch of antique Victorian; a romantic floral in navy and burgundy; an elegant "mountain" retreat; or a touch of coastal Carolina with the "Charleston" look. After a restful evening, start your day with a gourmet breakfast and friendly conversation.

Approved by: AAA, SCBBA

From Rt.29, turn onto E. North Street. Follow to Williams Street, turn right. Turn left onto Pettigru and look for the Inn on the right.

McClellanville, SC

B&B

8913 N. Hwy 17, P. O. Box 190, 29458
(803) 887-3708
Innkeepers: Jackie & Lee Morrison

$

Laurel Hill Plantation

The original Laurel Hill, an 1850's plantation house listed on the National Register of Historic Places, was destroyed by Hurricane Hugo on September 21, 1989. Nestled in a nook by a picturesque tidal creek, the spacious reconstruction has been designed to retain the romance of the past while affording the convenience of the contemporary. Wrap-around porches overlook a sweeping panorama of Cape Romain's salt marshes, islands, waterways, and the Atlantic Ocean. The Inn is a perfect blend of yesterday's nostalgia and today's comfort in a setting of magnificent coastal vistas.

Approved by: AAA, SCBBA

Located on Highway 17; 30 miles north of Charleston, 25 miles south of Georgetown, and 60 miles south of Myrtle Beach.

Monteagle, TN

B&B

Monteagle Assembly, 37356
(615) 924-4000, Fax (615) 924-3236
Innkeepers: Wendy & Dave Adams

$/
$$$

Adams Edgeworth Inn

Enjoy this place of rare magic, a century old Inn resting in its own Victorian village on top of a mountain. Experience the charm of fireplaces, tall wooden trestle foot bridges over the creeks, and porches with rocking chairs. Follow pine needle trails through ancient forests, play tennis or golf, enjoy concerts, plays, and lectures or rest and read. This almost 100-year-old Victorian is furnished in the English Manor style and houses an extensive collection of fine art. Dinner is an elegant affair with fine cuisine served by candlelight on Wedgewood china like that used by Queen Elizabeth.

Approved by: AAA, IIA, Mobil

From I-24 take Exit 134. Turn right. In the center of the village go left through the arch marked with a Monteagle Assembly sign. Turn right at the bottom of the hill and take immediate right at Chestnut Hill. Follow signs to Inn.

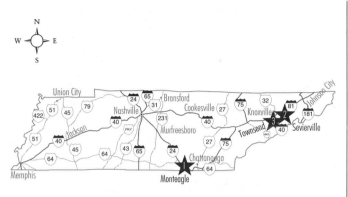

1. Adams Edgeworth Inn......p 180
   North Gate Inn......p 181
2. Blue Mountain Mist Country Inn.......p 182
   Von-Bryan Inn......p 182
3. Richmont Inn......p 183

Relay Numbers: TTY (800) 848-0298, VCE (800) 848-0299

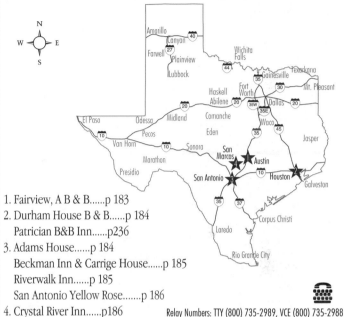

1. Fairview, A B & B......p 183
2. Durham House B & B......p 184
   Patrician B&B Inn......p236
3. Adams House......p 184
   Beckman Inn & Carrige House......p 185
   Riverwalk Inn......p 185
   San Antonio Yellow Rose.......p 186
4. Crystal River Inn......p186

Relay Numbers: TTY (800) 735-2989, VCE (800) 735-2988

Monteagle, TN

B&B
&

P. O. Box 858, 37356
(615) 924-2799
Innkeepers: Nancy & Henry Crais

North Gate Inn

$

From the moment that you walk under the bright blue awning into the lattice-walled Sun Room you know that this will be a happy place to spend a few days. The varied, light-filled common areas beckon you to your own private spot and entice you to curl up with a good book for a memorable afternoon. Every guest room is light, airy, and most of all comfortable; they are rooms that you can live in. Your hosts will treat you like family; they truly want you to remember your stay as time away from time. Visit this century-old neighborhood and return to a simpler and easier way.

Approved by: AAA

From I-24 take Exit 134. Turn right and go .3 miles to a brick building on the left. Go through the stone gates and follow the signs to the Inn.

12R 5S

BYOB

12

V,M

Sevierville

B&B

1811 Pullen Road, 37862
(800) 497-2335, Fax (615) 453-1720
Innkeepers: Norman & Sarah Ball

$/
$$

Experience the silent beauty of mountain scenery while rocking on the big wraparound porch of this Victorian style farmhouse. Relax in common rooms filled with antiques or individually decorated guest rooms. Enjoy many special touches such as old-fashion claw foot tubs, high antique headboards, and quilts. Nestled in the woods behind the Inn are five country cottages designed for romantic getaways. Each with Jacuzzi® and fireplace. Lots of visiting takes place in this homey atmosphere, yet the Great Smoky Mountains National Park and Gatlinburg are only 20 minutes away.

Approved by: AAA

Blue Mountain Mist Country Inn

From I-40, take 407 Exit to Sevierville, then turn left at first traffic light onto Highway 411. Go to 3rd light, and then turn right onto Middle Creek Road. Go 4 miles, then turn left onto Jayell Road. Then proceed 1 1/2 miles. Inn is located on the left side.

6R 2S

BYOB

10

V,M,X
DV

Sevierville

B&B

2402 Hatcher Mountain Road, 37862
(800) 633-1459, Fax (615) 428-8634
Innkeepers: D. J. & JoAnn Vaughn

$/
$$$

You will experience the joys of the Great Smoky Mountains in this mountaintop, log Inn. Watch the mist form, flow, and fade from the patchwork valley below. Be dazzled by the first light and spellbound by the sky at sunset. The Inn's atmosphere is casual and pleasant with its fine wood surfaces, cathedral ceilings, skylights, and big windows framing the views. Relax in the spacious rooms with whirlpools and steam showers. A variety of games, a piano, an extensive collection of books, and original art are here to enjoy. A breakfast buffet or a breakfast basket on the grounds will begin your day.

Approved by: AAA

Von-Bryan Inn

From I-40 take Exit 407 to Pigeon Forge. Turn onto 321(S) and go 7.2 miles to Hatcher Mountain Rd. Turn right and drive to the top of the mountain and the Inn.

Photos: Pro Studio

Townsend, TN

Richmont Inn

B&B

220 Winterberry Lane, 37882
(615) 448-6751, Fax (615) 448-6480
Innkeepers: Jim & Susan Hind

$$$

Situated on the "peaceful side of the Smokies," this Appalachian cantilever barn is beautifully furnished with 18th century English antiques and French paintings in the living-dining rooms. Graciously appointed guest rooms have sitting areas, king beds, wood-burning fireplaces, spa tubs for two, and private balconies. Wherever you look there are breathtaking mountain views. French and Swiss cuisine are featured at breakfast and there are flavored coffees and gourmet desserts by evening candlelight. The Inn is just 10 minutes to the Great Smoky Mountains. Art and craft shops are nearby.

Approved by: Mobil

From Townsend on Hwy. 321(N) or (S), take Old Tuckaleechee and Laurel Valley Roads through stone entrance to Laurel Valley. Bear right through stone entrance on the paved road to the crest of the hill. Turn left to the Inn.

Austin, TX

Fairview, A Bed & Breakfast

B&B

1304 Newning Avenue, 78704
(800) 310-4746, or (512) 444-4746
Innkeepers: Nancy & Duke Waggoner

$$/
$$$

Surrounded by huge live oak trees, this turn-of-the-century, Texas Colonial Revival home offers gracious and elegant accommodations. Carefully selected antique furnishings give each of the oversized guest rooms or suites its own unique style and romance. Stroll through the lavishly landscaped gardens and return to the Inn for a leisurely breakfast or afternoon refreshments. The Great Room, the Parlor, or the adjacent rose garden are wonderful places to unwind, visit with other guests, and plan the evening. The knowledgeable hosts will help you enjoy this active city.

Approved by: Mobil

From IH 35, take Riverside Drive West to Congress Avenue and turn left. Follow to Academy Drive, turn left. Turn right onto Newning Avenue. Inn is on the right.

Houston

Durham House Bed & Breakfast

B&B

921 Heights Boulevard, 77008
(800) 722-8788, Fax (713) 868-7965
Innkeeper: Marguerite Swanson

$$

What a delightful surprise it is to find downtown Houston skyscrapers only five minutes away from this Queen Anne Victorian Inn listed on the National Register of Historic Places. Romantic but practical, the Inn is as suitable for sweethearts as it is for corporate guests desiring individualized services and special dietary considerations. The Inn boasts a garden gazebo, player piano, front porch swing, and spacious solarium for your use. Urban sophistication, antique furnishings, and Texas hospitality harmoniously combine to make your stay here truly memorable.

Approved by: AAA, ABBA

Follow I-10(W) to Heights/Studemont exit. Proceed on feeder road to the first traffic light, turn right onto Heights Blvd.

San Antonio

Adams House

B&B

231 Adams Street, 78210
(800) 666-4810, Fax (210) 223-5125
Innkeeper: Betty Lancaster

$$

This is a restored, three-story, brick Victorian Italianate house, built in 1902 by German immigrants. Located in the King William Historic District, it showcases finely crafted, red-pine woodwork. Four large, airy verandas with tables and rockers and a backyard terrace shaded by towering pecan trees offer a choice of private retreats. The Inn is within walking distance of the River Center-Convention Center and the lively downtown Riverwalk area. The Riverwalk winds through the neighborhood and offers a scenic and quiet place for walking or jogging. The bus and the trolley are nearby.

Approved by: ABBA

From IH-37 exit at Durango and go west to South Alamo. Turn left onto South Alamo and at the 3rd traffic light turn left onto Adams. From IH-10 exit at South Alamo and go east to Adams Street. Turn right onto Adams. The Inn is on the corner of Adams and Stieren.

San Antonio

Beckmann Inn & Carriage House

B&B
222 E. Guenther Street, 78204
(800) 945-1449, or (210) 229-1449
Innkeepers: Betty Jo & Don Schwartz

$$/
$$$

Enjoy warm and gracious hospitality in an elegant Victorian home built in 1886. The Inn is located in the King William Historic District just across the street from the start of the Riverwalk and minutes from the Alamo by the trolley. The beautiful wraparound porch welcomes guests to colorfully decorated rooms featuring ornately carved, antique Victorian queen-size beds, and private baths. A gourmet breakfast with a special breakfast dessert is served in the formal dining room. The Inn is perfectly located to allow you to experience all that San Antonio has to offer.

Approved by: AAA, Mobil

From airport, follow IH-37(S). Exit Durango/Alamodome and turn right. Turn left on S. St. Mary's Street, turn right on King William, left on Guenther.

San Antonio

Riverwalk Inn

B&B
&
329 Old Guilbeau Road, 78204
(800) 254-4440, Fax (210) 229-9442
Innkeepers: Johnny Halpenny & Jan & Tracy Hammer

$$$

Comprised of five two-story log homes, circa 1840, that have been restored on the Downtown San Antonio Riverwalk, this Inn is decorated in period antiques creating an ambiance of "country elegance". You will "rock til you drop" on the 80-foot long porch lined with rocking chairs. You will love Aunt Martha's evening desserts and the local story-tellers that join you for breakfast. Not only are you close to all the excitement of the Riverwalk, but you also have the convenience of telephones, television, and refrigerators. The experience here is truly Texas tradition with a Tennessee flavor.

Approved by: AAA

From IH 37, exit at Durango and turn right. Cross Alamo and St. Mary's Streets and turn right onto Aubrey. The Inn is on the corner of Aubrey and Old Guilbeau.

San Antonio

B&B

229 Madison, 78204

(800) 950-9903, or (210) 229-9903

Innkeepers: Jennifer & Cliff Tice

$$/
$$$

San Antonio Yellow Rose

This 1879 home built by Charles Mueller, a German immigrant, is a brick Victorian with a mansard roof and large porches. The guest rooms are distinctively decorated with antiques and each has a private bath and television. The large living room and dining room are decorated with 18th century furnishings and provide plenty of space to relax. The Inn is located in the King William Historic District, just two blocks from the Riverwalk. You will enjoy a full breakfast, off-street parking, and convivial hosts who willingly share their knowledge of the city.

Approved by: ABBA

From IH-10, 35, 37, or Highway 281, take Durango to South St. Mary's. Turn south. Take the second right onto Madison. The Inn is on the right in the second block.

San Marcos

B&B

326 W. Hopkins, 78666

(512) 396-3739, Fax (512) 353-3248

Innkeepers: Mike & Cathy Dillon

$/
$$$

Crystal River Inn

Near the crystal-clear San Marcos River for all watersports, the Inn is famous for escape packages such as murder mysteries, outlet shopping, romantic interludes, and ballooning. Three different buildings meet needs from honeymoon privacy to business travel, with such varying amenities as fireplaces, phones, TV, canopied beds, sunken tubs, and mini-kitchens. Every guest experiences designer decor, antiques, flowers, classical music, a library, twinkle lights, and topiaries. Breakfast is gourmet glamour served in bed and in the atrium, veranda, or fountain courtyard.

Approved by: Mobil

Off I-35, take Exit 205. Go west into town. Inn is located 3 blocks past court house on the right.

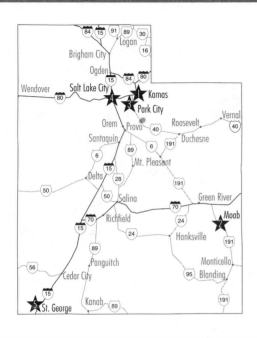

Relay Number: (800) 346-4128

5R

BYOB

10

V,M

Kamas

B&B

P. O. Box 849, 84036
(800) 658-0643, Fax (801) 783-2910
Innkeepers: Patricia & John Skomars

Patricia's Country Manor

$/
$$

You will love this old fashioned Bed & Breakfast located at the "Gateway to the Uinta Mountains". Just minutes from the renown ski areas of Deer Valley, Park City, and Wolf Mountain and from world class golf courses including the Wasatch Mountain State Park course is this lovely old house. There is a common great room with a fireplace, television, and VCR; a family room with another fireplace and a sunroom looking out over the grounds. You will enjoy the covered patio area and the outside hot tub. Home-style breakfasts feature delectable sweet rolls served in Victorian elegance.

Approved by: BBIU

From the Salt Lake City airport travel east on I-80 for 32 miles. Take Exit 148 to Hwy. 40(E). From Hwy. 40(E) take Exit 4 and follow signs to Kamas. The Inn is on the NW corner of 100 North.

Moab

B&B

185 North 300 East, 84532
(801) 259-2974
Innkeepers: Richard & Marjorie Stucki

Sunflower Hill Bed & Breakfast

$/
$$

You will enjoy the simple pleasures of a country retreat nestled in the heart of the canyonlands. This turn-of-the-century farmhouse and cozy garden cottage welcome you with country charm and honest-to-goodness comfort. Unique guest rooms offer quaint antiques, fanciful stenciling, and luxurious beds with colorful linens. You may wander through lush flower gardens and wooded pathways or relax in a steaming hot-tub surrounded by pines. In the morning a sumptuous breakfast buffet is served from an antique sideboard. This serene spot is three blocks from downtown.

Approved by: AAA, BBIU

Take highway 191(S). At first traffic light, (4th light on 191(N)), turn east onto 100(N). Go three blocks. Turn left onto 300 East. Inn is 4th house on left.

Salt Lake City

B&B

57 South 600 East, 84102
(800) 524-5511, Fax (801) 596-1316
Innkeepers: Mark Brown & Keith Lewis

Anton Boxrud B & B Inn

$$

As you arrive at this Inn, you cannot help but realize that you are in one of Salt Lake City's historic neighborhoods. This "Grand Old Home", an example of the Victorian Eclectic school of architecture, is located 1/2 block from the Governor's Mansion and just six blocks from Temple Square and City Center. Whether you are enjoying a cozy fire, a soothing soak in the hot tub after a great day of skiing, or simply relaxing on a cool summer evening on the front porch after a day of sight-seeing, you will feel the Inn's invitation to unwind with its uncomplicated hospitality.

Approved by: AAA, BBIU

From I-80 and I-15, take City Center Exit (600 South). Turn left at 700 East and left at South Temple. Turn left at 600 East. The Inn is on the left.

3R 1S

BYOB

20

V,M

Salt Lake City

B&B

936 East 1700 South, 84105
(800) 969-0009, Fax (801) 484-7832
Innkeepers: Cill Sparks & Jeri Parker

$-
$$$

Wildflowers

This is an 1891 Victorian home surrounded by blue spruce and an abundance of wildflowers. Listed on the National Register of Historic Places, it is 5 minutes from downtown and 35 minutes from skiing. In their careful restoration, the owners have kept the delights of the past and added the comforts of the present. Hand carved staircases, stained glass windows, claw leg bathtubs, original chandeliers, private baths, a deck, a putting green, and a reading room make up the present Inn. When you add to all of this the personal service and gourmet breakfast you have a very special Inn.

Approved by: AAA, BBIU

From I-80(W) exit onto 1300 East. Turn left onto 1700 South. The Inn is on the left.

12R 2S

BYOB

25

V,M,X
DV,DN,JCB

St. George

B&B

217 North 100 West, 84770
(800) 600-3737,or (801) 628-3737
Innkeepers: Jay Curtis & Jon Bowcutt

$/
$$$

Seven Wives Inn

This delightful Inn is featured on the walking tour of St. George and is just across the street from the Brigham Young home. The house is decorated with antiques collected in America and Europe. The bedrooms are lovely and are each named for one of the seven wives of the Innkeeper's polygamous great-grandfather. A gourmet breakfast is served in the elegant dining room that gives you a hint of the past. There is a swimming pool for your enjoyment and you will be near eight different golf courses. The Zion and Bryce national parks are close for year-round recreation.

Approved by: AAA

From I-15, exit onto St. George Blvd. Turn right onto 100 West. The Inn is on the corner of 100 West and 200 North.

Vermont

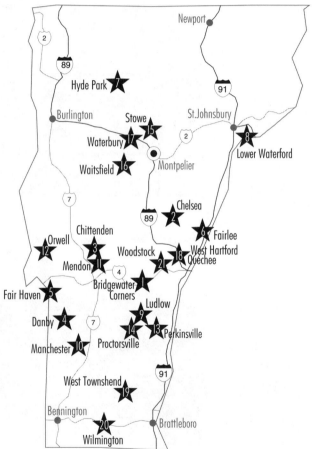

6R

Chelsea

MAP
B&B

P.O. Box 37, Main Street, 05038
(800) 441-6908, or (802) 685-3031
Innkeepers: Jay & Karen Keller

Shire Inn

$$/
$$$$

This Inn is set in the historic-registered town of Chelsea and is a reward for venturing off the beaten track. Day trip from this ideal, central location to some of the best places Vermont and New Hampshire have to offer. Constructed in 1832 with Vermont brick and granite, the Inn offers you a warm, comfortable parlour; guest rooms with canopied beds, fireplaces, and private baths; gourmet dining; and a 22-acre setting on the White River. Enjoy a romantic, relaxing getaway here in scenic, central Vermont, anytime of the year.

Approved by: IIA

From I-91, take Exit 14 (Thetford). Proceed VT-113 (N) 25 miles to VT 110. Turn left and go 150 yards to Inn. From I-89, take Exit 2 (Sharon). Turn left. Continue to VT-14. Turn right. Continue for 5 miles to VT-110 (N). Go 13 miles to Inn.

8R

Chittenden

MAP

Chittenden Dam Road, 05737
(800)707-0017, or (802) 483-6213
Innkeepers: Ed and Rosemary McDowell

Tulip Tree Inn

$$$/
$$$$$

"Backwoods luxury" best describes this Country Inn which is secluded in a quiet corner of the Green Mountain National Forest. There are eight comfortable guest rooms, all with private bath and most with Jacuzzi®. Hearty Vermont, country breakfasts; fine, country dining by the light of candles; and an award-winning wine list make this an ideal place for those who appreciate the finer things in life. Ed and Rosemary take great care to be sure that each visit is an experience to treasure. Any season is the time to visit and rekindle your love affair with life.

Approved by: AAA, Mobil

From Route 4 east of Rutland or Route 7 north of Rutland, follow the signs to Inn.

Danby

B&B

RR 1, Box 66F, 05739
(802) 293-5567
Innkeepers: Paul & Lois Dansereau

$/
$$

Built in 1891 by Vermont's first millionaire, the Inn has rooms in the mansion as well as the carriage house. All guest rooms are furnished with period antiques and most have queen-size beds. A collection of antique kitchen utensils decorates the dining room where a Vermont country breakfast and dinner are served. Relax by the fire or enjoy the front porch while lingering over afternoon tea and treats and planning your next hike, antique search, or ski trip. Located in a picturesque village with the Green Mountain National Forest across the valley, the views are spectacular.

Approved by: AAA, Mobil

Silas Griffith Inn

Follow Rt. 7, 15 minutes north of Manchester. Turn left at the Danby sign and left onto Main Street.

Fair Haven

B&B

Route 22 A South, 05743
(800) 253-7729
Innkeepers: Cindy & Doug Baird

$/
$$

You will rediscover romance in this 1843, Greek-Revival Inn listed on Vermont's historical register. Common rooms include the Keeping Room with fireplace, the BYOB Tavern, the Gathering Room with library, and the Parlor with a complimentary cordial bar. Air conditioned guest rooms and suites are appointed in Colonial and Victorian styles. Amenities abound! A bountiful breakfast buffet will start your day and a delicious confection at turn-down time will beckon you toward a wonderful night's sleep. There is an on-site antique shop, bicycles, and a canoe.

Approved by: AAA, Mobil

Maplewood Inn & Antiques

Take Exit 2 off US Route 4. Proceed through downtown Fair Haven to 22 A (S), one mile south of village. Inn is on your left.

Hyde Park

B&B
MAP

RFD 1, Box 1879, 05655
(800) 639-2903, or (802) 888-3834
Innkeepers: Richard Pugliese & Stanley Corklin

$-
$$

Fitch Hill Inn

This large, circa 1794, colonial federalist-style farm has spectacular views of the beautiful Lamoille River Valley and the surrounding Green Mountains and is only 15 minutes north of Stowe. The aroma of fresh-ground, Green Mountain coffee awaits you in the morning as raspberry cream cheese-filled French toast sizzles on the grill. Candlelight dinners are available by reservation and should not be missed. The antique-filled guest rooms are romantic and inviting and assure a relaxed visit in a friendly, Vermont atmosphere.

Approved by: AAA

Take I-89 to Exit 10. Follow SR 100(N) for 19 miles to Morrisville. After Morrisville, turn left on SR 15 and proceed 11/2 miles west to Fitch Hill Rd. Inn is 1/3 mile up the hill.

Lower Waterford

MAP
B&B

Route 18, 05848
(800) 762-8669, Fax (802) 748-8342
Innkeepers: John and Maureen Magee

$$/
$$$$$

Rabbit Hill Inn

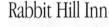

A tiny, enchanted hamlet...an historic district untouched by time...is the setting of this 1795, award-winning, Country Inn classic. The Inn is elegantly stylish and romantic and renowned for exceptional service. You'll enjoy pampered relaxation amid canopied beds, in-room fireplaces, Jacuzzis® for two, and unusual turn-down service. Outstanding cuisine in two, stunning, candlelit dining rooms is accompanied by chamber music. Enjoy a film in the library, share laughter in the Irish Pub, and above all experience personal, caring touches.

Approved by: AAA, IIA, Mobil

From I-91 (N or S), take Exit 19 to I-93 (S). Take Exit 1. Turn right onto Route 18 (S): Continue for 7 miles to Inn. From I-93 (N), take Exit 44 onto Route 18 (N). Continue 2 miles to the Inn.

Ludlow

MAP

86 Main Street, 05149
(800) 468-3766, Fax (802) 228-8830
Innkeepers: Deedy & Charlie Marble

The Governor's Inn

$$$-
$$$$$

It is pure pleasure to be a guest at The Governor's Inn. The Marbles have made innkeeping an art form. They love what they do and you will too. Both graduated from L'ecole du Mougin, Roger Verge (FR) and present their famous cuisine on museum-quality, antique China. In fact, Deedy and Charlie share everything in their collections with guests: precious knife rests, Waterford crystal, magnificent chocolate pots, polished silver, and whimsical breakfast bells. "It makes me feel like Royalty," one guest remarked. You will love it here!

Approved by: IIA, Mobil

Photo: jurgen schultz

Ludlow is located where 100 and 103 cross paths. The Inn is 1/2 mile from the juncture. From I-91, 23 miles (N), just off the Village Green.

Manchester

B&B

West Road, 05254
(800) 372-2761, or (802) 362-2761
Innkeepers: Jim and Pat Lee

Birch Hill Inn

$$/
$$$

The original wing of this Inn was built in 1790, and at one time the farmhouse was a stage coach stop. The grandparents of the present Innkeeper purchased the property in 1917. At that time, they doubled the size of the house. Magnificent white birches were planted after the construction. Today they draw gasps of admiration from visitors to the Inn. Lush lawns and gardens add to the beauty of the natural landscape. This is a restful and beautiful retreat where a personal warm welcome is offered to all.

Approved by: IIA

In Manchester Center, at the Junction of Routes 7A and 30, take Route 30 (N) for 2.7 miles to Manchester West Road. Go left (south) for 3/4 of a mile.

18R 12S

V,M,X
DV

Manchester Village

MAP

Historic Route 7A, Box 408, 05254
(800) 370-0300, or (802) 362-1792
Innkeepers: Anne & Jay Degen

$$$-
$$$$$

You will be enchanted as you enter and experience the creative whimsy and fanciful fun woven throughout this "French Country Inn". Rose chintz fabrics, lace, antiques, and baskets of flowers create a casual yet elegant atmosphere. Hot cider, crackling fires, and the cozy tavern overlooking the ice rink and mountains beckon you to relax in winter. The pool, fountains, marble terrace, 100-foot front porch with rockers, and tennis court draw you outside in the summer. The Rose Room features romantic, candlelight dining with a sophisticated country menu and fine wines.

Approved by: AAA, Mobil

Village Country Inn

Photos: George & Roberta Gardner Accociates

The Inn is on Rt. 7A in the center of Manchester Village.

12R

16

V,M

Mendon

MAP
B&B

Woodward Road, 05701
(802) 775-2290, Fax (802) 773-0594
Innkeepers: Sue & Harris Zuckerman

$$/
$$$$$

Down a winding country road, set amidst 13 acres, this rambling 1840's farmhouse estate was once General John Woodward's summer retreat. Today, this Inn offers guests warmth, pampering, and exceptional gourmet fare. From enticing rooms with hand-made quilts, antiques, some whirlpools, and blazing fires—to sumptuous breakfasts, majestic mountains views, and candlelit dining with soft music, the atmosphere is relaxed, welcoming, and peaceful. An added treat is Gruffy, a carrot-loving pony, and his petite companion, Minnie, a lovable miniature horse.

Approved by: AAA, Mobil

Red Clover Inn

Photos: George W. Gardner

Take I-91 (N) to Exit 6, Route 103. Follow signs to Rutland. Take Route 7 through Rutland to Route 4 (E). Go 5.2 miles to Woodward Road, then turn right. Go 1/4 mile to Inn on left side.

Orwell

B&B

Route 22A, P.O. Box 36, 05760
(802) 948-2727, Fax (802) 948-2015
Innkeepers: Joan & Murray Korda

$$$

Family owned and operated, the Historic Brookside Farms estate includes an 18th century guesthouse/antique shop, 300 acres of scenery, manicured grounds, and a stately 18th century, Greek Revival Mansion. On the National Register of Historic Places, the Mansion and Guesthouse provide a spectacular architectural history. Filled with art, music, history, an enormous library, and antiques dating back to the 17th century, it is a veritable museum. The Korda family, carrying on five generations of innkeeping, provide guests with gourmet dining and country hospitality.

Approved by: AAA, IIA

Historic Brookside Farms

From I-87 (N), take Exit 20 (Glens Falls). Left on Route 9 to Route 149 (E) to Route 4 (E) to Route 22A. Continue for 13 miles. From I-89 (N), take White River Junction Exit to Route 4 (W) to 22A (N) to Orwell.

Photos: Tad Merrick

Perkinsville

MAP

Route 106, 05151
(800) 477-4828, Fax (802) 263-9219
Innkeepers: Mary Louise & Ron Thorburn

$$$/
$$$$$

Woven with love, congeniality, tradition, music and poetry, this Colonial Sampler is a special place. The Inn is nestled in the lap of Vermont history and offers 21 scenic acres, a swimming pond, and horse-drawn sleigh and carriages. There are individually-decorated guest rooms and suites with canopy beds and working fireplaces. A wonderful afternoon tea, five-course dinners, and a bountiful breakfast buffet is served daily. A tavern, extensive wine cellar, and duo grand pianists during dinner round out the experience. This is a unique setting for weddings.

Approved by: AAA, ABBA, IIA, Mobil

The Inn At Weathersfield

Northbound on I-91, take Exit 7 onto Route 11 to Route 106, then go 5.5 miles to Inn.
Southbound on I-91, take Eixt 8 onto Route 131 to Route 106, then turn left and go 3 miles to Inn.

Proctorsville

MAP
B&B

Depot Street, P.O. Box 218, 05153
(800) 253-8226, or (802) 226-7744
Innkeepers: Kirsten Murphy and Marcel Perret

$$$

Golden Stage Inn

A tradition of hospitality continues in this 200-year-old Inn, a former stagecoach stop. The white clapboard house was also a stop on the Underground Railroad and the home of actress/writer Cornelia Otis Skinner. The wraparound porch offers a view of the Okemo Valley. An outdoor pool overlooks four acres of lawns and gardens. Flowers provide a panorama of color from April through October. The warmth of Grandmother's quilts, a full cookie jar, antiques, greenery, favorite books, and a blazing fire will comfort you as you enjoy hors d'oeuvres before a five-course, candlelit dinner.

Approved by: AAA

Photos: jurgen schultz

Take I-91 to Vermont Exit 6. Go left onto Route 103. Continue for about 17 miles, then turn right at Proctorsville sign. Take the first drive on the right.

Stowe

B&B

717 Maple Street, 05672
(800) 729-2980, Fax (802) 253-7425
Innkeeper: Andy Aldrich

$$-
$$$

Brass Lantern Inn

This is a traditional B&B in the heart of Stowe, Vermont. The Inn combines an 1800 farmhouse and carriage barn, and its restoration won an award in 1989. The Inn is decorated in period decor and furnished with antiques. All guest rooms are individually air conditioned and heated and have private baths. Most guest rooms, common rooms, and the patio, have spectacular views of Vermont's highest mountain, Mt. Mansfield. Some rooms and the guest living room have a fireplace. Afternoon tea is offered on the patio or fireside depending on the season.

Approved by: AAA, ABBA, Mobil

From I-89, take Route 100 (N) to Stowe Village. Continue 1/2 mile north on Route 100 from village center. The Inn is located on the left.

Waitsfield

B&B

East Warren Road, 05673
(802) 496-2276, Fax (802) 496-8832
Innkeepers: Jack & Doreen Simko & Anne Marie DeFreest

$$/
$$$

This is the Inn that lives in your imagination. A place that is rich in history, elegant, luxurious, and charming, without the least bit of pretension. Enjoy exquisite guest rooms with roaring fireplaces, relaxing steam showers, Jacuzzis®, and comfortable canopied beds. Wake to a scrumptious breakfast of Blueberry Belgium waffles and cinnamon coffee. In winter, walk out the door of the Inn and ski 30K of groomed cross country trails. Rosignol equipment rentals, snowshoes, and instruction are available. In summer, explore 85 acres of lush gardens, meadows, woodlands, and ponds.

Approved by: AAA, Mobil

Inn At Round Barn Farm

I-89 to Exit 9. Take Route 100B to Waitsfield (14 miles from exit). Turn left at Bridge Street/East Warren Road, then take a right at fork after Covered Bridge. Inn is 1 mile up on left.

Waitsfield

B&B

Route 100, 05673
(800) 426-3986, Fax (802) 496-7558
Innkeepers: Susan & Lawrence McKay

$-
$$$

Enjoy "relaxed elegance" by the Mad River. The Inn is situated on 52 pristine, country acres in Central Vermont's most beautiful valley. All summer sports are near, as well as world-class, alpine skiing at Sugarbush, Mad River Glen, and Stowe. Antiques fill each room. Oriental rugs, fireplaces, museum-quality art, and the music of Vivaldi and Mozart add to your pleasure. You'll awaken to the aroma of freshly-baked muffins and enjoy whimsical, gourmet breakfasts. Swim off the Inn's private river banks, snooze in a hammock, walk the nature paths, and soak in the hot tub.

Approved by: AAA, Mobil

Newtons' 1824 House Inn

Drive 10 miles south of I-89 Exit 9 to Route 100 B. Take Exit 10 to Route 100.

Waterbury

Grünberg Haus Bed & Breakfast

B&B Route 100 South, RR 2, Box 1595, 05676-9621
(800) 800-7760
Innkeepers: Mark Frohman & Christopher Sellers

$/ $$$

This romantic Austrian Inn rests on a quiet hillside in Vermont's northern Green Mountains and is perfect for trips to Stowe, Montpelier, Waterbury, and Burlington. Choose from an antique-filled guest room with wonderful views from the carved wood balconies, a secluded cabin hidden along wooden trails, or the spectacular carriage house with skywindows, balconies, and modern kitchen. Ski expertly-groomed XC trails and help gather fresh eggs; then relax in the BYOB pub or by the fire or Jacuzzi®. Each morning, enjoy Innkeeper Chris playing the grand piano during breakfast.

Approved by: Mobil

From I-89, travel south 4.5 miles on Route 100. Located on the east side of Route 100.

West Hartford (Quechee)

The Half Penney

B&B Box 84, Handy Road, 05084
(802) 295-6082
Innkeepers: Gretchen & Robert Fairweather

$$/ $$$

If your idea of a trip to Vermont includes following a dirt road through meadows and woods to a circa 1803 Inn on the Appalachian Trail, where cheerful rooms with picturebook views await you; where your day starts with a bountiful breakfast in front of a blazing fire in winter or by the old stone patio in summer, then you'll love this Inn. Only minutes from Woodstock and Quechee, Vermont and Hanover, New Hampshire, you are convenient to everything. Visit museums or historic sites; hike, kayak or canoe, cross-country ski or sit in front of the fire, and enjoy.

Approved by: AAA

From Quechee, take the Quechee-West Hartford Rd. 4.9 miles to Handy Rd. From I-89(N), Exit 2, take Rt. 14(S), 5 miles. Go over the West Hartford bridge and up the hill, Handy Rd. is on the right. The Inn is 1/2 mile.

West Townshend

B&B
MAP

Windham Road, Box 44, 05359
(800) 944-4080, Fax (802) 874-4702
Innkeepers: Grigs & Pat Markham

Windham Hill Inn

$$$$

Created from an historic 1825 homestead, the Inn offers a 160-acre, Green Mountain hillside setting with spectacular views of the West River Valley. Award-winning ambiance, fine dining, and a friendly welcome are offered year-round to guests desiring a quiet, country getaway. In winter, skiing is featured at the Inn's onsite, cross-country, learning center. In summer, hike on the Inn's trails or at two beautiful, nearby, state parks. After a full day, return to an exceptional dining experience at this delightful Inn.

Approved by: AAA, IIA

Turn uphill off Route 30 across from West Townshend country store. Turn right in 1.2 miles, and follow signs.

Wilmington

B&B

Route 9 West, 05363
(802) 464-3351
Innkeepers: Del & Charlotte Lawrence

Nutmeg Inn

$$/
$$$

This small elegant Country Inn was originally built in the mid-1770's. Rooms all have private baths and top-of-the-line oversize beds, central air, and in-room phones. Most offer color cable TV and a wood-burning fireplace. The attached barn was renovated into lovely suites. An extensive plate collection graces walls and cabinets throughout the Inn. A lovely, perennial garden beckons you to the back yard to sit and relax. Hiking trails from the back yard lead to beautiful views of the valley and beyond.

Approved by: AAA, ABBA

Nineteen miles west of I-91 (Exit 2) on Route 9 (W). Inn is 3/4 mile west of traffic light at junction of Route 9 and Route 100 in Wilmington.

Wilmington

B&B

Smith Road, 05363
(800) 859-2585, or (802) 464-2727
Innkeepers: Bill & Mary Kilburn

$$$

Trail's End, A Country Inn

This unique Country Inn is tucked away on ten acres. It has flower gardens, an outdoor heated pool, a clay tennis court, and a pond stocked with trout. The delightful rooms all have private baths. Four guest rooms and two suites have canopy beds, fireplaces, and whirlpool tubs. Each room is decorated in a different color scheme. Brass, white wicker, and antiques create a chic, country atmosphere. A full menu breakfast is served every morning, and afternoon refreshments are offered. The hosts' warm hospitality and attention to detail are evident throughout.

Approved by: AAA, ABBA, Mobil

Photos: A. Dannenberg

Take Exit 2 off I-91 to Route 9. At junction of Route 9 and Route 100 in Wilmington take Route 100 north for 4 miles. Trail's End is 1/2 mile east of Route 100. Follow State sign to the Inn.

Wilmington

B&B

P. O. Box 757, Route 9, 05363
(800) 541-2135, Fax (802) 464-5222
Innkeeper: Robert Grinold

$$/
$$$$$

The White House of Wilmington

This is a Victorian mansion set on the crest of a high, rolling hill surrounded by towering hardwoods and overlooking the town. Built in 1915 as a summer home for a lumber baron, the magnificent structure boasts 14 fireplaces throughout. Three intimate dining rooms offer romantic candlelight dining and award-winning Continental cuisine. The patio lounge offers a view of spectacular sunsets. The indoor pool, whirlpool, and sauna offer relaxation for the hiker or skier and the outdoor pool is ideal in summer. Enjoy 45 km of groomed, cross country terrain. A rental shop and lessons are available.

Approved by: Mobil

The Inn is at the junction of Rt. 9 and Rt. 100, 20 minutes west of Brattleboro. The Inn is on the right, just before entering Wilmington.

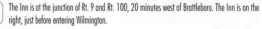

27R 2S

35

V,M, DV, X

Kedron Valley Inn

EP
MAP
B&B

Woodstock
Route 106, 05071
(802) 457-1473, Fax (802) 457-4469
Innkeepers: Max & Merrily Comins

$$/
$$$$

The Kedron's scenic location outside bustling Woodstock entices you to relax, rediscover romance, and count the stars. The queen canopy beds, fireplaces, private decks, and award-winning cuisine of this Victorian Inn beckon seductively as you slip away from the cares of your daily life. Enjoy the museum-caliber quilt collection. Meander through art galleries, historic estates, antique stores, and Vermont's new National Park, or sample the plentiful outdoor sports. One of the oldest Inns in the state, it is a wonderful hideaway in a valley of the Green Mountains.

Approved by: AAA, ABBA, Mobil

Left Photo: Doug Mindell.   Right Photo: Jon Gilbert Fox.

Follow Route 89 or Route 91 to Route 4 (W) to Route 106 (S).

8R

25

V,M,X

Village Inn Of Woodstock

B&B
MAP

Woodstock
41 Pleasant Street, 05091
(800) 722-4571, or (802) 457-1255
Innkeepers: Anita & Kevin Clark

$/
$$$

Driving through Woodstock's picturesque Historic District, the Inn's striking raspberry cream color embraces you. The Inn is replete with Victorian architecture, including embossed tin ceilings and stained glass windows. Outside, the perennial garden is the perfect place to relax. There is something for everyone; quiet country walks, romantic dining, unique shops, antiquing, and more. Chef Kevin prepares scrumptious breakfasts and is famous for his Roast Vermont Turkey dinners. You will love the warm touches that Anita has given all the rooms.

Approved by: AAA

The Inn is located on U.S. Rt. 4; the main east/west route through town. From I-91 take Exit 9 (Rt.12) to Rt. 4 into Woodstock. From I-89 take Exit 1(Rt. 4) into Woodstock.

Woodstock, VT

The Woodstocker B&B

B&B

61 River Street, 05091
(800) 457-3896, or (802) 457-3896
Innkeepers: Jerry & JaNoel Lowe

$$/
$$$

Nestled snugly at the foot of Mt. Tom in one of America's prettiest towns stands this Inn. Jerry and JaNoel offer hearty greetings as they escort you to one of nine elegant, romantic chambers, all with private bath. Each boasts its own stereo and you are invited to bring your favorite cassettes or CDs. Mornings begin with Jerry's sumptuous four-course gourmet breakfast. Afternoon refreshments feature wonderfully decadent chocolate chip cookies. A short stroll beside the river and across the covered bridge brings you to quaint shops, galleries, and fine restaurants.

Approved by: AAA, ABBA, Mobil

Take Exit 1 from I-89 (N) (Woodstock/Rutland-Route 4). Travel west on Route 4 for10 miles to Woodstock. Pass through the village. After crossing the bridge, the Inn is on the right.

Ashland, VA

Henry Clay Inn

B&B

114 North Railroad Avenue, 23005
(800) 343-4565, Fax (804) 798-0048
Carol Martin, Ann-Carol Houston & Judy Kostenbauder

$$-
$$$

You may relax in rocking chairs on the grand front porch or enjoy the view of Randolph-Macon College and the trains from the second floor balcony. The Inn consists of 15 guest rooms, including a luxury suite, all furnished with antique reproductions. The Drawing Room accommodates receptions, reunions, seminars, or meetings. Also, the Inn houses the Art Gallery displaying original works by local artists, and the Gift Gallery, which provides unique, specialty items and showcases local crafts. The restaurant serves home-cooked breakfasts, lunches and dinners.

Approved by: AAA, BBAV

From I-95 take Exit 92 to Route 54 (W). Follow Route 54 about 1 1/4 miles into the center of Ashland (to the railroad tracks). Inn is located across the tracks and to the right.

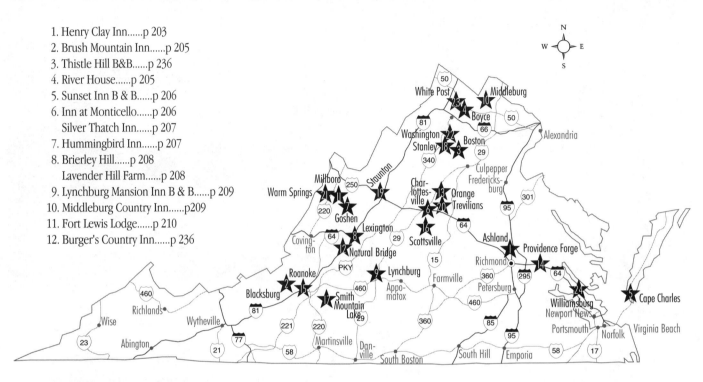

Relay Numbers: TTY (800) 828-1120, VCE (800) 828-1140

Blacksburg

Brush Mountain Inn B&B

B&B

3030 Mt. Tabor Road, 24060
(703) 951-7530
Innkeeper: Mode Johnson

$

Nestled among towering trees on 20 acres adjacent to the Jefferson National Forest, this newly-built, rustic B&B offers great views of the mountains from an oak-timber-frame great room with a 20-foot stone fireplace. Knotty pine floors, walls, and ceilings are throughout. A cozy area next to the wood stove provides views of the forest and wildlife. Decks and porches, which surround the cedar house, have rocking chairs for relaxing, reading, or ruminating. Local artwork and antiques decorate the house and are for sale. It is secluded with country charm.

Approved by: BBAV

Take Exit 118 on I-81 to Blacksburg. From downtown Blacksburg, go 2 miles (N) on N. Main Street. Turn right on Mt. Tabor Road, and go 5 miles to B&B.

Boyce

The River House

B&B

Route 1, Box 135, 22620
(703) 837-1476, Fax (703) 837-2399
Innkeepers: Cornelia & Donald Niemann

$$-
$$$

Listed in the Virginia Landmarks Register and the National Register of Historic Places, the Inn earned its position through a varied and lengthy past. In 1780, the present ground floor served as slave quarters. During the Civil War, Stonewall Jackson chose the property for encampment and crossing the Shenandoah River while the house served as a field hospital. Twentieth-century occupants continued farming, then established two restaurants, a tavern, and now a B&B. Comfortably and eclectically furnished, the Inn rests in the foothills of the Blue Ridge Mountains.

Approved by: AAA, BBAV

From I-81, take Exit 313A (E) onto Route 50 (E). Continue for 13 miles. Look for sign on right, directly across Route 50 from the origin of County Road 622, and just before Shenandoah River bridge.

Cape Charles

B&B

108 Bay Avenue, 23310
(800) 331-3113, or (804) 331-2424
Innkeepers: Al Longo & Joyce Tribble

$/
$$

Sunset Inn Bed & Breakfast

This waterfront, 1915 Victorian home faces the west on the beautiful Chesapeake Bay. It is newly renovated and eclectic in decor with large rooms with Hunter fans. You will enjoy the atmosphere of a by-gone era with all the comforts of today. Watch ships and birds as you snuggle into a comfortable rocker on the breezy front porch or from the shelter of the common room with its large bay-view windows. Unwind, relax, get in touch with yourself or your companion, and relish being away from the hustle and bustle of the daily world. You will love the unspoiled beauty of the Eastern Shore.

Approved by: BBAV

From US 13 take Rt. 184(W) to the Chesapeake Bay. Turn right; the Inn is on the right.

Charlottesville

B&B

Route 19, Box 112, 22902
(804) 979-3593
Innkeepers: Carol & Larry Engel

$$/
$$$

The Inn At Monticello

A charming country manor built in the mid-1800's, the Inn sits cradled in the valley of Thomas Jefferson's own Monticello Mountain. A bubbling brook graces the landscape; boxwood and azaleas ornament the grounds. Romantic guest rooms, elegantly appointed with antiques, canopy beds, and fireplaces, invite you to snuggle in. Each morning a country gourmet breakfast, prepared with the best of seasonally-available specialties, is served in the kitchen or, weather permitting, outside on the stone terrace. The croquet set is ready, and the hammock is gently swinging.

Approved by: AAA, BBAV

From I-64, take Exit 121A, if coming from the west, Exit 121 if coming from east. Then take Highway 20 (S). Continue to stoplight at foot of Visitor's Center. Go .03 mile south. Inn is located on the right.

Photos: Joseph E. Garland

Charlottesville

B&B

3001 Hollymead Drive, 22901-7422
(804) 978-4686, Fax (804) 973-6156
Innkeepers: Vince and Rita Scoffone

Silver Thatch Inn

$$$

Turn an ordinary evening into an extraordinary night! Dine and spend the night in one of these romantic rooms. Charlottesville's oldest Country Inn, circa 1780, is a rambling, white-clapboard home. Some rooms have canopy beds and fireplaces, all have private baths. Guests use the adjacent swimming pool (in season) and tennis courts. A truly special dining experience awaits you in the candlelit dining rooms. Modern American cuisine is offered, featuring healthy and eclectic entrees. Specialties are homemade desserts and an award-winning wine list.

Approved by: AAA, BBAV, IIA

        Eight miles north of the center of Charlottesville. One-third mile east of U.S. Route 29 on Route 1520.

Goshen

B&B

Wood Lane, P.O. Box 147, 24439
(800) 397-3214
Innkeepers: Diana & Jeremy Robinson

The Hummingbird Inn

$$

This unique, Carpenter Gothic villa offers accommodations in an early Victorian setting. Rooms are furnished with antiques and combine an old-fashioned ambiance with modern convenience. Architectural features include wraparound verandas on the first and second floors; original, pine floors; a charming rustic den dating from the early 1800's; a solarium; and a music room. A wide trout stream defines one of the property lines, and the old, red barn was once the town livery. Full breakfasts feature unique area recipes.

Approved by: BBAV

       From I-64 at Lexington, go west to Exit 43. Route 780 (N) 9.3 miles to Route 39. Left 1 mile into Goshen, then bear left on Alt. 39 around corner. Turn left after crossing railraad tracks.

Lexington

B&B   Route 6, Box 21, 24450 $/
MAP   (800) 422-4925, Fax (703) 464-8925 $$
Innkeepers: Barry & Carole Speton

This Inn is situated on eight acres of hillside meadowland near the western edge of Lexington. Spacious verandahs on three sides of the house offer a restful opportunity to take in views of serene farmland, the Blue Ridge and Allegheny Mountains, and the Shenandoah Valley. Tea in the English tradition (Carole and Barry are both from Vancouver, Canada) is served in the dining room or on the verandah. The house is furnished with antique pieces that the Spetons brought with them from Vancouver together with floral prints and English watercolors. A sumptuous, candlelight dinner is available.

Approved by: BBAV

Brierley Hill

From 81(S) take Exit 188B (60 West). Follow to Lexington and continue to Borden Rd. Turn left. Drive one mile to the Inn. From 81(N) take Exit 191, then Exit 55 to Business Lexington. Turn right onto Nelson (60 West) and proceed west to Borden Rd. Turn left and continue one mile to Inn.

Lexington

MAP   Route 631, Box 515, 24450 $
B&B   (800) 446-4240, or (703) 464-5877
Innkeepers: Cindy & Colin Smith

The Inn is located on a working farm just west of Lexington in the Shenandoah Valley. There is much to do on the farm, including walks to take in the panoramic mountain view, fishing, birding, relaxing on the porch, and visiting the sheep and goats. Nearby Lexington offers historic homes and museums, plays and concerts, Washington and Lee University, and Virginia Military Institute. The gourmet dinners at the Inn have gained a large repeat clientele. The Inn offers a variety of packages, including horseback riding, cooking courses, and outdoor theater.

Approved by: BBAV

Lavender Hill Farm

From I-81 (N) or (S), take I-64 (W) at Lexington to Exit 50 (2nd exit after leaving I-81). Turn left off exit ramp, left at stop sign, and immediately left onto Route 631. Inn is located 1.2 miles on left.

Lynchburg

B&B

405 Madison Street, 24504
(800) 352-1199, or (804) 528-5400
Innkeepers: Bob & Mauranna Sherman

$$/
$$$

Lynchburg Mansion Inn B & B

You will enjoy lap-of-luxury accommodations in this 9,000 square foot, Spanish Georgian mansion restored with your every modern comfort in mind. From the bubbling spa to romantic fireplaces; from sumptuous suites to very private bathrooms; from attentive evening turndown service to full silver service breakfast, this is a truly heavenly experience. In this small, Central Virginia city, surrounded by the Blue Ridge Mountains and rolling countryside, you may hike, bike, visit important historic sites, experience antique and outlet shopping, and participate in city festivals.

Approved by: AAA, BBAV

From Rt. 29, exit Main Street/Downtown. Go west on Main Street to Fifth Street (Bus. or Alt. 29) and turn left onto Fifth. Go four blocks and turn right onto Madison Street. The Inn is on the next corner of 4th and Madison.

Middleburg

MAP

209 E. Washington Street, 22117
(800) 262-6082, Fax (703) 687-5603
Innkeepers: John & Susan Pettibone

$$$-
$$$$

Middleburg Country Inn

In the historic town of Middleburg, the Inn offers casually elegant accommodations amidst a country setting. Built in 1780 as the original Episcopal rectory, the Inn is centrally located allowing you to walk to everything...designer boutiques, antique shops, art galleries, and restaurants. Day trips into Virginia Hunt Country take you to historic plantations and the finest antique shops. Inn guests are not only entitled to a full country breakfast but also a five-course dinner served in the Inn dining room.

Approved by: AAA, Mobil

Photos: Allen Studio

From Washington, D.C., west on Route 66 to Exit 57B for Route 50 (W), Inn on Route 50 opposite of Exxon. From Winchester and Route 81, take Exit 50 (E) to Middleburg.

Millboro

MAP

HCR 3, Box 21A, 24460
(703) 925-2314, Fax (703) 925-2352
Innkeepers: John & Caryl Cowden

This is a 3200-acre mountain farm where you can get away from the daily routine and experience the earth, the sky, and the river. At the heart of this beautiful place is a unique Country Inn decorated with wildlife art and locally handcrafted furniture. A silo with bedrooms "in the round" and historic, hand-hewn log cabins with stone fireplaces are perfect for romance. Spacious decks and the "lookout" atop the silo open to views of the meadows and rugged cliffs that tower above the river. The restored Lewis Mill showcases Caryl's legendary home cooking. Save room, dessert is a must!

Approved by: IIA

Fort Lewis Lodge

$$$

From Staunton take Rt. 254(W) to Buffalo Gap. Follow Rt. 42 to Millboro Springs and Rt. 39(W) for .7 miles to Rt. 678; turn right. Follow for 10.8 miles and turn left onto Rt. 625. Drive .2 miles to the Lodge on the left.

Orange

B&B

155 West Main Street, 22960
(703) 672-4893, Fax (703) 358-4422
Innkeepers: Pete & Phebe Holladay

$$/
$$$

This 1830 Federal style house was purchased by Dr. Holladay, Pete's grandfather, in 1899. As his family grew, major additions were made between 1910 and 1917. It was restored in 1989 by Pete and Phebe and has received a beautification award. Rooms are furnished with family heirlooms. The location and configuration of each room influenced the choice of furnishings and colors. You'll find blue, peach, rose, green, and even one with barn-red trim. Returning guests often request their favorite room by its color.

Approved by: BBAV, Mobil

Holladay House

Photos: Scott Painley

From Washington DC, go west on I-66 to Gainsville. Go south on Route 29 to Culpeper, then south on Route 15 (16 miles) to Orange. (90 minutes total.) From Richmond, go west on I-64 to Zion Crossroad. Go north on Route 15 to Orange. (75 minutes total.)

Providence Forge

B&B

4500 N. Courthouse Road, 23140
(804) 966-9836, or (804) 966-5858
Innkeepers: Howard & Joyce Vogt

$$

Located on 47 beautiful acres, this is a fully restored, 1750's farmhouse decorated with various period antiques. The plantation once included over 1000 acres and has witnessed much history marching through it in the past 300 years. The Inn is convenient to major highways, Williamsburg or Richmond are less than 30 minutes away, and the James River Plantations and fine dining are even closer. Yet with all of these areas of interest, you can easily return to the peace of the country at night. While visiting, you will enjoy walking the trails, tossing a game of horseshoes, or relaxing on the porch.

Approved by: BBAV

Jasmine Plantation B & B

From I-64 take Exit 214. Drive south on VA. State Route 155 for 2.4 miles towards Providence Forge. The Inn will be on the right.

Roanoke

B&B

381 Washington Avenue, S.W., 24016
(703) 344-5361
Innkeepers: Bill & Sheri Bestpitch

$/
$$$

This lovely 1890's Victorian home offers an exceptional, lodging alternative in the heart of the historic district, adjacent to downtown Roanoke and five minutes from the Blue Ridge Parkway. You'll find Rococo Revival, Renaissance Revival, and Eastlake style furnishings; Victorian playing cards; antique, English china, and original brass light fixtures. Although Mary herself has long been forgotten, there are those who believe her spirit is not gone.

Approved by: AAA, BBAV

The Mary Bladon House

I-81 to I-581 south to Exit 6 (Elm Avenue). Turn right onto Elm, and proceed to fourth traffic light. Turn left onto Franklin Road, then take the third right onto Washington Avenue. The Inn is on the right at the end of the first block.

7R 5S

25

V,M

Photo: Muncy Fine Photography

Scottsville

High Meadows Inn

B&B MAP
♿

High Meadows Lane, Route 4, Box 6, 24590
(800) 232-1832, or (804) 286-2218
Innkeepers: Peter Sushka & Mary Jae Abbitt

$$$

This 19th century Inn, located in the foothills of the Blue Ridge Mountains, is on the National Register of Historic Places. The spacious rooms are decorated with period antiques and art and offer fireplaces, porches, soaking and whirlpool tubs. There are 50 tranquil acres of romantic flower gardens, rolling meadows, footpaths in the forest, and spectacular sunsets. You will love the European supper baskets enjoyed by the pond, in the gazebo, or in the vineyard. Following the twilight tradition of Virginia wine-tasting, linger over a fine candlelight dinner, and dream!

Approved by: AAA, IIA

From I-64 in Charlottesville, take Exit 121(S) and proceed on Rt. 20(S) for 17 miles. After crossing Rt. 726, go 3/10 mile and turn left onto High Meadows Lane. The Inn is at the top of the hill.

6R 1S

BYOB

20

V,M

Smith Mountain Lake, VA

The Manor at Taylor's Store

B&B

Route 1, Box 533, 24184
(800) 248-6267, Fax (703) 721-5243
Innkeepers: Lee & Mary Lynn Tucker

$$/
$$$

This is an historic, 120-acre estate located in the foothills of the Blue Ridge Mountains. An easy 20 miles off of the Blue Ridge Parkway near Roanoke, Virginia, the Inn is at Smith Mountain Lake which is Virginia's premier lake resort area. Lee and Mary Lynn specialize in preparing "heart-healthy" gourmet breakfasts that draw rave reviews. Six, private, spring-fed ponds on the estate invite hiking, fishing, canoeing, swimming, and just relaxing in the lovely gazebo. A Colonial period garden is also a favorite spot to wander and relax amidst the seasonal beauty.

Approved by: AAA, BBAV

Take State Route 220 (S) from Roanoke to Route 122. Inn is Between Burnt Chimney and the Booker T. Washington National Monument on Route 122 about 1.6 miles north of Burnt Chimney on the right.

Stanley

MAP

Route 2, Box 375, 22851
(703) 778-2285, Fax (703) 778-1759
Innkeepers: Jetze & Marley Beers

$$$

Jordan Hollow Farm Inn

This is a 200-year-old, restored, colonial, horse farm. It has 150 acres of rolling pastures and woodlands located in the heart of the Shenandoah Valley with lovely views of the Blue Ridge Mountains. This cozy, full-service Inn, has delightful guest rooms which all open out to either a sundeck or private porch. Miles of well-marked walking, riding, and carriage trails are available on site. The "Farmhouse Restaurant" serves delightfully prepared food. The Inn is two hours west of Washington, D.C. and 6 miles from Luray Caverns and Skyline Drive.

Approved by: AAA, IIA, Mobil

From Stae Road 340 Business in Luray, go south 6 miles. Turn left onto 624, left onto 689, and right onto 626.

Staunton

B&B

28 North New Street, 24401
(800) 334-5575
Innkeepers: Joe & Evy Harman

$/
$$

Frederick House

Separate buildings and private entrances give you a unique experience; complemented by comfortable, oversized beds, ceiling fans, modern bathrooms, cable, remote TV, phones, plush robes, and antiques. A gourmet breakfast is served in Chumley's Tearoom. You may choose from quiches, hot and cold cereals, breakfast pies, homemade waffles, fresh-baked bread, and fresh fruit. Special dietary requests are accommodated. Enjoy walking to Mary Baldwin College or to a variety of fine restaurants, specialty shops, and antique shops all within five historic districts.

Approved by: AAA, Mobil

From I-81 Exit 222, take 250 (W) approximately 2.7 miles.

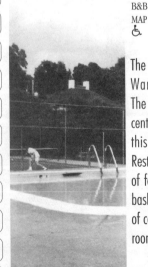

Trevilians

MAP
B&B

Route 3, Box 430, 23093
(800) 277-0844, Fax (703) 967-0102
Innkeepers: Michael & Laura Sheehan

Prospect Hill Plantation Inn

$$$$$

This restored 1732 plantation is located just 15 miles east of Charlottesville, which is home to Thomas Jefferson's Monticello and the University of Virginia. Lodgings are in the manor house and renovated out-buildings including the carriage house, slaves quarters, and plantation kitchen. Accommodations feature working fireplaces, private verandahs, and Jacuzzis®. Enjoy breakfast-in-bed, afternoon tea, and complimentary local wines. You are invited to stroll the grounds or relax beside the fire before a five-course dinner.

Approved by: AAA, IIA

Photos: George Salivonchik

        From I-64, take Exit 136. Turn right off ramp onto15 (S). Go 3/4 miles to intersection. Turn left on 250 (E) and go 1 mile. Turn left on 613. Inn is 3 miles on left.

Warm Springs

B&B
MAP

Box 359, Route 645, 24484
(703) 839-2231, Fax (703) 839-5770
Innkeepers: McWilliams Family

The Inn At Gristmill Square

$$

The Inn At Gristmill Square, in the picturesque village of Warm Springs, is a designated historic site. The restored gristmill, with working waterwheel, is the centerpiece of the five 19th century buildings that make up this handsome Inn created in 1972. The Waterwheel Restaurant offers delectable Continental dining, plus plenty of fellowship in the Simon Kenton Pub. Every morning a basket of fresh homemade breads, juice, and a steaming pot of coffee are delivered to your room. Many of the 16 guest rooms include a working fireplace.

Approved by: IIA, Mobil

       Turn west from Route 220 onto Route 619 (Court House Hill). Proceed 500 yards to Inn.

Washington

Foster-Harris House

B&B

P.O. Box 333, Main Street, 22747
(800) 666-0153
Innkeeper: Phyllis Marriott

$$$

The Inn is a tranquil, turn-of-the-century home in the historic village of "Little" Washington with wonderful views of the mountains and surrounding estates. The streets of the village are laid out exactly as they were surveyed by George Washington, more than 225 years ago. The Innkeeper, formerly a Washington, D.C. caterer and delicatessen owner, rises early each day to prepare a sumptuous breakfast. Afternoon refreshments may be taken in the parlor, on the porch, or beneath a grand old plum tree. There are beautiful flower gardens in season.

Approved by: BBAV

I-66 (W), Exit 43A, Route 29 (S). At Warrenton, take 211 (W) 23 miles. Right at Washington sign. Go to stop sign, turn left. Inn is located 3 blocks on right.

Washington

Gay Street Inn

B&B

Gay Street, P. O. Box 237, 22747
(703) 675-3288
Innkeepers: Robin & Donna Kevis

$$/
$$$

This charming, restored, 1860 farmhouse is perfect for relaxing and is an ideal base for enjoying all the pleasures of the Virginia countryside. The cozy rooms are delightfully furnished and offer unique cotton quilts in summer and flannel sheets and down comforters in the winter. Following a hearty breakfast featuring buttermilk muffins, seasonal fruit or home-grown melons, and a special entree, plan your day of sitting on the porch, antiquing, visiting the many nearby wineries, or the Shenandoah National Park which is only 20 minutes away. There is world-class dining steps away.

Approved by: BBAV

From Rt. 29(S), go to Warrenton. Follow Rt. 211(W) for 25 miles to Washington, VA. From Rt. 29(N), go to Madison. Follow Rt. 231(N) to Sperryville and take Rt. 211(E) for six miles to Washington, VA.

3R 1S

BYOB

V,M

Washington

B&B
&

Main Street & Piedmont Avenue, Box 427, 22747
(703) 675-3207, Fax (703) 675-1340
Innkeepers: Jean & Frank Scott

$$/
$$$

This was General Jubal Early's headquarters during the Civil War and is now the perfect headquarters for your visit to the Virginia Blue Ridge. The Inn is located in the heart of artistic "little" Washington, Virginia, within an easy drive to Civil War Battle sites, Skyline Drive, Luray Caverns, and many other recreational opportunities including world-renown dining. The village offers fine art, crafts, and artisans shops. You will enjoy heirloom antiques and collectibles, afternoon refreshments, delicious breakfasts, and the ambiance of the relaxed grace of Old Virginia.

Approved by: AAA, BBAV

The Heritage House

From Washington, D.C., take I-66 to Exit 43A. Follow Route 29 to Warrenton. Follow Route 211 from Warrenton to Washington, VA.

9R 1S

10

V,M,X
DN

White Post

B&B

P.O. Box 119, 22663
(800) 638-1702, Fax (703) 837-2004
Innkeepers: Alain & Celeste Borel

$$$-
$$$$$

This is a true South-of-France "Auberge" in Virginia Hunt Country. This 1753, stone, farm house is the setting chosen by the Innkeepers for their Auberge. The Inn features award-winning cuisine. "Works of Art" from Chef Alain's kitchen are often created from his head using home-grown vegetables and fruit. Rabbits, pheasant, quail, and fresh fish are purchased from local farmers. The Auberge has three dining rooms and ten beautiful guest rooms. It offers a gourmet breakfast, picnic baskets for two, romantic candlelight dining, and Sunday Brunch.

Approved by: IIA

L'Auberge Provencale

D.C. Beltway to: 66 (W) to exit 23 - 17 (N) to Route 50 (W) to Route 340 (S) for 1 mile.

3R 1S

Williamsburg

B&B

605 Richmond Road, 23185
(800) 899-2753, or (804) 229-0205
Innkeeper: Fred Strout

$-
$$$

Applewood Colonial B&B

The Inn was named because its owner has a collection of over 300 apple items, including an apple checker board. It was built in 1929 by a Colonial Williamsburg restorer, who added many of the fine details used in the historic area. The house has a Flemish-bond brick exterior, a handsome 18th century-style portal, and dentil crown moldings in the interior. Your Innkeeper serves a deluxe, continental, candlelit breakfast, with apples, of course!

Approved by: AAA, BBAV

From I-64, take Exit 238. Go 2 lights to Route 132 (S), and continue to second light. Go 1 block past stoplight, and turn right on Scotland. Go 4 blocks to Richmond Road, then turn right. Go 1 block. Inn is located on the right.

5R 1S

Williamsburg

B&B

501 Richmond Road, 23185
(800) 776-0570, Fax (804) 253-7667
Innkeepers: Barbara & Phil Craig

$/
$$

Colonial Capital Bed & Breakfast

The Inn is located in the Architectural Preservation District, only three blocks from the Historic Area and across the street from the College of William and Mary. From the columned portico, through the entry foyer, to the bright and airy guest rooms, guests immediately sense warmth and comfort. Each room has a cozy-canopied bed and private bath. The large, plantation parlor feeds into a columned, screened-in porch, shaded patio, and deck. Its woodburning fireplace creates an inviting place. A full breakfast, with a gourmet touch, is served as well as afternoon tea and Williamsburg wines.

Approved by: AAA, BBAV

From I-64, take Exit 238 to Route 132 (S), to Lafayette Street. Turn right, then take 4th left onto Virginia Avenue. Go 2 blocks to corner at Richmond Road. Inn is located on the right.

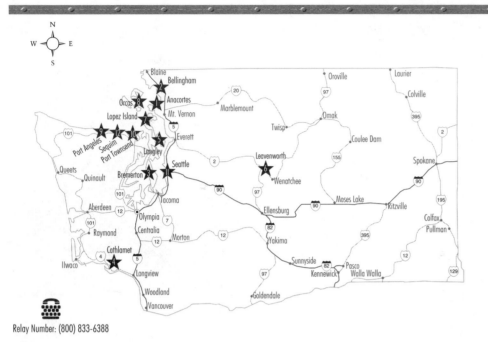

Relay Number: (800) 833-6388

6R

BYOB

V,M,DV

Anacortes

B&B

2902 Oakes Avenue, 98221
(800) 238-4353, or (360) 293-9382
Innkeepers: Dennis & Patricia McIntyre

$-
$$

Channel House

You will take home memories of quiet conversation, sun-filled rooms, blue water, and the silhouette of the islands at sunset. Channel House is a 1902 classic, heritage home in Craftsman style, overlooking Guemes Channel. It is less than two miles from the ferry terminal. In two sitting rooms you'll find Pat's Oatmeal Raisin Cookies, coffee, and tea. After a wonderful dinner at one of Anacortes's fine restaurants, you can return to the Channel House for conversation, a game of Scrabble®, or a soak in the hot-tub.

Approved by: WBBG

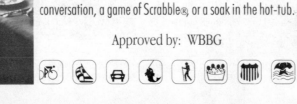

From I-5, take the #230 (Highway 20) Exit. Follow Highway 20 (W) 18 miles to Anacortes. Bear right onto Commercial Avenue, and turn left at 12th Street. 12th Street changes into Oakes Avenue.

1R 2S

BYOB

10

V,M

Bellingham

B&B

4421 Lakeway Drive, 98226
(800) 562-2808, Fax (360) 734-2808
Innkeepers: Vermont & Donna McAllister

$$$/
$$$$

Schnauzer Crossing B&B

You will be warmly welcomed at this luxurious Inn above twelve mile Lake Whatcom. Accommodations include the Queen Room with modern private bath and lake view, the Master Suite, and the Cottage. Each offers a king bed, fireplace, Jacuzzi® tub, sunroom or deck, and lake or garden view. Delight in the lakeside ambiance, country quiet, and bird song. There is a lovely garden with raspberries and blueberries for the picking! Enjoy the down comfort, fresh flowers, breakfast bounty, outdoor spa, and, of course, the Standard Schnauzers "Chuck & Barbel!"

Approved by: WBBG

I-5 to 253 Lakeway Drive Exit. Turn east (away from town), and travel 2.8 miles to intersection of Lakeway, Euclid and Cable. Turn left on Lakeway. Inn is located on the left down gravel drive.

5R

15

V,M

Bremerton

B&B

2390 Tekiu Road NW, 98312
(360) 830-4492, Fax (360) 830-0506
Innkeepers: Cecilia & Phillip Hughes

$$/
$$$$

Willcox House Country Inn

Overlooking Hood Canal, this historic 1930's Country House Inn is situated in a forest setting between Seattle and the Olympic Peninsula. The mansion estate offers park-like grounds, a private saltwater beach, a pier with floating dock, and spectacular views from all rooms. Comfortable period pieces and antiques are featured in guest rooms as well as in the great room, billiard room, pub, library, and dining room. There is an afternoon wine and cheese hour and a prix fixe lunch and dinner are available by reservation. The Inn is just 17 miles west of Bremerton on the Hood Canal.

Approved by: AAA, IIA

From Bremerton, go west on Kitsap Way, 1.4 miles to Northlake Way and fork left. Go 1.1 miles and fork left on Seabeck Hwy. Go 2.9 miles, turn left on Holly. Go 4.9 miles, turn left on Seabeck-Holly Rd. Drive 5.2 miles and fork right on Old Holly Hill. Turn right on Tekiu. Go 1.2 miles.

Langley

B&B

3273 E. Saratoga Road, 98260
(360) 221-5483
Innkeepers: Norma & Jack Metcalf

$$

Log Castle Bed & Breakfast

Imagine a secluded beach with a castle made of logs festooned with vines of flowering yellow clematis. This unique lodge has it all; an arched wood-and-stained-glass doorway; a large, stone fireplace; private porches with swings for two; and even an eight-sided turret rising from the center of the house. Each of the four rooms has its own beautiful view. The Metcalfs designed and built the Inn themselves, and they love sharing it with their guests. Their warm welcome and delightful breakfasts make this a place to visit again and again.

Approved by: WBBG

From I-5, take the Mukelteo/Whidbey Island Exit. Drive onto the ferry at Mukilteo. Go to Langley (6 miles from ferry), and turn left on Second Street. Go straight out of town 1 1/2 miles to Inn.

Lopez Island

B&B

Route 2, Box 3402, 98261
(360) 468-3636, Fax (360) 468-3637
Innkeepers: Robert Herrmann & Christopher Brandmeir

$-
$$$

Inn at Swifts Bay

The Inn at Swifts Bay is one of the finest Bed and Breakfast Inns in the San Juan Islands of Washington State. This elegantly-maintained, "northwest" style B&B sits on three wooded acres, with a private beach just minutes away. Bald eagles fly overhead, and otters play in the waters offshore. Whale watching for the orca whale can be arranged in season. In the winter, the emphasis turns inward with two fireplaces, 200 videos, and 500 books that turn every day into a Sunday. Quiet and secluded, this is the perfect island getaway.

Approved by: AAA, Mobil, WBBG

Eighty miles north of Seattle on Highway 5 to Anacortes and San Juan Ferry.
Destination: Lopez Island.

4R

Orcas

B&B

P.O. Box 32, 98280
(360) 376-2500
Innkeepers: Sam & Kim Haines

$$- $$$

WindSong

$$- $$$

Your stay here promises to be memorable. The rooms and common area are delightfully furnished, and showcase the work of local artisans. This large, 1917 schoolhouse is now country elegant and aims to be your home away from home. Spacious, comfortably appointed rooms and queen-size beds with down comforters make for luxurious sleeping. A four-course, sumptuous, farm breakfast features fresh juice sorbets, homemade granola, and home-baked muffins or breads. A pastoral setting near West Sound Marina, a llama farm, and the ferry landing complete the scene.

Approved by: WBBG

From ferry landing, go 2 1/2 miles north on Horseshoe Highway. Turn left onto Deer Harbor Road.

2R 2S

BYOB

10

V,M

Port Angeles

B&B

146 Wildflower Lane, 98362
(360) 457-4174, Fax (360) 457-3037
Innkeepers: John & Madeleine Lanham Chambers

$$/ $$$

Domaine Madeleine

Minutes from Olympic National Park, the grounds of this Franco-American estate are so quiet you could hear an oyster yawn! You'll discover a scholarly, artistic, nurturing, salon-like exchange of ideas here. Madeleine assists those wishing to practice their foreign language or cooking skills. John, a botanist, will show you his Monet garden replica, Zen gardens, and oriental pond. You may play the harpsichord he built. Wake up to the aroma of French bread baking and enjoy a multi-course epicurean breakfast.

Approved by: AAA, Mobil

Three miles west of Sequim on Highway 101, right on Carlsborg 1.8 miles. Turn left on Old Olympic Highway, and proceed 3.7 miles. Turn right on Matson, and go .8 miles. Turn left on Finn Hall, and go 1 mile.

Port Angeles

B&B

1108 South Oak, 98362
(360) 452-3138
Innkeepers: Jane & Jerry Glass

The Tudor Inn

$-
$$

In 1910, an eccentric English dentist built this half-timbered, historic Tudor-style home. He even built his own coffin on the third floor from a locally selected Redwood. Today, the Inn is furnished with English and European antiques. Each bedroom reflects individual personality with hand-painted decorations and views of the mountains, the Strait of Juan de Fuca, or the landscaped English gardens. This beautiful spot is centrally located for day trips to the Olympic National Park and the west coast beaches. Afternoon tea is served daily and the generous breakfast is fresh and healthy.

Approved by: AAA, Mobil, WBBG

Follow Hwy. 101(S) on Lincoln St. through downtown to 11th St. Turn right onto 11th St. and drive 2 blocks to Oak St. The Inn is located on the corner of 11th and Oak.

Port Townsend

B&B

313 Walker at Washington, 98368
(800) 300-6753, Fax (360) 385-2097
Innkeepers: Rob & Joanna Jackson

F.W. Hastings House Old Consulate Inn

$/
$$$$

Experience the gracious hospitality of the Victorian past in this beautifully restored Queen Anne masterpiece. The Founding Family Mansion-on-the-Bluff offers incredible views of Mount Rainier, Port Townsend Bay, and the Olympics. Evenings you will retire to your king-bedded room or suite with private bath, antique furnishings, and custom linens. Awaken each morning to a lavish breakfast served with breath-taking views of the bay. Return to afternoon tea and refreshments and evening conversation accompanied by sherry and port. You may also share a friendly game of billiards or Scrabble®.

Approved by: AAA, WBBG

Take Bainbridge Ferry to Highway 305 to Highway 3. Cross the Hood Canal Bridge to Highway 19. Go north 23 miles to Port Townsend. Go past first stop light, turn left onto Washington Street. Go to the first corner which is Walker.

Port Townsend

Ravenscroft Inn

B&B

533 Quincy Street, 98368
(360) 385-2784, Fax (360) 385-6724
Innkeepers: Leah Hammer & John Ranney

$/
$$$

The Inn stands high on a bluff overlooking historic Port Townsend, the Olympic Peninsula's Victorian seaport. This romantic hideaway is a colonial built in the Charleston single house style. Guests are offered a unique combination of colonial hospitality mixed with a comfortable, casual feeling. Each morning enjoy a sumptuous repast accompanied by music on the grand piano. You will find this a delightful vacation spot meeting all of your needs; comfort, scenic beauty, theatre, fine dining, boating, kyaking, and hiking in the National Parks and the Hoh River Rain Forest.

Approved by: WBBG

Please call for directions.

Sequim

Greywolf Inn

B&B

395 Keeler Road, 98382
(360) 683-5889
Innkeepers: Peggy & Bill Melang

$$

Hidden away in a crescent of towering evergreens, this Northwest country estate sits atop five acres overlooking sunny Dungeness Valley. Located in the rain shadow of the mighty Olympic Mountains, it is the ideal starting point for year round adventure on the Olympic Peninsula. Enjoy hiking, fishing, golf, and more. After a day of activity, unwind with a leisurely stroll down a meandering woodswalk, soak in the enclosed Japanese style hot tub, or curl up by the flickering fire. Then retire to one of Greywolf's cozy, comfortable theme rooms for the perfect ending to an exciting day.

Approved by: AAA, Mobil, WBBG

 A scenic, 2-hour drive from Seattle via Highway 101. One mile east of downtown Sequim and 4/10 mile north of Highway 101.

Wisconsin

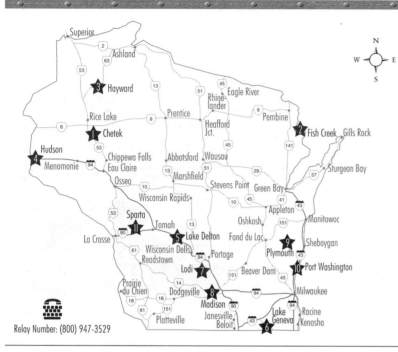

Relay Number: (800) 947-3529

9R 5S

EP

Fish Creek

4225 Main Street, P. O. Box 160, 54212
(414) 868-3517, Fax (414) 868-2367
Innkeepers: Andy & Jan Coulson

Established in 1896, the Inn is a landmark in this historic, unspoiled, bayside village in the heart of Wisconsin's Door Peninsula. Guests are escorted to antique-filled bedrooms and cottages, many with working fireplaces. Famous for its unique, traditional, Door County fish boils, where locally caught Lake Michigan whitefish is cooked before your eyes over an open wood fire, the Inn is also known for hearty breakfasts, lunches, and candlelight dinners. The Inn is close to all kinds of year-round recreational and cultural activities from golf to wind-surfing, antiquing to summer stock theatre.

Approved by: IIA, WBBHHIA

White Gull Inn

$$/$$$

Take I-43 from Milwaukee to Green Bay. Follow Highway 57 to Sturgeon Bay. Take Highway 42(N) to Fish Creek. Turn left at bottom of hill to the sign of the White Gull Inn.

V,M,X DN,DV

Hayward

Corner of 4th Street & Kansas Avenue, 54843

B&B   (715) 634-3012 $/ $$

Jan Hinrichs Blaedel & Wendy Hinrichs Sanders

Lumberman's Mansion Inn

Built in 1887, this Queen Anne-style Victorian was known by locals as the "Lumberman's Palace." Come relive the grand days of the lumbering era. The antique furnishings, modern comforts, breakfasts featuring regional specialties, and many little extras will make your stay memorable. The Inn is located one block from Main Street with its unique gift shops and classic, small town ambiance, yet it is surrounded by a year-round recreational paradise. Hospitality, service, cleanliness, charm, quality, history, friendliness, privacy, and relaxation are guaranteed!

Approved by: AAA, WBBHHIA

One block off Main Street on 63 (N), turn north on Kansas Avenue and go to 4th block.

Hudson

B&B   1109 3rd Street, 54016 $$$

(715) 386-7111

Innkeepers: Sharon & Wally Miller

Jefferson-Day House

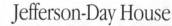

Twenty minutes east of St. Paul and Minneapolis and 30 minutes from the Mall of America, this 1857 Italianate Inn offers a peaceful retreat on a quiet, tree-lined street of historic homes just two blocks from the scenic St. Croix River. Hudson offers a variety of art and antique shops, fine dining, an historic museum, and the Phipps Theatre for the Arts. The Inn features Maxfield Parrish and Atkinson Fox prints and Fiesta and Roseville Pottery. All guest rooms have private baths, air-conditioning, queen-size beds, double whirlpools, and three have gas fireplaces. The suite offers private dining in the sunroom.

Approved by: WBBHHIA

From Highway I-94, take Exit 1 and go north on Second Street. Turn right onto Myrtle, then turn left onto Third Street. The Inn will be on the left.

Lodi

Victorian Treasure B&B

B&B

115 Prairie Street, 53555
(800) 859-5199, Fax (608) 592-4352
Innkeepers: Todd & Kimberly Seidl

$/
$$$

Experience timeless ambiance, thoughful amenities, and caring Innkeepers at this classic Bed & Breakfast Inn. The Inn features 1897 Queen Anne architecture; a wraparound front porch; stained and leaded glass; pocket doors; gas and electric chandeliers; and more. The Innkeepers are experienced, gourmet cooks, who are fussy about the details and genuinely interested in exceeding guest's expectations. The Inn is located in the scenic Lake Wisconsin recreational area, between Madison and the Wisconsin Dells.

Approved by: WBBHHIA

From I-90/94, take Highway 60 (W) Exit to Lodi. At Highway 113, continue straight 1 block. Turn right on Prairie Street.

Madison

Annie's Bed & Breakfast

B&B

2117 Sheridan Drive, 53704
(608) 244-2224, Fax (608) 242-9611
Innkeepers: Anne & Lawrence Stuart

$
$$

Opened as Madison's first Bed & Breakfast in April of 1985, Annie's is a rustic, cedar-shake house in a quiet residential neighborhood. It overlooks a beautiful valley and is just a block away from the eastern shore of Lake Mendota. Tall green spruces, shaggy birch trees, and extensive gardens surround the house, gazebo, and lily pond. Enjoy the surrounding meadows, wildlife marsh, and woods. The accommodations are deluxe, with intriguing little surprises tucked into each suite. You'll find great attention to detail here.

Approved by: AAA, Mobil, WBBHHIA

Four blocks north on Sheridan Drive from McPherson Street.

Madison

Mansion Hill Inn

B&B

424 N. Pinckney Street, 53703
(800) 798-9070, Fax (608) 255-2217
Innkeeper: Kris Schoenbrun

$$
$$$$

Capturing the spirit of its renowned past, this Inn is filled with tall, round-arched windows, ornate cornices, handcarved marble, and beautiful hardwoods. The four-story spiral staircase leads to a panoramic view of the city. Elegance abounds in the exquisite guest rooms and suites. Special amenities include afternoon refreshments, evening turndown service, 24-hour valet service, continental breakfast, fireplaces, private baths, and whirlpool tubs. The Inn is located in the heart of Madison, near the Capitol and the University campus. Perfect for business or pleasure.

Approved by: AAA

South on Highway 151 (E. Washington Avenue) to Capitol Square. Bear to right until Wisconsin Avenue. Turn right, and continue to Gilman Street. Turn right, and proceed 1 block. Inn is on right side.

Plymouth

Yankee Hill

B&B

405 Collins Street, 53073
(414) 892-2222
Innkeepers: Peg & Jim Stahlman

$
$$

This Inn, with its two historic homes, welcomes you into the solitude of a quiet Wisconsin, agricultural town in the heart of the scenic Kettle Moraine recreational area. One home is an 1891 Queen Anne style, while the second, is listed on the National Register of Historic Places, and has a modified Italianate-Gothic architectural styling. Both homes have common rooms in which to socialize with guests. Rooms have individualized decor with period and unique antiques. Nurture your relationships at Yankee Hill and walk to excellent shopping and dining experiences in Plymouth.

Approved by: WBBHHIA

Photo: Ken Pannier

Fifty miles north of Milwaukee. Fifteen miles west of I-43 on State Highway 23 to Plymouth. Exit County Highway "O" south to Eastern Avenue. Turn right and go 1 1/2 blocks. Turn left on Collins Street and continue for two blocks.

Photo: Mark Pastor

Port Washington, WI

308 W. Washington, 53074
(414) 284-5583, Fax (414) 284-2283
Innkeepers: Connie Evans & Craig Siwy

B&B

Port Washington Inn

$$

This 1903 Victorian home boasts original stained glass, light fixtures, wallcoverings, and woodwork. A spacious foyer leads to a high-ceilinged parlor where you may relax after dinner with a book from the cozy library. The menu-board at the foot of the staircase describes the morning feast of fresh fruits, homemade coffeecakes, and casseroles. Linger on the suite's private balcony or lounge in the wicker rockers on the porch and savor the hilltop view of Lake Michigan. The harborside community of Port Washington will charm you and historic Cedarburg is just 10 miles away.

Approved by: WBBHHIA

I-43(N) to Exit 96, turn right onto Route 33 for two miles. Turn left onto Franklin. Continue two blocks to Washington. Inn is three blocks west of Franklin.

Wyoming

1. A. Drummond's Ranch B & B......p 229
2. The Wildflower Inn......p 229
3. Window on the Winds.......p230

Relay Numbers: TTY (800) 877-9965, VCE (800) 877-9975

Cheyenne

B&B
AP

399 Happy Jack Road, 82007
(307) 634-6042
Innkeeper: Taydie Drummond

$/
$$

A. Drummond's Ranch B & B

The view of Long's Peak in the Colorado Rockies takes your breath away as you discover this treasure tucked into the hillside on 120 acres. You are welcome to bring your horse and explore Medicine Bow National Forest's 55,000 acres. If you like, create an "Adventure at Your Pace" package to include guided mountain biking, hiking, or cross-country skiing tours. Enjoy fresh flowers in your room and fine dining on linen, silver, and china. Whether relaxing or discovering Cheyenne and Laramie, only 25 minutes away, a stay here is a retreat to tranquillity.

Approved by: AAA, Mobil

Highway I-80(E) to Exit 323. Go left over I-80, left onto Happy Jack Rd. Drive 1 6/10 miles past entrance to Curt Gowdy State Park. Turn right at 4th dirt road with small sign, "Private Road". House is 1/4 mile on left. I-80(W) to I-25(N) to Exit 10B. Go west 4/10 mile, turn left on dirt road.

Jackson

B&B

P.O. Box 3724, 83001
(307) 733-4710, Fax (307) 739-0914
Innkeepers: Ken & Sherrie Jern

$$$

The Wildflower Inn

The Inn is a gorgeous log home on three acres with aspens, ponds, mountain views, and of course wildflowers. The Inn has a wonderful and warm Jackson Hole feeling. Each room is decorated with log furniture, down comforters, private bathrooms, decks, and terrific views. Guests can visit around a crackling fire, soak in the hot tub while looking out on the distant mountains, or relax quietly in a nearby hammock. Skiing, tennis, golf, hiking, fishing, and superb restaurants are only minutes away. A delicious country breakfast is served around the large antique table and the conversation is lively.

Approved by: Mobil

From Highway 22, take 390(N) for 2.5 miles. Turn left on Shooting Star Lane, just past the Jackson Hole Racquet Club.

Pinedale, WY

Window on the Winds

B&B

10151 Highway 191, 82941
(307) 367-2600, Fax (307) 367-2395
Innkeepers: Leanne McClain & Doug McKay

$

You will enjoy this rustic log home decorated in Western and Plains Indian decor. Comfortable lodge-pole pine, queen beds, a large common room with breathtaking views of "the Winds," and a hot tub are offered for your enjoyment. The hosts are archaeologists, who enjoy sharing their unique perspective on the cultural heritage of the area. Pinedale is at the base of the Wind River Mountains in Western Wyoming. It is on a major route to Jackson, Grand Teton, and Yellowstone National Parks. Enjoy comfort and friendliness in a warm and casual atmosphere.

Approved by: AAA

1 1/2 miles west of Pinedale, on Highway 191.

Victoria, BC

Prior House Bed & Breakfast Inn

B&B

620 St. Charles Street, V8S 3 N7
(604) 592-8847, Fax (604) 592-8223
Innkeepers: Candis & Ted Cooperrider-Gornall

$$$/
$$$$

Formerly a private residence of the English Crown, this grand Bed & Breakfast Inn has all the amenities of the finest European Inns. You'll enjoy antique-filled rooms with ocean and mountain views, fireplaces, marble Jacuzzi® baths, goose down comforters, sumptuous breakfasts, and afternoon tea. The Inn is in one of the city's most prestigious neighborhoods, near the Government House, Parliament Buildings, and the Royal British Columbia Museum. When you visit the beautiful city of Victoria, you will fall in love with life at this incredible Inn.

Approved by: AAA, Mobil

South on Highway 1 or 17 into Victoria downtown. Turn left on Fort, and travel 1 mile to St. Charles. Turn right.

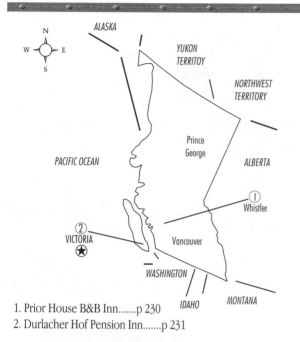

ALASKA

YUKON TERRITOY

NORTHWEST TERRITORY

Prince George

PACIFIC OCEAN

ALBERTA

① Whistler

VICTORIA ②

Vancouver

WASHINGTON

IDAHO

MONTANA

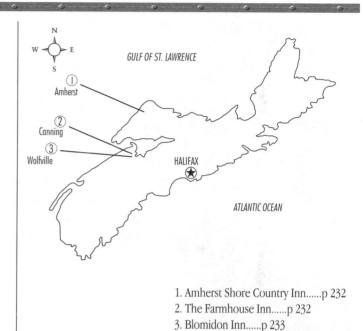

GULF OF ST. LAWRENCE

① Amherst

② Canning

③ Wolfville

HALIFAX

ATLANTIC OCEAN

Whistler, BC

MAP
B&B
♿

7055 Nesters Road, Box 1125, VON 1BO
(604) 932-1924, Fax (604) 938-1980
Innkeepers: Peter & Erika Durlacher

Durlacher Hof Pension Inn

$
$$$$

This is an enchanting Austrian Mountain hideaway featuring hospitality and European traditional cuisine. Goose down comforters, private baths, and a beautiful lounge create a feeling of warmth. Enjoy tastefully decorated rooms with balconies and unsurpassed mountain views. Evening meals are served family-style featuring Austrian comfort food. A bountiful breakfast will keep a skier going all day! Afternoon coffee and just-from-the-oven kuchen (coffee cake) are wonderful!

Approved by: AAA

Photos: Jane Weitzel

From Highway 99 (S) and Nester's Subdivision, take the 2nd left after Whister Village entrance.

Amherst

Amherst Shore Country Inn

EP
MAP

RR #2, B4H 3X9
(800) 661-ASCI, or ((902) 661-4800
Innkeeper: Donna Laceby

$-
$$$

Here you may escape to the quiet, natural beauty of Nova Scotia's Northumberland Strait. Choose a comfortable room, a luxurious suite, or a rustic cottage to suit your mood. The century-old Inn specializes in home-style, gourmet dining and ocean views. Each evening a four-course dinner is served that features the freshest of Nova Scotia ingredients. The menu changes every night and reservations are a must. There is no need to worry about calories since the Inn offers miles of peaceful beach just a two minute walk from your room.

Approved by: AAA

          Take Hwy. 366 from Amherst to the Inn.

Canning

The Farmhouse Inn

B&B

1057 Main Street, P. O. Box 38, B0P 1H0
(800) 928-4346, Fax (902) 582-7900
Innkeepers: Ellen & Doug Bray

$

This lovely, 18th century home is filled with country accents and antiques. It is located in the Annapolis Valley on the access route to The Lookoff, known for its incredible view, and Cape Blomidon and Cape Split, both favorites of hikers. Bird watchers who visit will be delighted by the nearby Bald Eagles. The Inn houses a craft and gift shop and after you have enjoyed a scrumptious breakfast, you will be able to create your favorite dishes at home using the Inn's own country breakfast cookbook. The guest rooms are delightful and all have private baths.

Approved by: AAA

       Take Exit 11 off Hwy. 101. Follow Rt. 1 into Wolfville to Rt. 358. Follow Rt. 358 through Port Williams into Canning. The Inn is on the left side of Main Street.

26R 4S

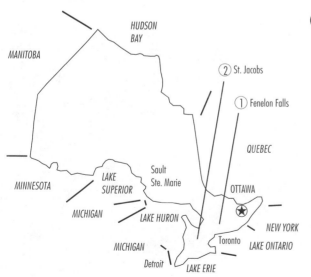

Wolfville, NS

B&B
MAP

127 Main Street, P. O. Box 839, BOP 1XO
(800) 565-2291, Fax (902) 542-7461
Innkeepers: Jim & Donna Laceby

Blomidon Inn

$/
$$

Sherman Hines

When you escape to the Annapolis Valley you may visit this beautifully restored, 19th century sea captain's mansion for a relaxed lunch or dinner of regional cuisine and a selection of local wines. If you are planning an overnight getaway, many of the rooms feature four poster beds and several have fireplaces or Jacuzzi®tubs. Much of the interior detail work is in exotic hardwood and dates back to the 1870's. The Inn is set on four acres of treed and terraced lawns and offers a tennis court and shuffle board. A stay here will let you experience the style and grace of the Victorian era.

Approved by: AAA, Mobil

Take Hwy. 101(W) to Exit 10. Follow Hwy. 1 to Wolfville and the Inn.

Ontario

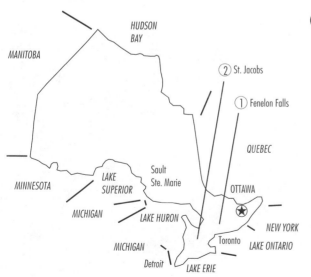

HUDSON BAY

MANITOBA

② St. Jacobs

① Fenelon Falls

QUEBEC

LAKE SUPERIOR

Sault Ste. Marie

MINNESOTA

OTTAWA

MICHIGAN

LAKE HURON

MICHIGAN

NEW YORK

Toronto

LAKE ONTARIO

Detroit

LAKE ERIE

7R 6S

Fenelon Falls

EP
B&B
&

RR #3, KOM INO
(705) 738-5111, Fax (705) 738-5111
Innkeepers: Patty & John Egan

$$$-
$$$$

Eganridge Inn & Country Club

The Eganridge Inn provides spectacular views of Sturgeon Lake. Located in a setting of pine and stone, this Inn includes the Dunsford House, which was built in 1837. The Dunsford building is one of North America's finest-preserved examples of a 2-story, hand-hewn log home. Challenging golf, award-winning continental cuisine, and the ultimate in luxurious accommodations will fulfill your highest expectations.

15

V,M,X

Approved by: IIA

Highway 7 through Lindsay to Highway 36. Go on 36 to Bobcayggon to Country Road 8 (4 miles west of Bobcayggon.)

12R

St. Jacobs

B&B

16 Isabella Street, NOB 2NO
(519) 664-2208, Fax (519) 664-1326
Innkeeper: Ella Brubacher

$$/
$$$

Jakobstettel Guest House

BYOB

This Victorian house has a history as rich as its decor. The Inn has gracious guest rooms and rests on five, treed acres. There is an outdoor pool, a tennis court, bikes, badminton, and a private rose garden. A wooded walking trail and other sports are available nearby. Steps away there are excellent dining choices, over 80 specialty shops, a maple syrup museum, and a Mennonite Meeting Place. Further down the road are numerous farmers markets and the Kitchener-Waterloo cultural attractions. Groups may rent the entire house and have access to the conference room for a productive, retreat.

12

V,M,X

Approved by: AAA

Hunsberger Photography

From Hwy. 401, exit Hwy. 8(W) to Kitchener. Take Hwy. 86(N) to Waterloo. Go approximately 16 kilometers to the lights on Road 17. Turn left and left again into the Village. Go over the bridge and take the second right onto Albert St. Go straight two blocks to the Inn.

Notes

State	City	Inn	Phone
AR	Eureka Springs	Heartstone Inn & Cottages	501 253 8916
AZ	Tucson	Casa Alegre Bed & Breakfast	602 628 1800
AZ	Tucson	La Posada Del Valle	602 795 3840
AZ	Tucson	Peppertrees B & B	602 622 7167
AZ	Tucson	SunCatcher	602 885 0883
CA	Carlsbad	Pelican Cove	619 434 5995
CA	Murphys	Dunbar House,1880	209 728 2897
CA	Napa	Beazley House	800 559 1649
CA	San Diego	Heritage Park B & B Inn	619 299 6832
CA	San Francisco	Alamo Square Inn	415 922 2055
CA	San Jose	Hensley House Bed & Breakfast	408 298 3537
CA	Santa Barbara	Simpson House Inn	805 963 7067
CA	Santa Monica	Channel Road Inn	310 459 1920
CA	Valley Center	Lake Wohlford B & B	800 831 8239
CO	Estes Park	Anniversary Inn	303 586 6200
CO	Steamboat Springs	Steamboat Valley Guest House	303 870 9017
CT	Tolland	Tolland Inn	203 872 0800
DE	Dover	Inn At Meeting House Square	302 678 1242
FL	Lake Buena Vista	Perri House Bed & Breakfast	800 780 4830
FL	Ocala	Seven Sisters Inn	904 867 1170
IL	Maeystown	Corner George Inn	618 458 6660
IL	Mossville	Old Church House Inn	309 579 2300
IL	Mount Carmel	Poor Farm B & B	618 262 4663
IL	Nauvoo	Mississippi Memories	217 453 2771
IN	Ligonier	Minuette Bed & Breakfast	219 894 4494
IN	Metamora	Thorpe House Country Inn	317 647 5425
KS	Council Grove	Cottage House	316 767 6828
LA	New Orleans	La Maison Marigny	504 488 4640
LA	St Francisville	Green Springs Plantation	800 457 4978
MA	Falmouth	Palmer House Inn	508 548 1230
MA	S. Egremont	Weathervane Inn	413 528 9580
MD	Annapolis	William Page Inn	410 626 1506
MD	Chesapeake City	Inn At The Canal	410 885 5995
MD	Keedysville	Antietam Overlook Farm	301 432 4200
MD	Tilghman Island	Black Walnut Point Inn	410 886 2452
ME	Castine	Pentagoet Inn	207 326 8616
ME	Deer Isle	Pilgrims Inn	207 348 6615
MI	Brooklyn	Chicago Street Inn	517 592 3888
MI	Fennville	Hidden Pond Bed & Breakfast	616 561 2491
MI	Holland	Dutch Colonial Inn	616 396 3664
MI	Saugatuck	Bayside Inn	616 857 4321
MI	Saugatuck	Park House	616 857 4535
MN	Hastings	Rosewood Inn	800 992 INNS
MO	Branson	Inn At Fall Creek	417 336 3422
MO	Jackson	Trisha's Bed & Breakfast	314 243 7427
MO	New Franklin	Rivercene B & B	800 531 0862
MO	St. Charles	Boone's Lick Trail Inn	314 947 7000
MO	St. Louis	Winter House	314 664 4399
MO	Warrensburg	Cedarcroft Farm	816 747 5728
MT	Columbia Falls	Bad Rock Country B & B	406 892 2829
MT	Columbia Falls	Turn In The River	800 892 2474
MT	Kalispell	Creston Inn Bed & Breakfast	800 257 7517
MT	Kalispell	Switzer House Inn	406 257 5837
MT	Somers	Osprey Inn	406 857 2042
MT	Three Forks	Sacajawea Inn	406 285 6515
NC	Asheville	Applewood Manor	704 254 2244
NC	Asheville	Colby House	704 253 5644
NC	Asheville	Richmond Hill Inn	800 545 9238
NC	Germanton	MeadowHaven Bed & Breakfast	919 593 3996
NC	New Bern	Harmony House Inn	919 636 3810
NH	Conway	Darby Field Inn	603 447 2181
NH	Hancock	John Hancock Inn	603 525 3318
NH	Snowville	Snowvillage Inn	603 447 2818
NH	West Chesterfield	Chesterfield Inn	603 256 3211
NJ	Cape May	Manor House	609 884 4710
NJ	Hope	Inn At Millrace Pond	908 459 4884
NJ	Spring Lake	Normandy Inn	908 449 7172
NJ	Spring Lake	Sea Crest By The Sea	908 449 9031
NM	Albuquerque	Casas De Sueños	505 247 4560
NM	Santa Fe	Water Street Inn	505 984 1193
NY	Averill Park	Gregory House Country Inn	518 674 3774
OR	Ashland	Romeo Inn	503 488 0884
OR	Klamath Falls	Klamath Manor	503 883 5459
OR	McMinnville	Steiger Haus	503 472 0821
OR	Oregon City	Jagger House Bed & Breakfast	503 657 7820
OR	Seaside	Riverside Inn Bed & Breakfast	800 826 6151
PA	Brackney	Indian Mountain Inn	717 663 2645
PA	Canadensis	Brookview Manor	717 595 2451
PA	Hanover	Beechmont Inn	717 632 3013
PA	New Hope	Wedgwood Inn	215 862 2520
RI	Westerly	Villa	800 722 9240
TX	Houston	Patrician Bed & Breakfast Inn	713 523 1114
UT	Park City	Old Miners' Lodge	801 645 8068
VA	Boston	Thistle Hill B & B	703 987 9142
VA	Natural Bridge	Burger's Country Inn	703 291 2464
VA	Staunton	Ashton Country House	703 885 7819
VA	Warm Springs	Meadow Lane Farm Lodge	703 839 5959
VT	Bridgewater Corners	October Country Inn	802 672 3412
VT	Fairlee	Silver Maple Lodge & Cottages	802 333 4326
VT	Ludlow	Andrie Rose Inn	802 228 4846
WA	Cathlamet	Country Keeper Bed & Breakfast	206 795 3030
WA	Langley	Eagles Nest	206 221 5331
WA	Leavenworth	All Seasons River Inn	800 254 0555
WA	Leavenworth	Run Of The River	509 548 7171
WA	Seattle	Prince Of Wales Bed & Breakfast	206 325 9692
WI	Chetek	Lodge At Canoe Bay	715 924 4594
WI	Lake Delton	Swallows Nest Bed & Breakfast	608 254 6900
WI	Lake Geneva	Eleven Gables Inn On The Lake	414 248 8393
WI	Sparta	Just-N-Trails	608 269 4522
WV	Charles Town	Hillbrook Inn	304 725 4223
WV	Lewisburg	General Lewis Inn	304 645 2600

Alphabetical Index

Alphabetical Index

Wendy and Jon Denn each have over 20 years of experience in the hospitality industry. Jon is the recipient of a Great Menu Award from the *National Restaurant Association* and 11 Adrian Awards from the *Hotel Sales and Marketing Association International*. He will be doing the biennial Inn Industry Study for the *Professional Association of Innkeepers International* in 1995. He was a Contributing Editor for *Hotel and Motel Management Magazine*, writing the "Dining Out" column for three years. He is the author of two other recent books, *The Fundamental Guide to Playing Pool* and *Rack 'Em Daddy!*, the only kids' book on how to play pool. Together, Wendy and Jon have previously published several successful Inn Travel Guides.

Wendy, forever an Innkeeper and an avid Inn traveller since childhood, has been working with Innkeepers in a variety of capacities for many years. She works with the Professional Association of Innkeepers International and writes "A Country Inn Perspective" column for *innkeeping* newsletter.

The Denn's are now Co-Director's at the Trinity Conference Center in West Cornwall, CT.; a private religious conference center operated by The Parish of Trinity Church, New York City.

This year a foster kitten, Max, joined their two dogs, Chessie and "Razzman", and a feline juvenile, TigerLily, who has shown Jon many computer keyboard sh oRT c uts. Max now runs the house and just ahead of "Razz"putin the Irrepressible.

For more information about the profession of Innkeeping, this publication, or the services of the
Professional Association of Innkeepers International, please contact the association at
P.O. Box 90710, Santa Barbara, CA 93190, (805) 569-1853.

For more information about this Guide, please write
Colburn Press at P.O. Box 356, Montvale, NJ 07645.

For comments about your stay at an Inn in this Guide,
please contact the appropriate inspection service(s); a list is on pages 5 and 6.